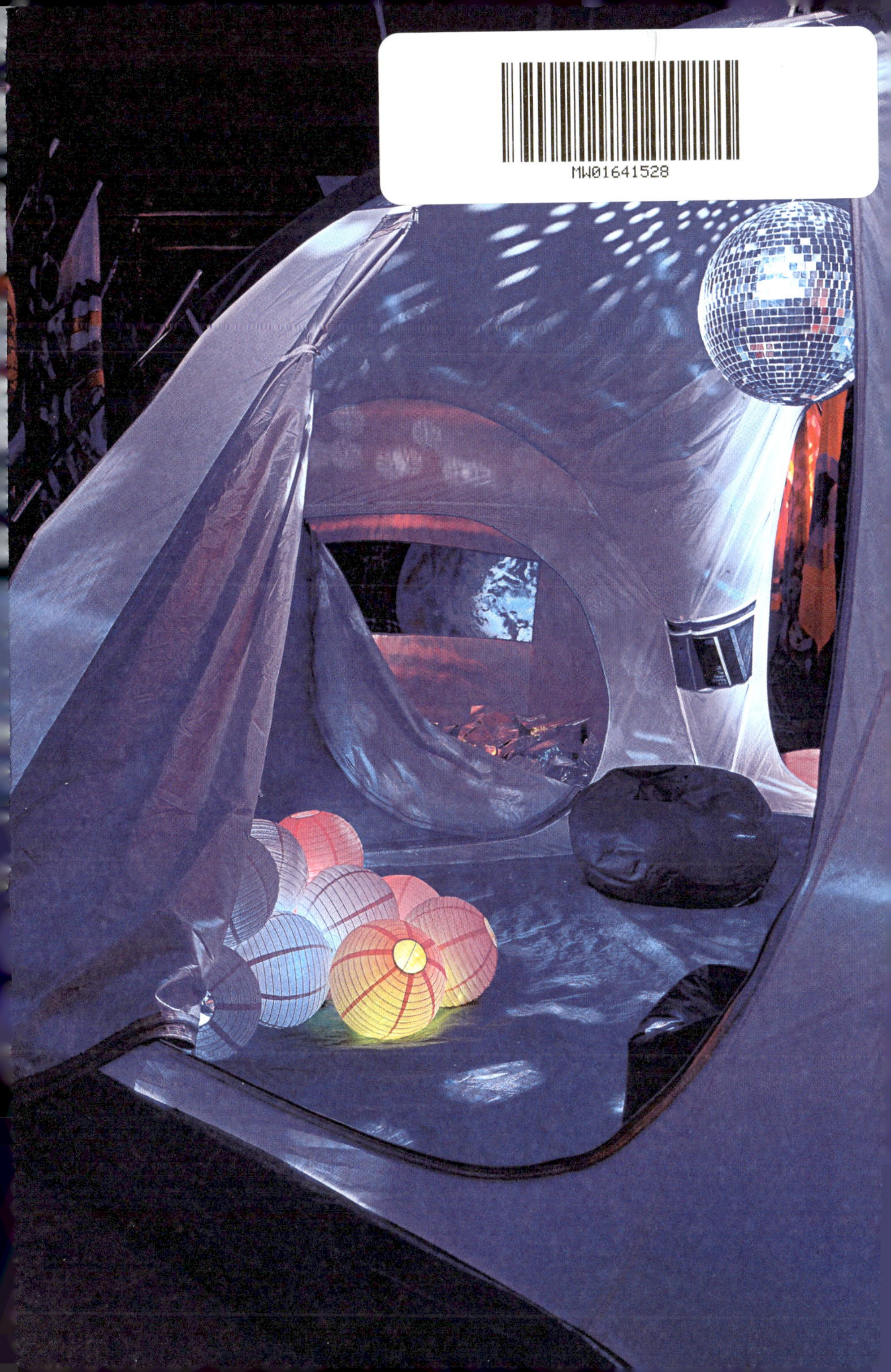

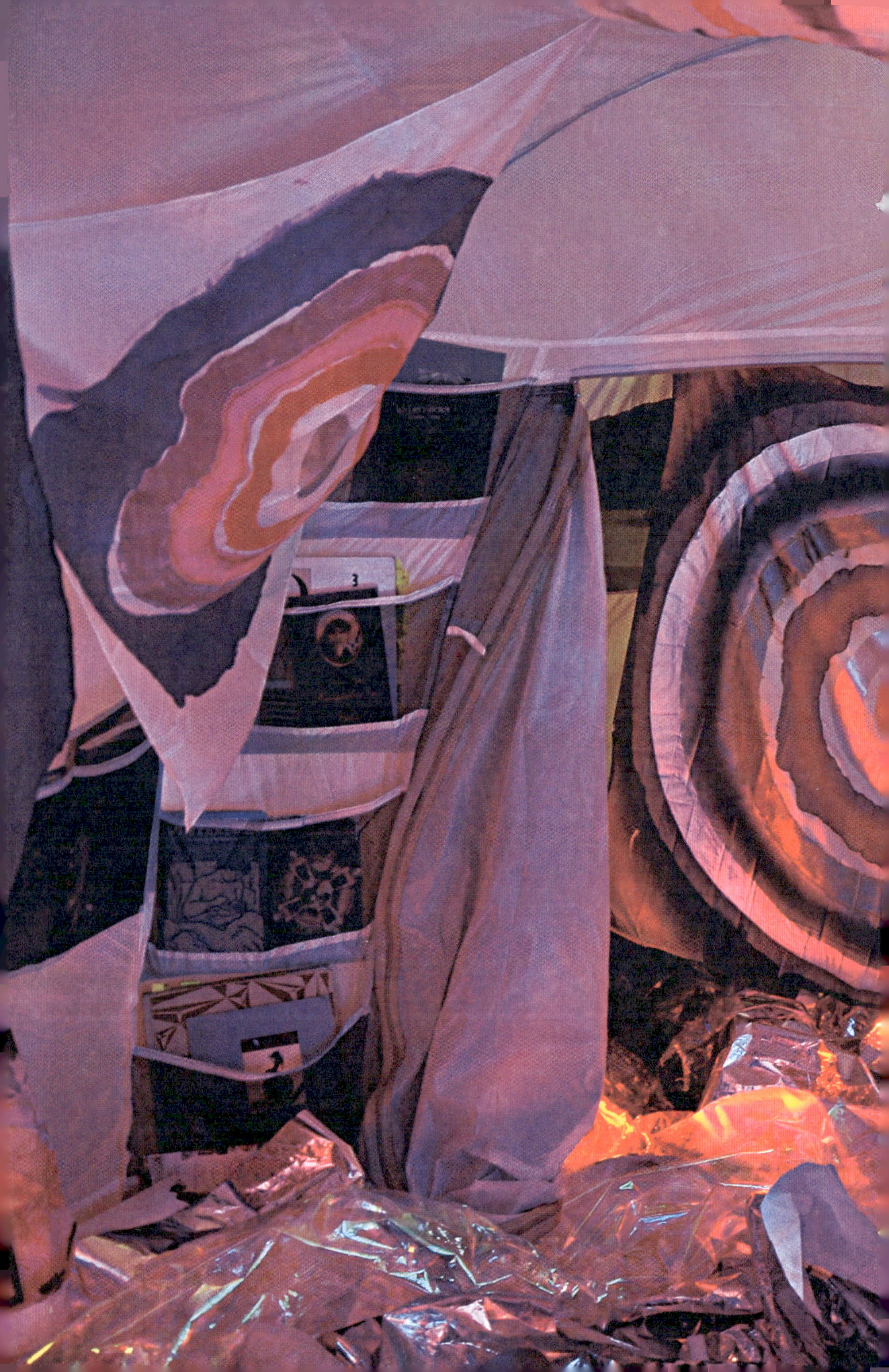

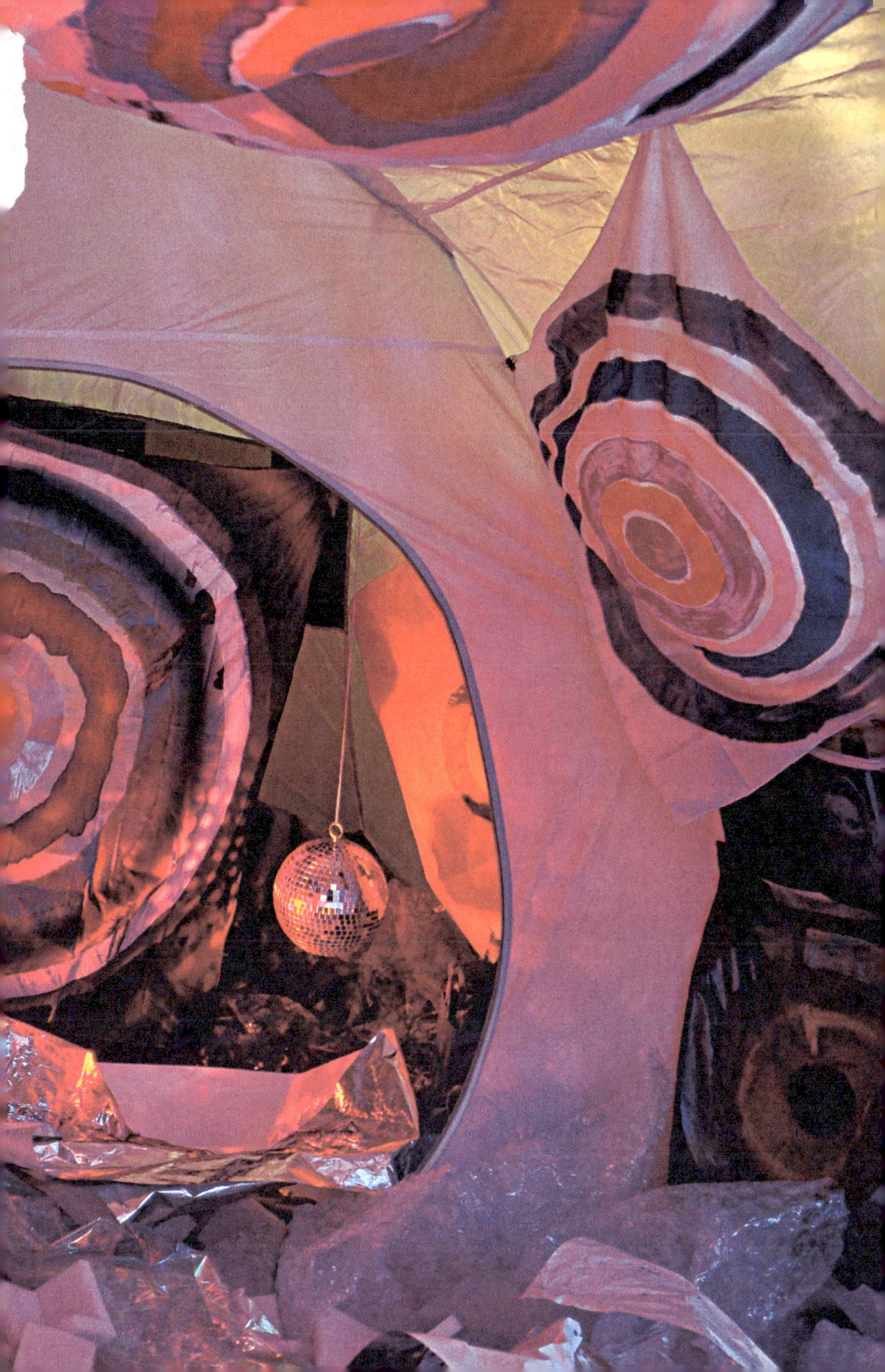

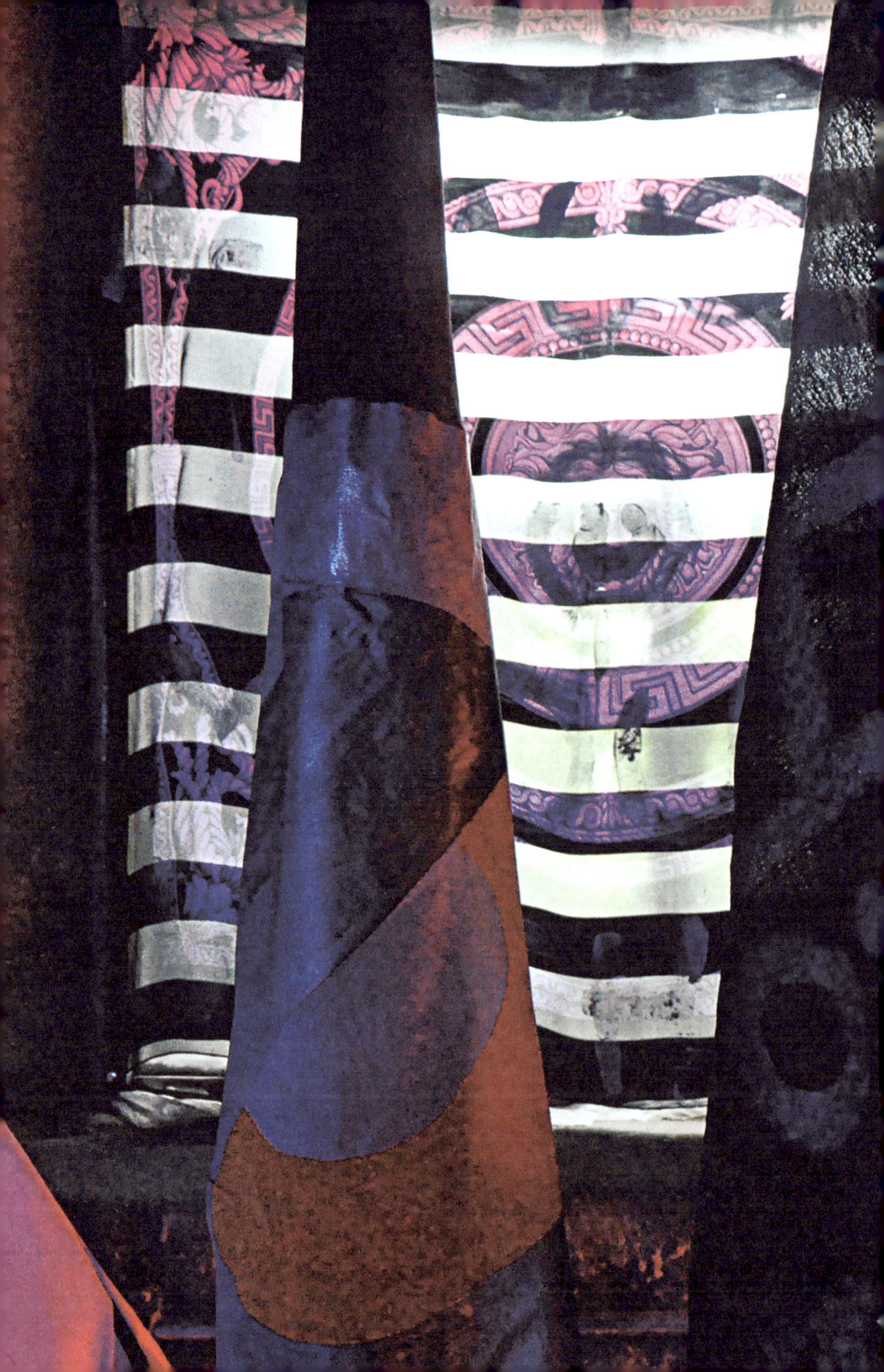

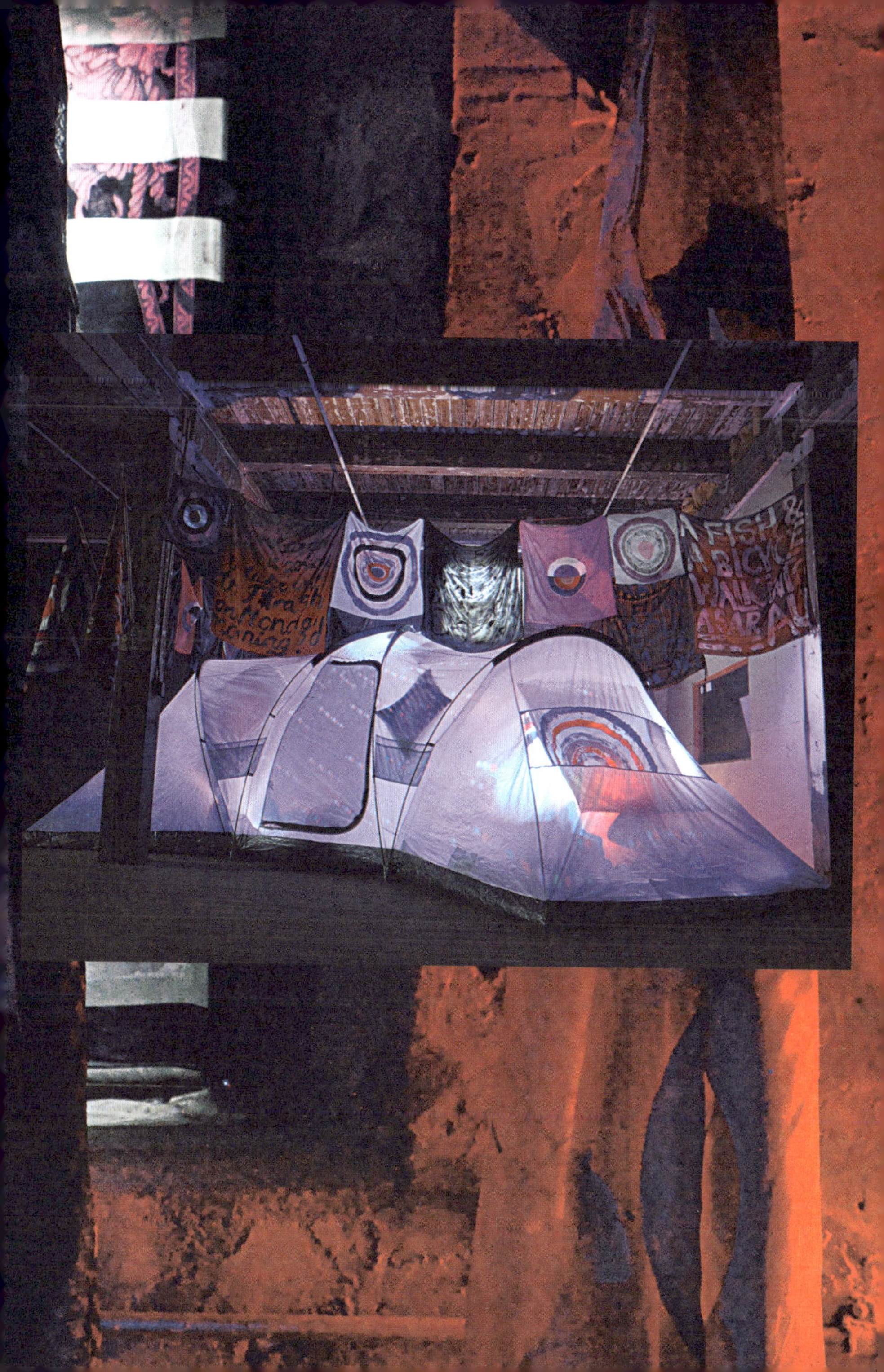
A FISH &

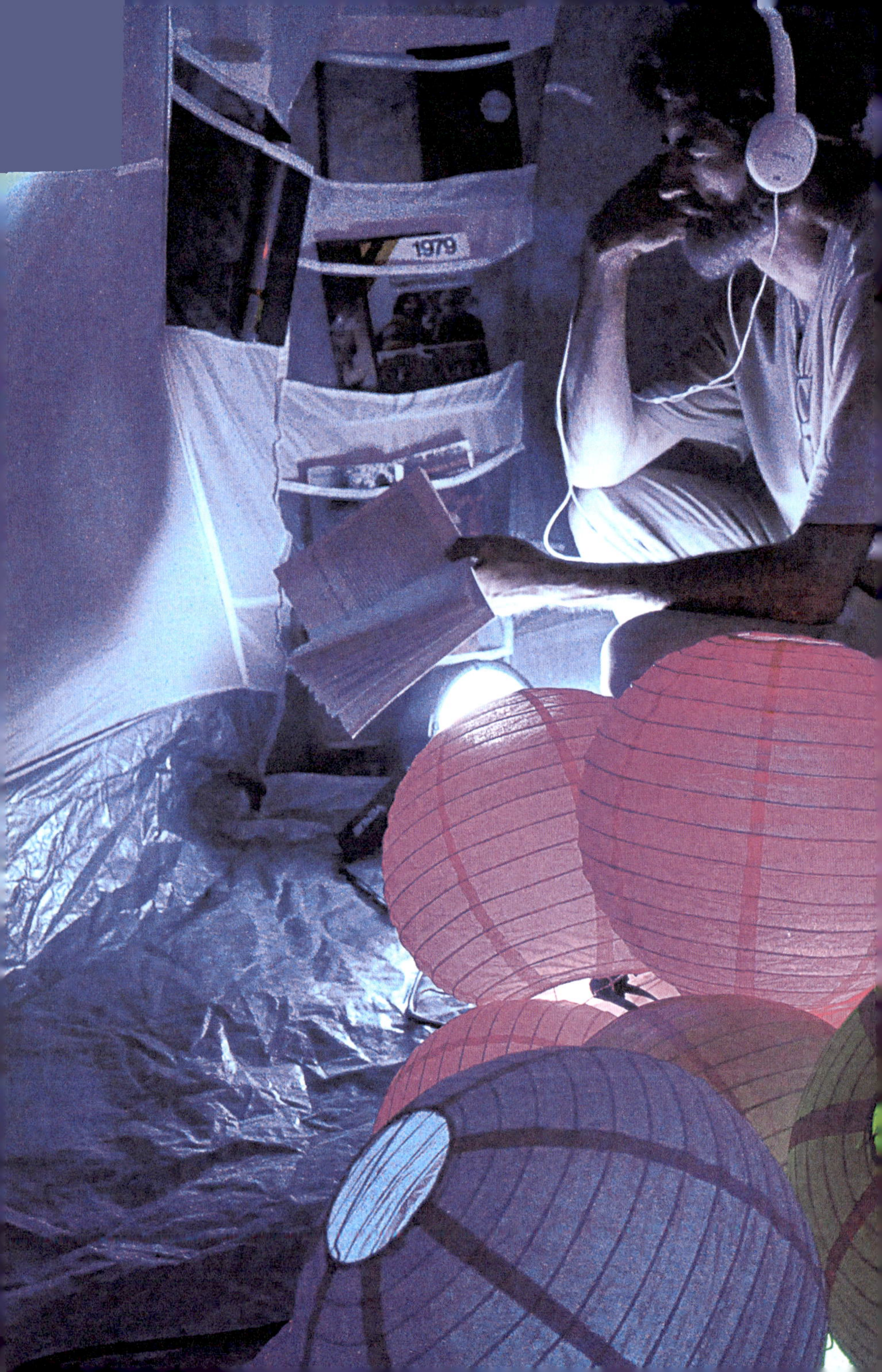
1979

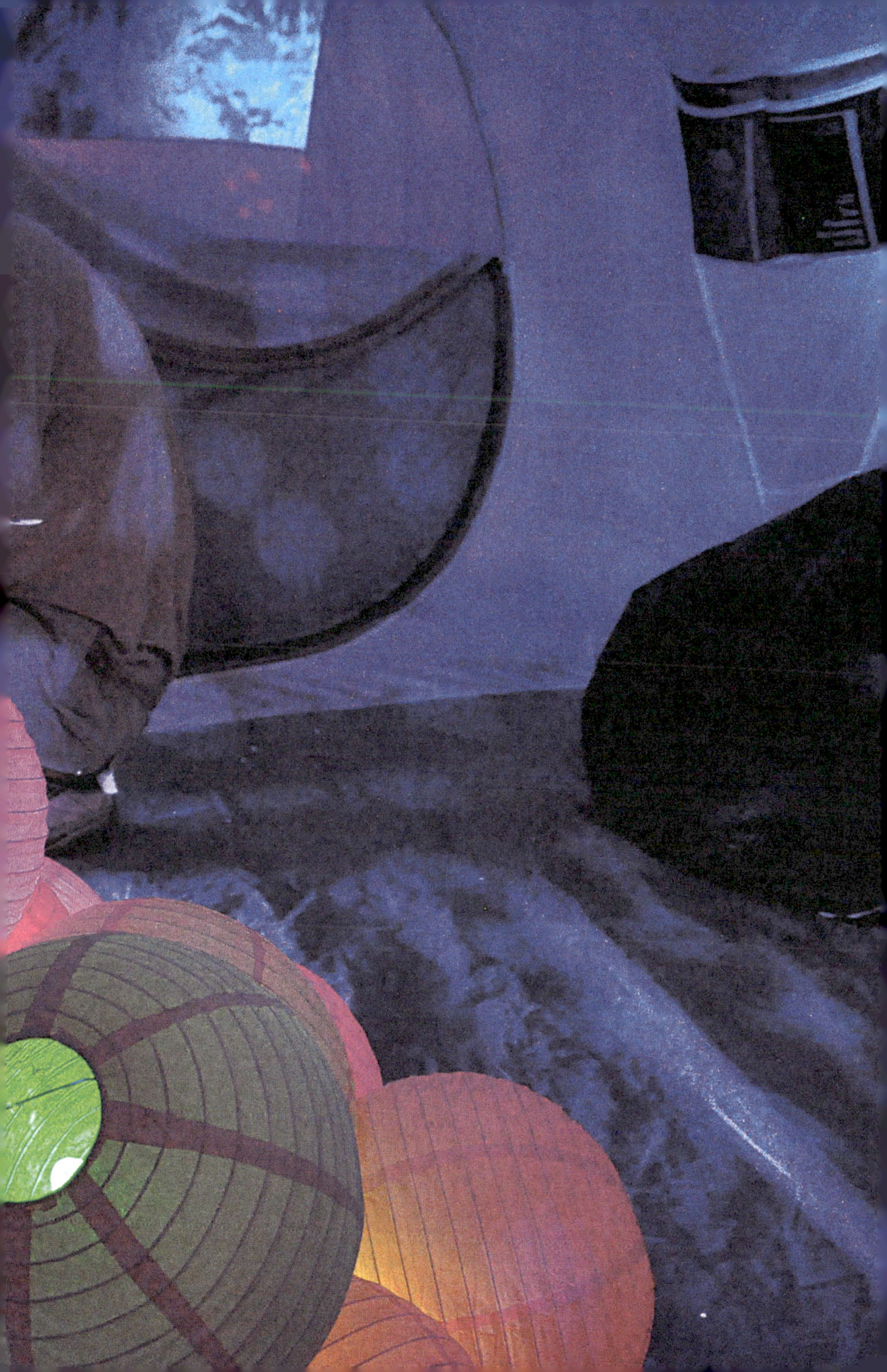

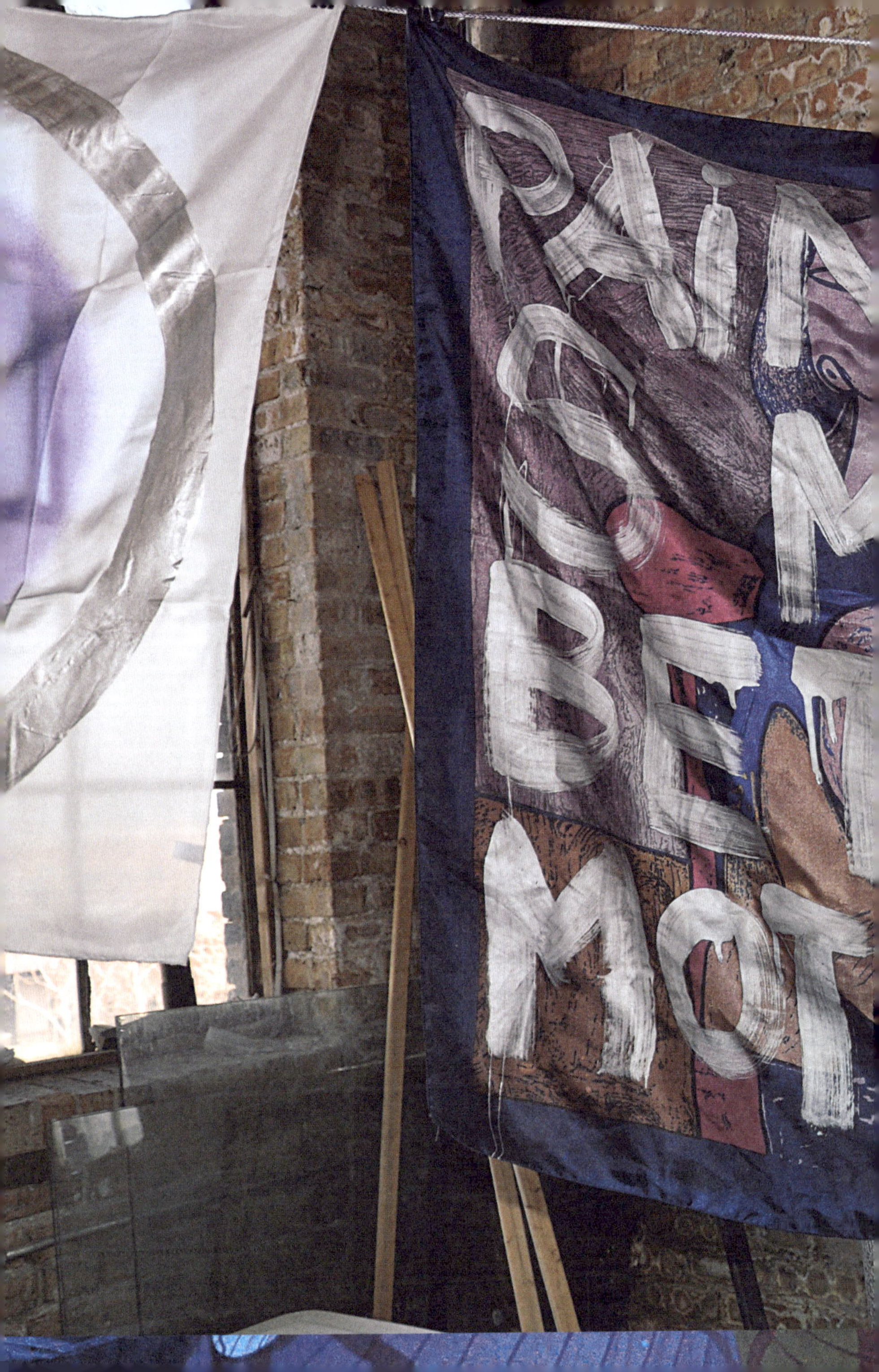

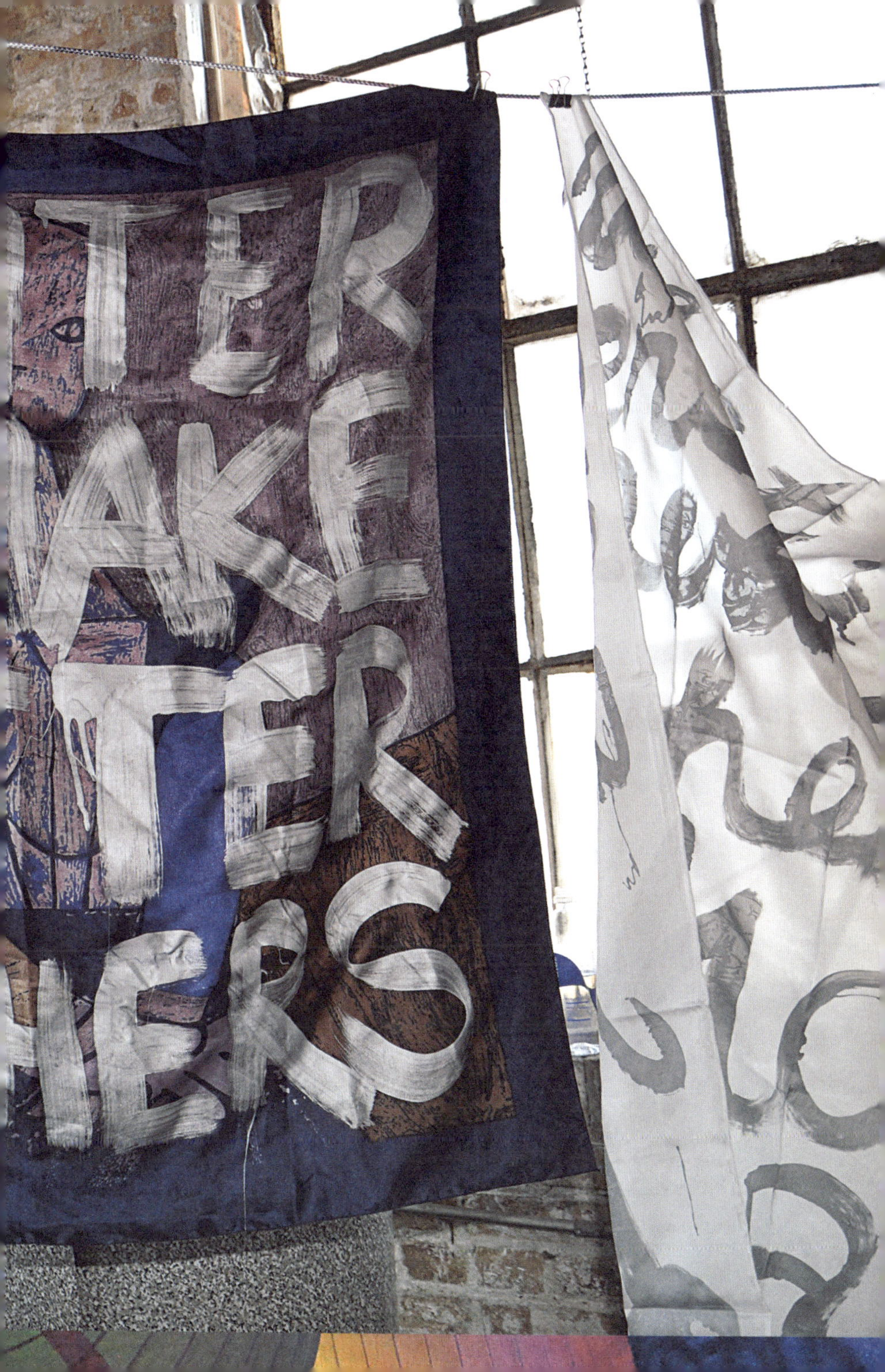

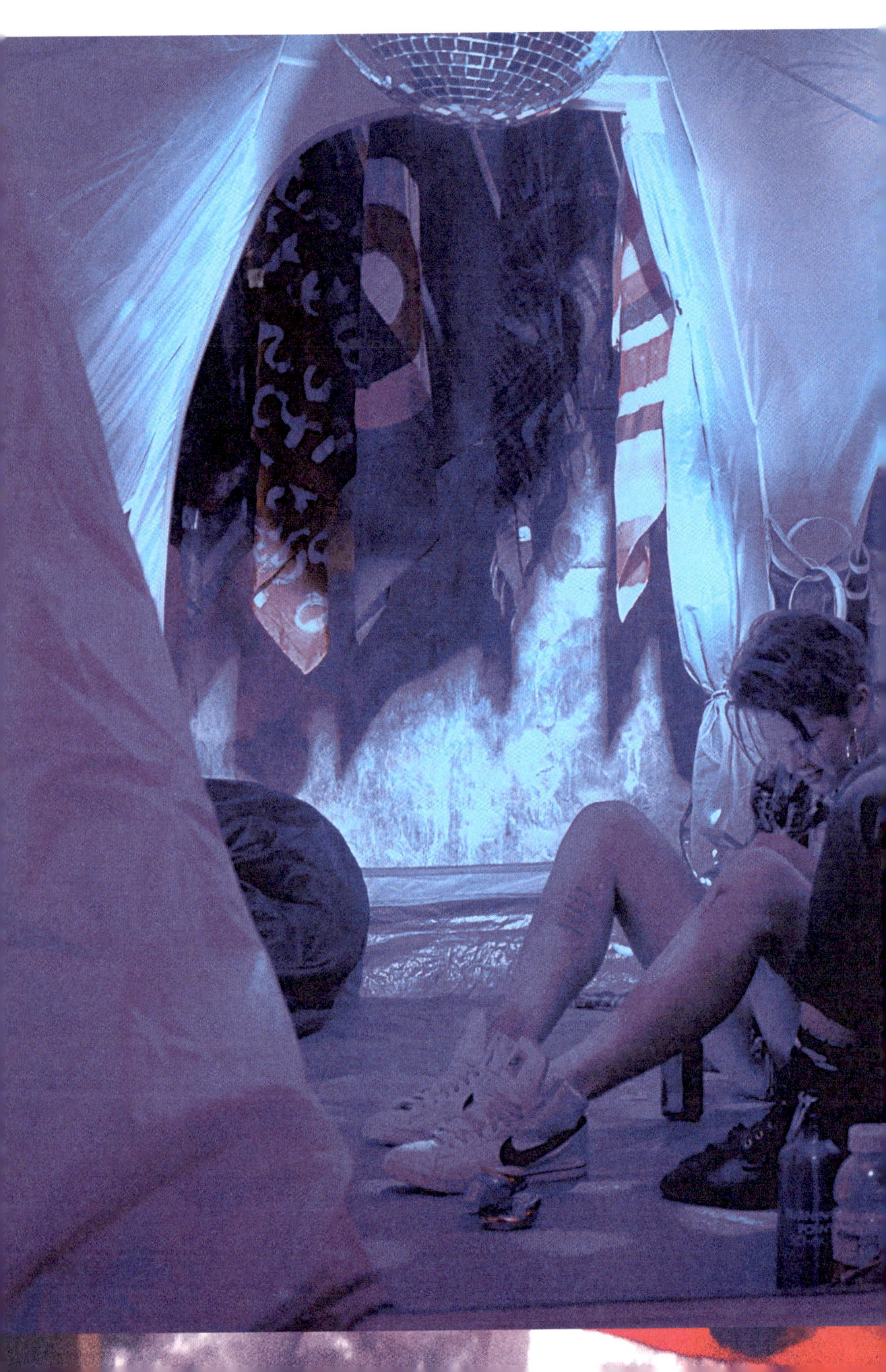

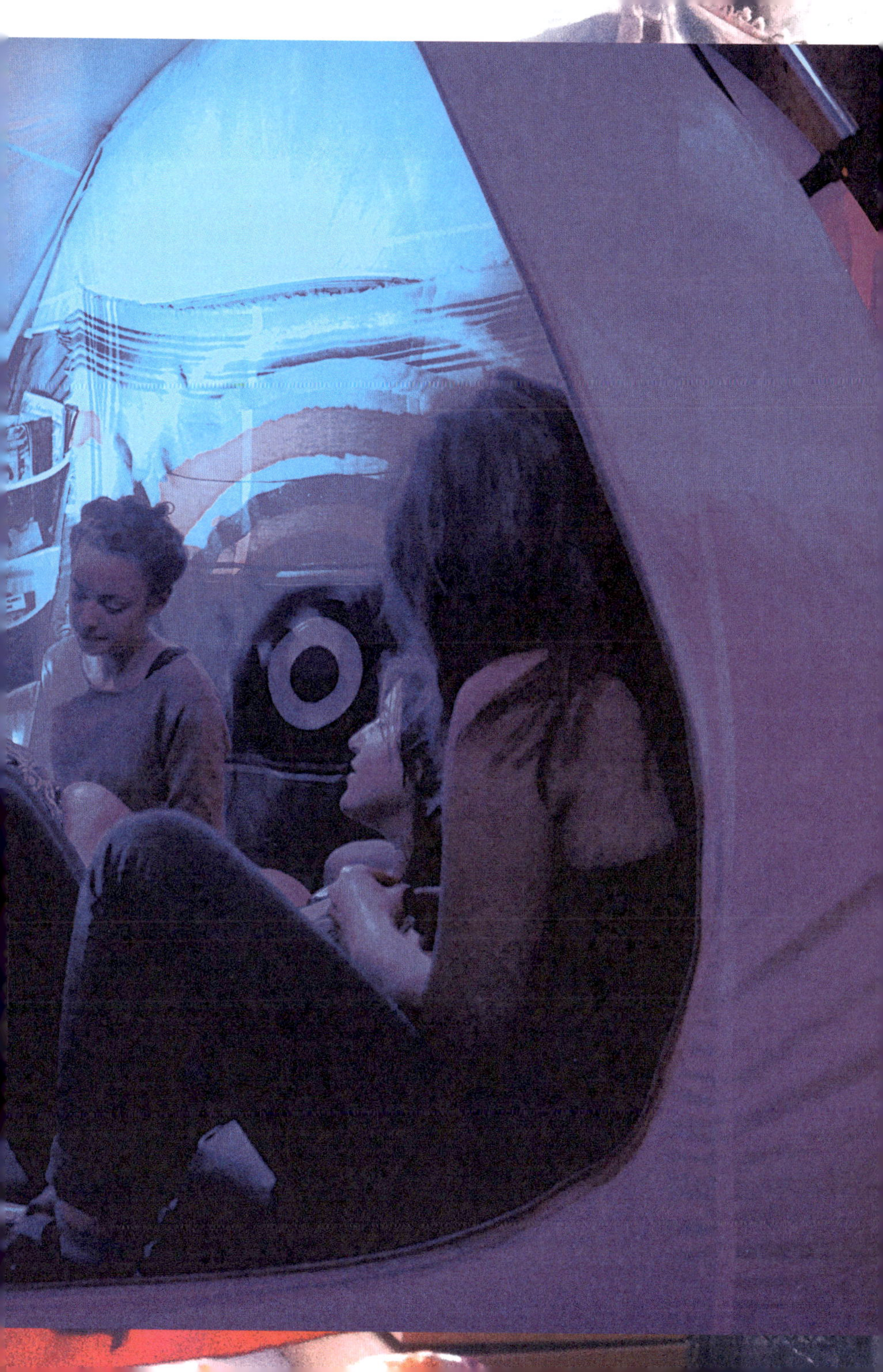

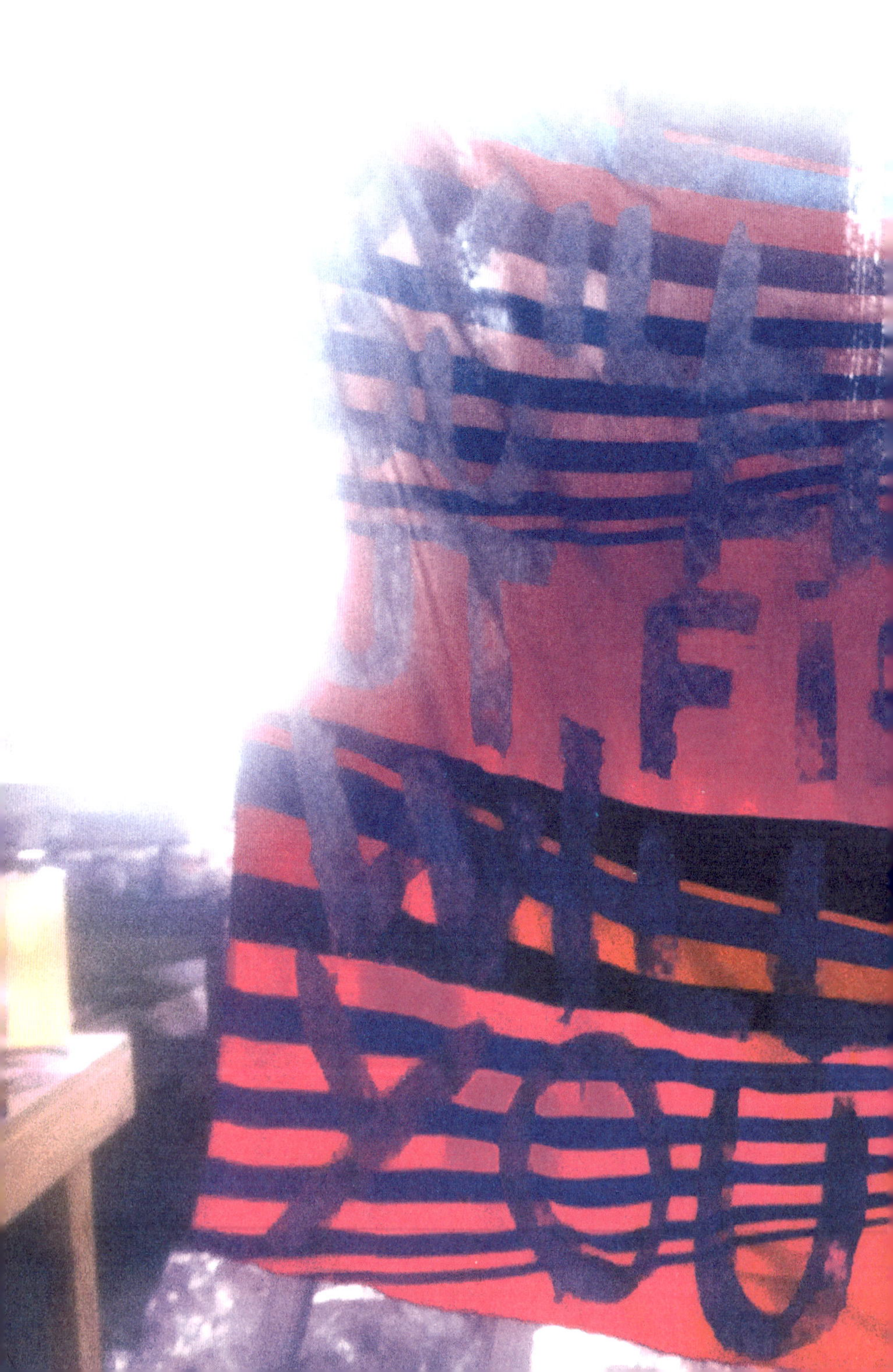

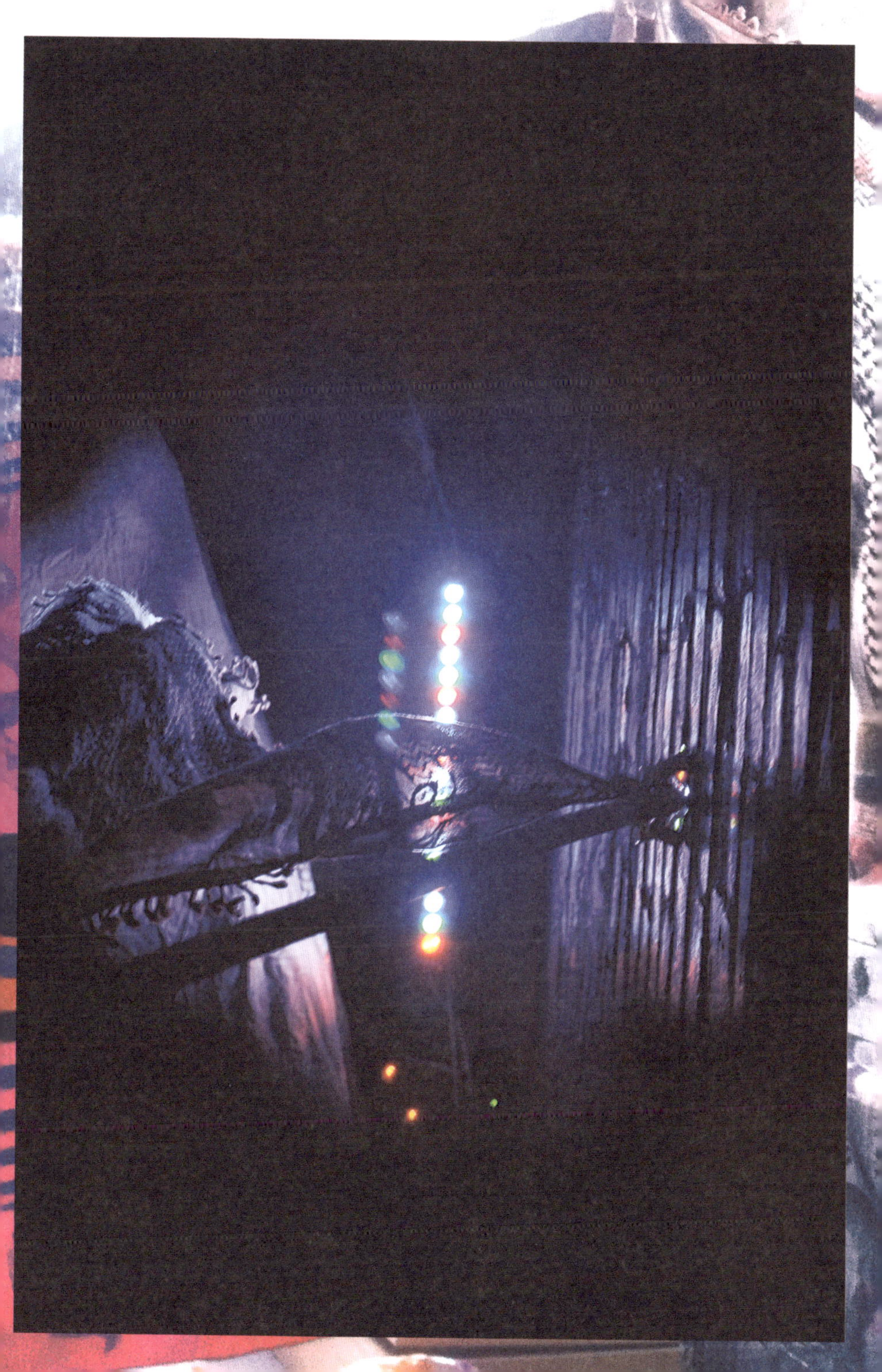

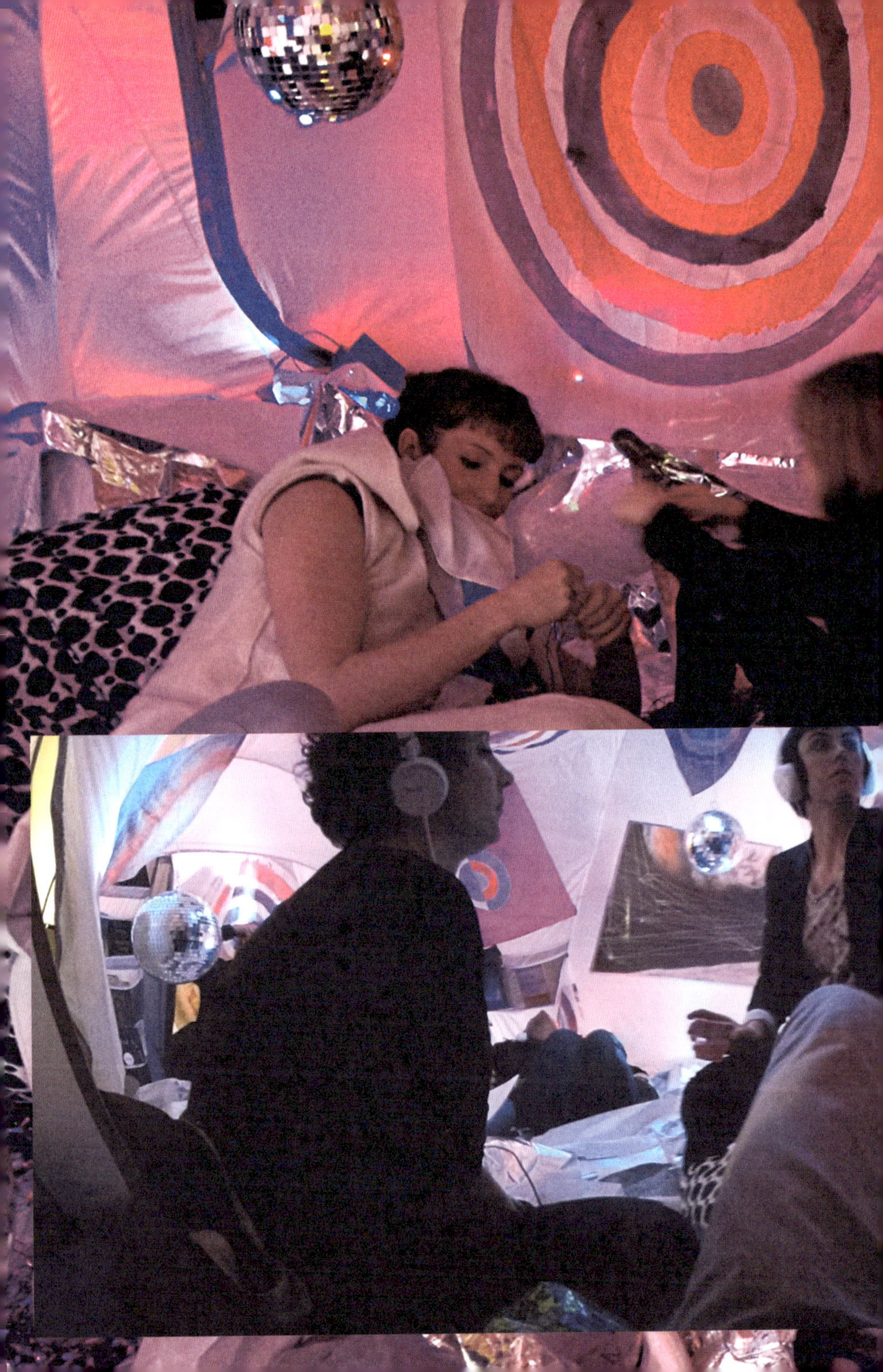

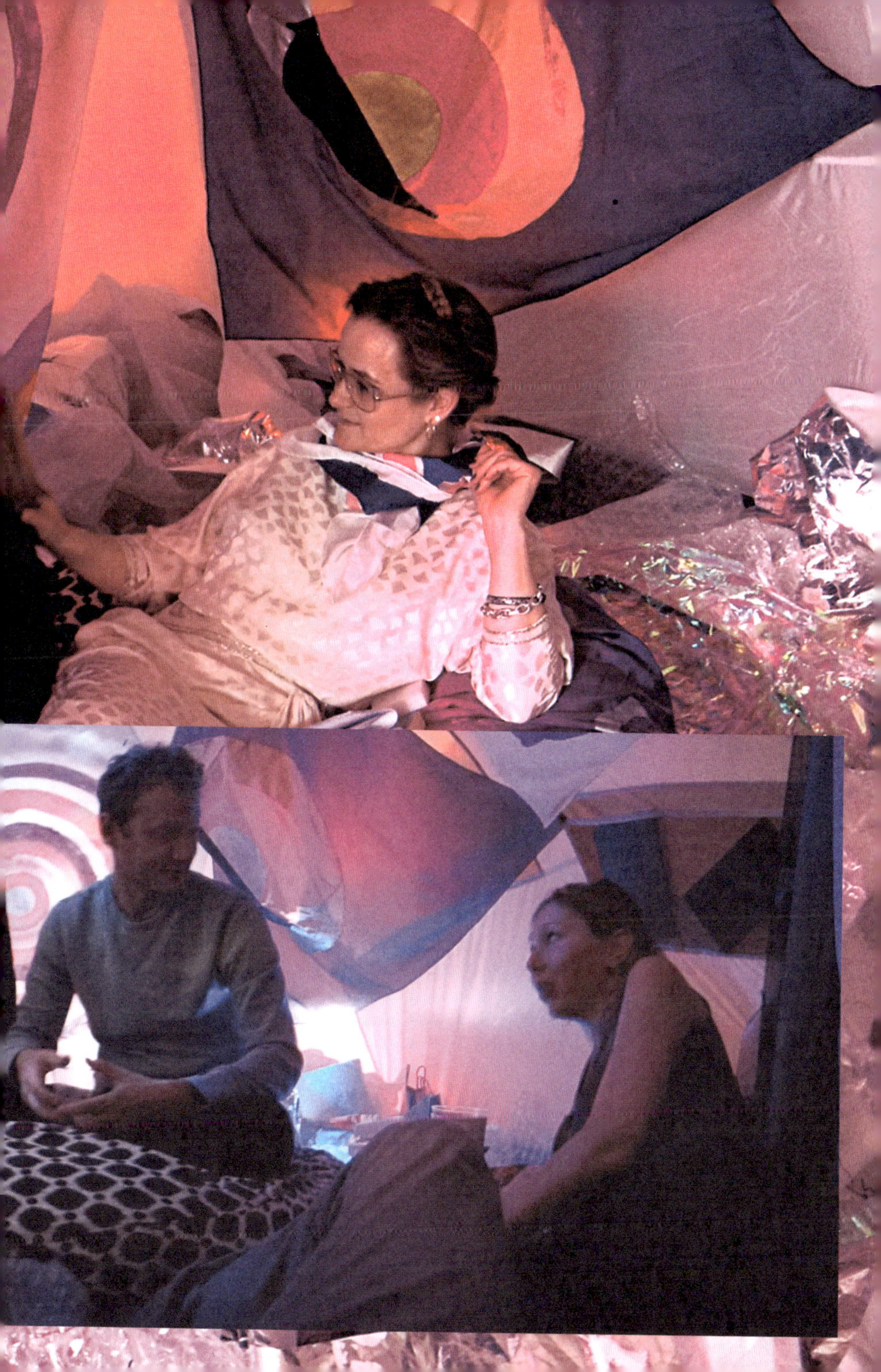

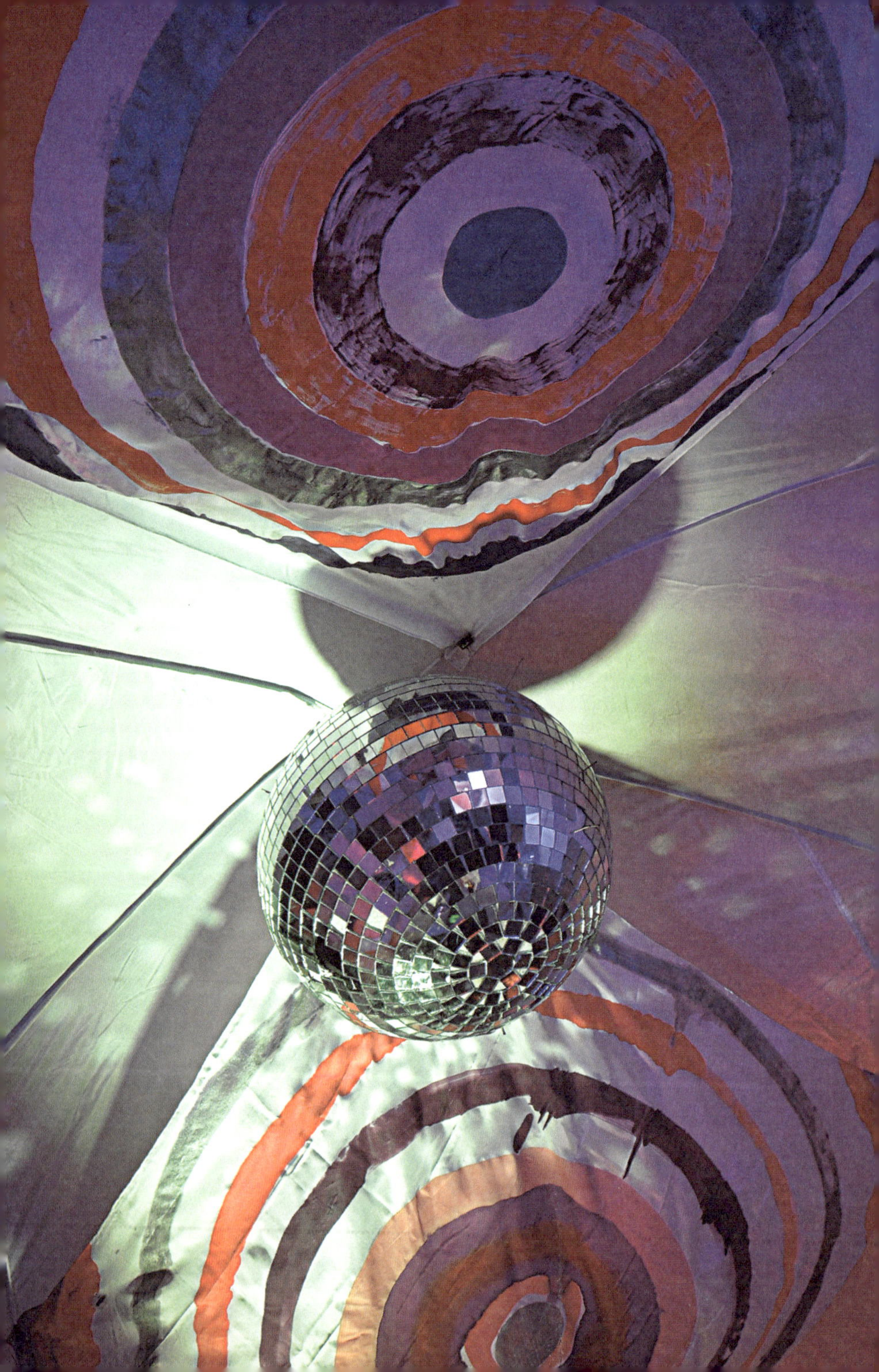

UMAMI

At the intersection of feminism, science fiction, and disco, **MOTHERNISM** aims to locate the mother-shaped hole in contemporary art discourse, therefore:

MOTHERNISM is not solely an ethical or political position, but also an aesthetic position.

MOTHERNISM aims to make mothers and mothering visible, audible, and palpable, outside but particularly inside of the visual arts.

MOTHERNISM aims to examine and challenge the perceived schism between the maternal and the artistic.

MOTHERNISTS strive for the highest degree of excellency, bearing in mind that the parameters of "quality" are not universal, but local.

MOTHERNISM is co-laboring with the forces.

MOTHERNISM is an orgy of organization.

MOTHERNISM is re-studio, re-modern, re-constructivist, and re-feminist.

MOTHERNISTS play in the expanded field between criticality and generosity.

MOTHERNISM begins to breathe while being drawn out.

All mothers being equal, not all mothers are alike nor are all **MOTHERNISTS** alike.

MOTHERNISTS get their daily food groups covered: eye candy, soul food, **UMAMI**.

UNITED MOTHERNIST
ARTIST MANIFEST
ILLUMINISMS

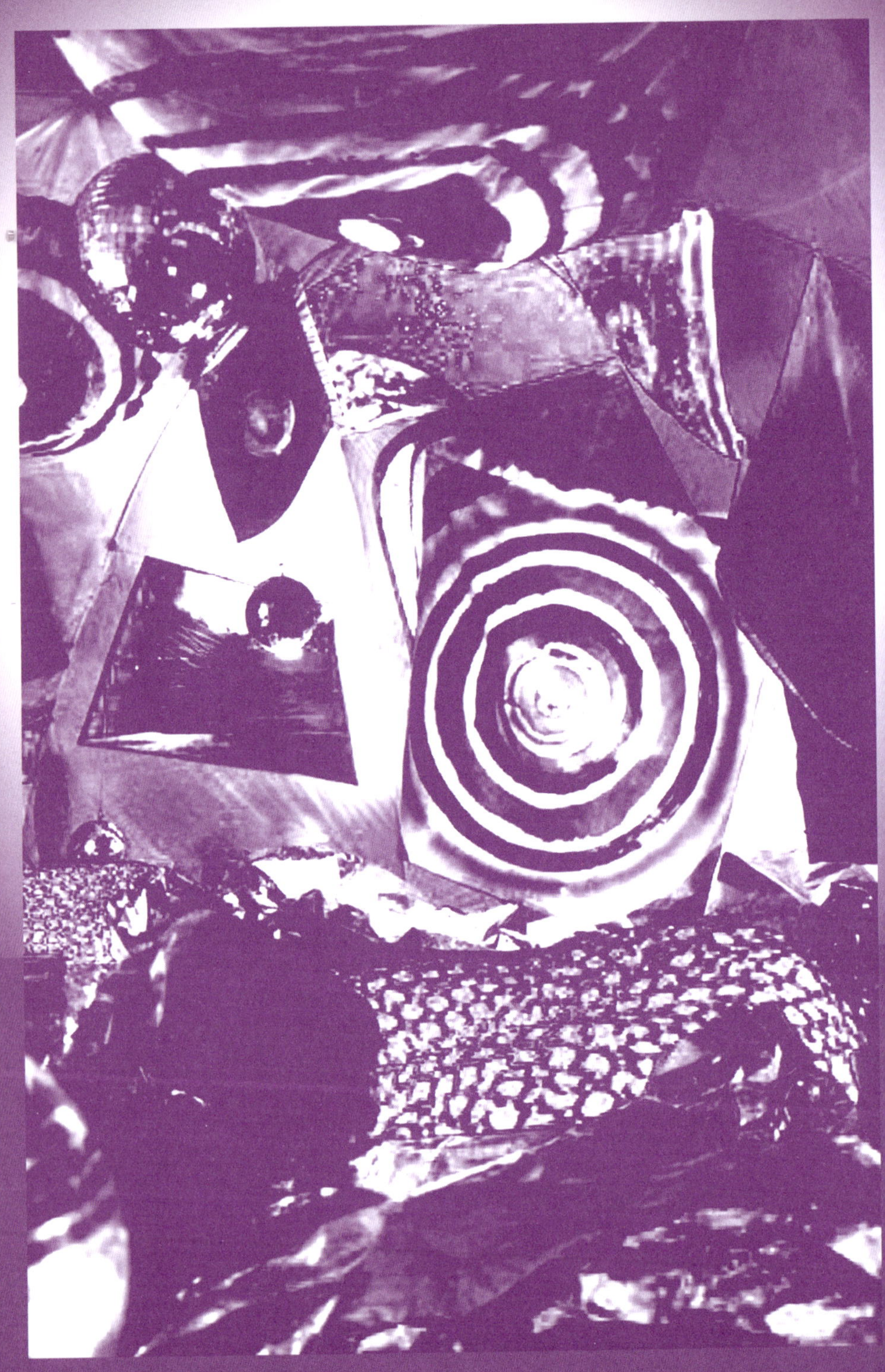

MOTHERNISM

By
LISE HALLER BAGGESEN

Thanks to all my doulas:
Caroline Picard, Michelle Grabner, Rebecca Duclos, Romi Crawford, Anette Trads, Emily Lansana, Amelia Charter, Kirsten Leenaars, Adelheid Mers, Brad Killam, Lester the Handyman, Kai Mah, Teena McClelland, Giacomo Tagliabue, Mairead Case, Julia V. Hendrickson, Dasha Filippova, Hamza Walker, Jennifer Reeder, Lori Waxman, Sonnenzimmer, Happy Collaborationists, Rikke Baggesen, Jonathan Ross, Adam Ross, Eleanor Ross, My Mother, Her Mother

Everybody and Anybody
in the SAIC VCS Department

Published by
Green Lantern Press
2337 North Milwaukee Avenue
Chicago, IL 60647, USA
www.press.thegreenlantern.org

and

Poor Farm Press
125 North Harvey Avenue
Oak Park, IL 60302, USA
www.poorfarmexperiment.org

Edition
First printing, edition of 1500

Publications director and editor
Caroline Picard

Editorial assistance
Mairead Case

Copy editor
Julia V. Hendrickson

Images
Images throughout this publication show *Mothernism* as it was installed at Co-Prosperity Sphere in Chicago, April, 2013, and at The Great Poor Farm Experiment in Manawa, Wisconsin, August, 2013. Photos by Lise Haller Baggesen and Jonathan Ross, except photos on page 14/15 by Teena McClelland and Giacomo Tagliambue. For more (visual) information, and for audio recordings of the original letters, please go to http://lisehallerbaggesen.wordpress.com/mothernism.

Cover and book design
Sonnenzimmer

Typefaces
Cousine, Fakt, FE Engschrift

ISBN 978-0-9884185-5-4

Printed in China

table of contents

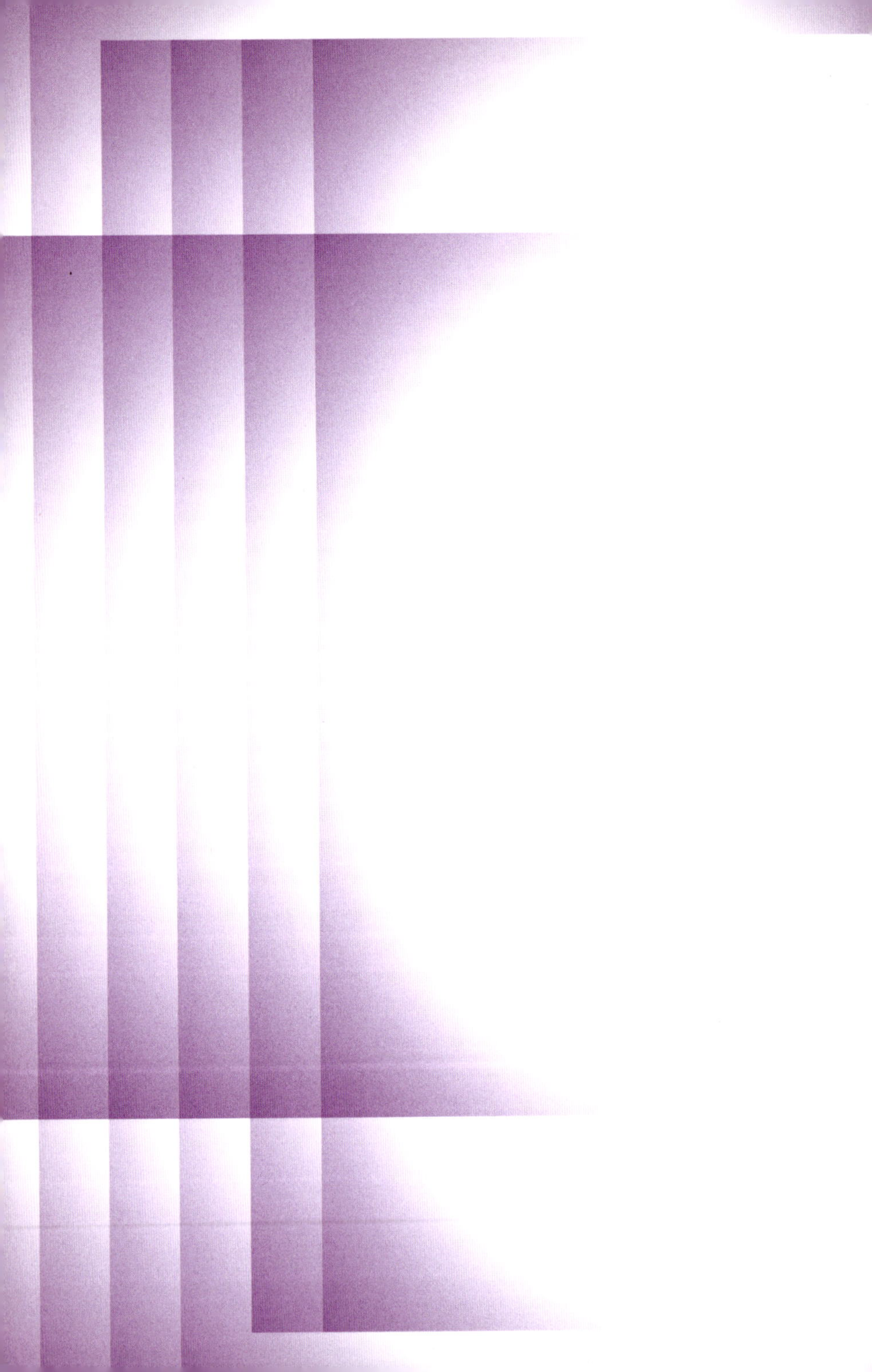

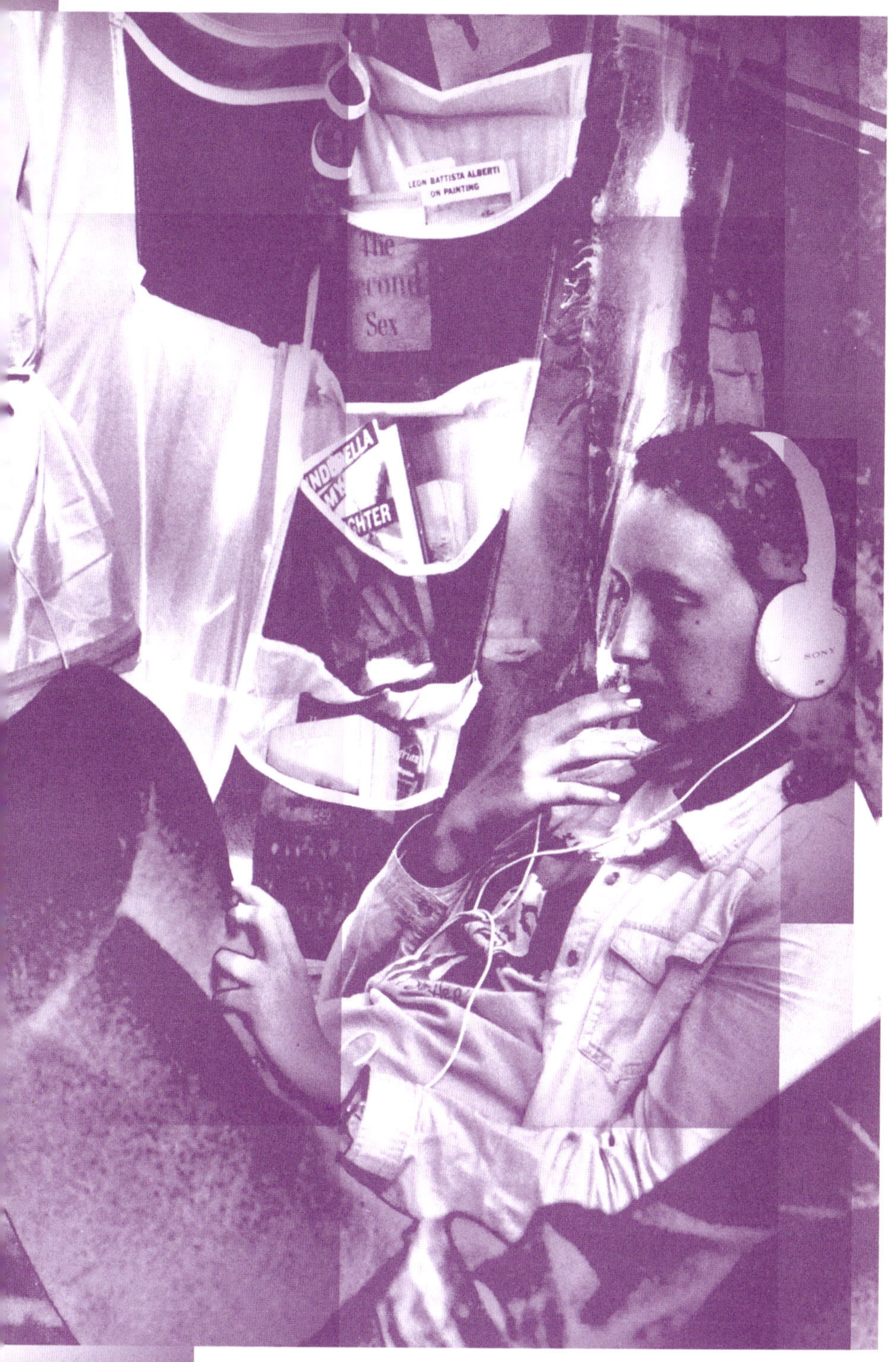
LEON BATTISTA ALBERTI
ON PAINTING
The
econd
Sex
SONY

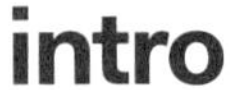

The Beat Goes On

The German Autobahn has its own particular rhythm.

There is no speed limit on this "highway from hell," this masterpiece of infrastructure invented and intended to export Third Reich ideologies to an ethnically cleansed Europe of the future. Although most of it has now been covered in tarmac—parts of its original construction, concrete slats laid out perpendicular to the driving direction as a giant pavement—are still visible and more importantly, audible.

On a good night, we drive the 800 km trip from Amsterdam to Copenhagen in eight hours flat, including our—typically long—breaks.

I rarely drive that fast. In fact, I fear speed as another might fear great heights, except I occasionally trick myself to snap out of that horizontal vertigo. On the road you can forget about your fears, or you can try to ignore them.

I got my driver's license at the tender age of 35 when I was pregnant again, and although I uttered an exclamatory *"Oh shit!"* when instructed to take my driving teacher's minuscule Peugeot onto the Amsterdam Ring way, my examiner let me pass.

I drive the slow part along the Dutch *snelweg*, but occasionally let my inhibitions slide. When the needle climbs past 140 km/h, my husband puts his hand on my thigh and says, *"Sweetie, you're speeding!"* and his eyes light up like the speed is a gift or a dare, like racy underwear…

At the German border we swap and I move to the passenger seat, manning the stereo. We listen to a lot of music on such a trip. As we drive deeper and deeper into the dark, the kids fall asleep in the back seat and local commuters check in for the night. The road gradually empties, and on long stretches of motorway we can average 160 km/h, occasionally climbing to 180 or even 200, 220.

240 is the fastest our old Volvo will go.

When the taillights of trucks before us approach too speedily, I close my eyes and try to sleep. I tune into the rhythm of the road and relax as it hypnotically takes over and translates the landscape underneath and around us to a pulse in my body: the regular dub of the car passing over the cracks between the cement slabs, the swoosh of the cars overtaking each other, the low humming of the road markings as we pass between lanes or the delayed echo of a stretch of soundproofed wall as we drive past countryside villages: this is the Euro beat.

Its mesmerizing, monotonous drone is captured most beautifully in Kraftwerk's minimalist masterpiece *Autobahn* from 1974, but in my opinion doesn't really gather momentum until a year later with the single "Love to Love you Baby." Produced by Giorgio Moroder, it is co-written by Pete Bellotte – and of course Donna Summer, who also did the vocals.

In my somnolent half state I imagine them driving late at night on the Autobahn near Munich, where Donna Summer found herself after touring Germany as part of the American cast for the musical *HAIR*. As they drive into the night, Giorgio taps his new drumbeat on the steering wheel (no, wait a minute, let's put Donna in the driver's seat!). So, Giorgio is tapping on the dashboard, like a click track, and Donna starts cooing, orgasmically: *"Oooooooooh, love to love you baby."*

She later said of herself as a performer:

> One of the most important aspects of my singing that Giorgio encouraged me to expand was my approach to a song. To this day I will approach a song as an actress approaches a script. I do not sing; I act. When I sing, I sing with the voice of the character in the song.[1]

It is a move often employed by singers, writers, and artists: a move, a gift, a truth or dare – to speak under the guise of a different persona, as though under hypnosis, not unlike the way spirits will manifest themselves through an entranced medium in a séance.

In this way, "The idea takes form by traversing the energy of bodies, when the message does not come 'from the artists body, but passes through it.'"[2]

As for me, I sing the song of Queen Leeba.

Leeba sings in the form of letters, to her dear "Dear."

Just like Leeba has some resemblance to me, Dear has some resemblance to my daughter. But also to my son and sometimes to my sister and sometimes to my mother – and sometimes to you, dear reader.[3]

She comes to me as a soul sister, a ghost of feminisms past, a visitation or a travel companion, and she teaches me to sing about things we wish we hadn't seen, and things that should have come

1 Donna Summer and Mark Elliot, *Ordinary Girl: The Journey* (New York: Random House, 2003), 102

2 Pascal Rousseau, "Premonitory Abstraction – Mediumism, Automatic Writing, and Anticipation in the Work of Hilma af Klint," in *Hilma af Klint – A Pioneer of Abstraction*, ed. Iris Müller-Westermann and Jo Widoff (Stockholm: Moderna Museet and Hantje Cantz, 2013), 169.

3 I don't have a feminist theory on motherhood. I only have these notes, these paragraphs, some insights. Curiously, they take the form of another woman's writing about motherhood.[...] We are part of a resistance. For necessity does not stop long enough for us to analyze. We have only brief illuminations, which we must record between interruptions, set down side by side, hoping to make sense of it all some day later.

Susan Griffin, "Feminism and Motherhood," in *The Mother Reader: Essential Writings on Motherhood*, ed. Moyra Davey (New York: Seven Stories Press, 2003), 35.

into view by now. But most of all she comes to me as an imaginary friend – because you need friends to get by in the art world.

She visits me in the form of a song and I sing her song, but I sing it my way. This way, our voices co-emerge as we sing, sometimes in unison, sometimes out of sync.

It is a song of Motherhood, of Feminism, of Disco, and of Art. It is a song of bodies, of spaces and of ideas for us to inhabit, to move in and out of, and to pass through. It is a song of protest and of hope, hoping one day to make itself redundant.

The song is sometimes a political parole and sometimes a secular chant.

It is sometimes a battle cry and sometimes a lullaby.

The song is called Mothernism:

MOTHER of INVENTION

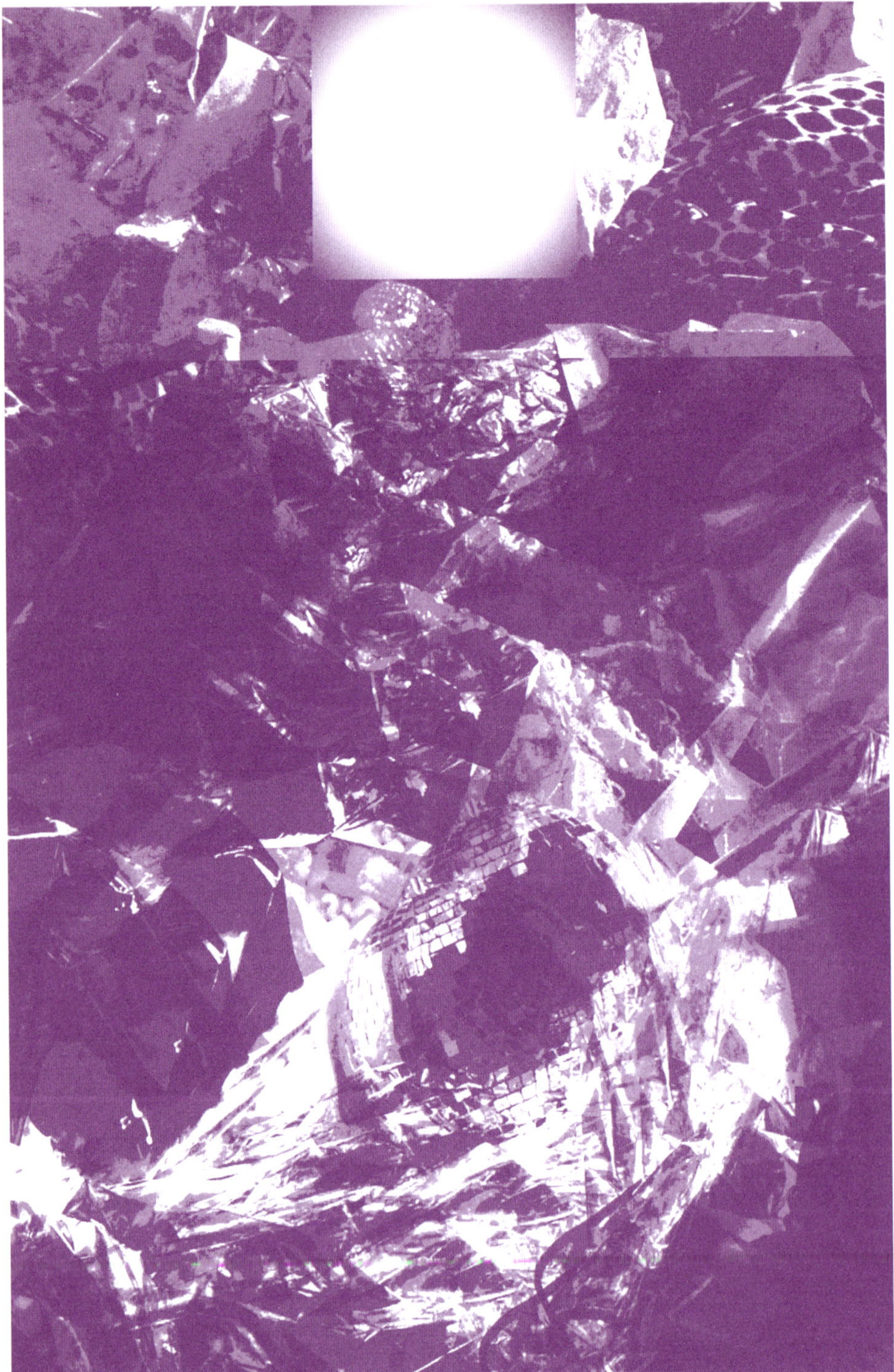

Dear,
You should never preach what you practice. You should strive for a more enlightened, better, brighter you. Just remember, when offered enlightenment, to ask yourself first: "Who is enlightened, by what, and why?"

You probably are a better, brighter me already. You are younger for sure. More symmetrical perhaps. In this day and age, people are surgically altered to look more like you and less like me.

When this is practiced in other parts of the world, we like to call it "female circumcision," or even "genital mutilation," but when it happens here, we call it *the Barbie*.[1]

I cannot tell you what to do, but remember it's true: symmetry is valuable, but pleasure is valuable too—*ooooh—oooooooh*:

> We're learning to live
> With somebody's depression
> And I don't want to live
> With somebody's depression
> But we'll get by I suppose
> It's a very modern world
> but nobody's perfect
> It's a moving world…[2]

I'm wearing purple underpants these days—as if I can only connect to the cosmos through my root chakra, like a giant Kundalini Cobra up my butt, like Cicciolina last time I saw her.[3]

---

1 Dr. Red Alinsod, a Laguna Beach-based urogynecologist who invented the Barbie surgery, which amputates the entire icky Labia Minora, explains:

> This results in a 'clamshell' aesthetic: a smooth genital area, the outer labia appearing 'sealed' together with no labia minora protrusion. Alinsod tells me he invented the Barbie in 2005. 'I had been doing more conservative labiaplasties before then,' he says. 'But I kept getting patients who wanted almost all of it off. They would come in and say, I want a 'Barbie.' So I developed a procedure that would give them this comfortable, athletic, petite look, safely.'

Katie J. M. Baker, "Unhappy With Your Gross Vagina? Why Not Try 'The Barbie,'" *Jezebel*, 18 January, 2013, http://jezebel.com/5977025/unhappy-with-your-gross-vagina-why-not-try-the-barbie (accessed 2 April, 2014).

2 David Bowie, "Fantastic Voyage," *Lodger* (RCA, 1979).

3 I googled *Cicciolina + Cobra* to see if I could actually find this image, but ended up via a bizarre shot of Brigitte Nielsen's cleavage on a Spanish speaking site dedicated to *Great tits of the 80's*… so I'm sorry: if you live by the web, you die by the web—something to keep in mind!

It was after her breakup with Jeff Koons and she was looking good. A little flustered, her cheeks a little hot, her cerulean gaze intransigent. As if she was facing the whole world while at the same time fixating her audience, her audience of one, and saying:

> 'Sup, Jeff? How are you doing? I'm good, you know,
> I'll get by, as you know, cause it's a moving world,
> and I've got a giant snake up my butt and you don't!

Jeff, I imagine, had his head too far up his own butt to take notice, and so it is in general, I fear, with the art world and cosmology. Like a cobra in the butt, this particular enlightenment gets too weird, too deep, too uncomfortable, too soon. And so, the art world could not really fathom Cicciolina, although it embraced her for a while.

Of the many arenas she passes through – pop music, politics, and pornography to name but a few – she seems to walk in and out of them remarkably unscathed. Even when the photographs suggest that "work" (that overworked euphemism for plastic surgery) was done, you bet it was for her pleasure![4]

In fact, Cicciolina, or Ilona Staller as is her "real" name, has turned her unorthodox pleasure principle into a provocative, personal and political strategy – from being the first woman to bare her breasts on Italian television, to campaigning naked on horseback in the streets of Rome for the Radical Party, to a five-year-tenure in the Italian Parliament (during which she used her va-va-voom to push a fairly serious liberal agenda, including sex positivism, women's liberation, and a radical environmentalism), to a court battle over her state pension as an elected official – which she received with the words: "I've earned it and I'm proud of it!"[5]

While in office, she publicly offered her sexual services to Saddam Hussein and Osama Bin Laden in return for peace in the Middle East, defending her actions with the argument: "My breasts have never done anyone any harm, while Bin Laden's war has caused thousands of victims."[6]

If her CV has a recurrent theme of "Make Love Not War," her divorce and subsequent custody battle with Jeff Koons was not so amicable, however.

---

4 As an example of how these spheres – political propaganda, pop music, and pornography – mesh in Cicciolina's universe, watch her sing "Political Woman" on *LIVE Rome*: http://www.youtube.com/watch?v=EuVG0F_oorM (accessed 28 March, 2014).

5 Palash Ghosh, "A Star is Porn: Whatever Became of Italy's Cicciolina," *International Business Times*, 27 February, 2013, http://www.ibtimes.com/star-porn-whatever-became-italys-cicciolina-1104912 (accessed 30 March, 2014).

6 AP/AFP, "Bush and Saddam Should Duel: Iraq's Challenge," *AP/AFP smh.com.au*, 5 October, 2002, http://www.smh.com.au/articles/2002/10/05/1033538810033.html (accessed 30 March, 2014).

The story begins in 1988 when, enchanted by a photo shoot of La Cicciolina posing in a kitschy Eastern European fairy tale set for an Italian porn magazine, Jeff Koons sent Staller an invitation to be his co-star for a series of billboards he had been commissioned to do for the Whitney Museum of American Art.

In her Italianate English, she later told *Vanity Fair*:

> One day I got the fax saying that Jeff Koons was a very important artist American who wants to meet Ilona Cicciolina…I think maybe this is a very strange thing, maybe best [to say] no. I bring this fax and make trash. But my ex-manager [said], 'No, no, no. We should respond because this artist might be doing good work.'[7]

Conceived on the set of Koon's seminal body of work *Made in Heaven*, a celestial romance blossomed, and soon wedding invites featuring a cute Annie Leibovitz portrait of the nude couple were sent out. They married in June of 1991 at a small reception with 40 close friends and family. Celebrity gossip would have it that the couple had already drifted apart at this stage, but that Koons needed the wedding—as a nod to traditional family values—to lend some credibility to his fictional persona and perhaps also just to drive home the point that sometimes reality *is* stranger than fiction.

Real feelings were nevertheless at stake, when out of this fantasy union came *a real boy!*

On October 29, 1992, at 8:30 in the morning, Ludwig Maximilian Koons was born at Mt. Sinai Hospital in New York. Koons, the proud father, recalls: "I was the first person to greet Ludwig and give him a kiss."[8]

Already estranged, the couple separated soon after and Staller brought the child with her to Rome, under the guise of an emergency family matter. When she failed to return, Koons followed them abroad to bring the child back to the US. With little Ludwig in his custody; he promptly filed for divorce upon his return. In a statement released by his New York office, he declared that: "The differences between our cultural and social standings are too great."[9]

What followed was a he said/she said wherein the couple repeatedly sued each other for child abduction, unpaid child support, and unfit parenting. Ludwig has lived with Staller in Rome since 1993, when she sent his bodyguard (appointed to ensure that neither party could remove the child from the jurisdiction of the state of

7 Ingrid Sischy, "Koons, High and Low," *Vanity Fair*, March, 2001, http://www.vanityfair.com/culture/features/2001/03/jeff-koons-200103 (accessed 28 March, 2014).

8 Sischy, "Koons, High and Low."

9 "Pop Artist Says Marriage To Ex-porn Queen Is Over," *Orlando Sentinel*, 28 February, 1992, http://articles.orlandosentinel.com/1992-02-28/news/9202280604_1_cicciolina-artist-jeff-koons-married (accessed 28 March, 2014).

New York) out for a pack of cigarettes, and fled with the toddler while he was gone.

Shortly thereafter Koons started *Celebration*—a series of paintings and high gloss sculptures of balloon animals and children's toys—an imagined homecoming for the little prince, who did not return. As Koons said: "I was trying to communicate to my son, when he's older, just how much I was thinking about him all the time."[10]

The irony of this tragic fairy tale is that in reality Cicciolina was a match for Koons, and not the "human readymade" he imagined her to be. In the magic kingdom she inhabited she was never ever going to let him be king of the castle!

Meanwhile, the photos that started it all are as potent and as iconic as ever.

Cicciolina (or should I say, the iconography of Cicciolina, for I, like most, have never met her in the flesh) has a cosmology and a pagan poetry of its own. With a floral wreath in her peroxide blond hair, she is an orgy of one, a technicolor bacchanalia to outrival Caravaggio's drab chiaroscuro.[11]

With a Cobra snake up her butt she is the *Mother of Invention*.[12]

Her (and Koons') cameo appearance in U2's video "Even Better Than The Real Thing" illustrates the complexity and the plasticity of Staller's carefully sculpted re-imagined body as it conflates with the plastic image of Cicciolina's re-imagined persona. As the lyrics suggest, she is both the "Real Thing" and "Even Better Than The Real Thing" simultaneously.[13]

And yes, I know it is not so cool to reference U2, but this is how it happened: U2 and Cicciolina were contemporaries, and they *were* a match made in some ironic heaven. With that video U2 propelled themselves to a new level of super stardom—from a band known for "keeping it real" to a hyper-band "keeping it hyper-real."

---

10 Sischy, "Koons, High and Low."

11 I met Jeff Koons at the reception for his retrospective at the Stedelijk Museum in Amsterdam. It must have been the fall of 1992, as I went there with my first and only Dutch boyfriend, a relationship that lasted all of four months. We travelled cross-country by train. I wore hot black hot pants with cherry Doc Martens up to my knees, and Jeff autographed my arm with a Sharpie, which made me feel, briefly, voluptuous in a sculptural kind of way but also, that Cicciolina's position is not as far out as you may think.

12 A premonition:

> You're highbrow, holy
> With lots of soul melancholy shimmering
> Serpentine sleekness was always my weakness
> Like a simple tune
> But no dilettante filigree fancy beats the plastic you
> Career girl cover
> Exposed and another slips right into view
> Oh looking for love in a looking glass world
> Is pretty hard for you…

Roxy Music, "Mother of Pearl," *Stranded* (Polydor Records, 1973).

13 U2, "Even Better Than The Real Thing (Original Music Video)," 1992, *YouTube*, http://www.youtube.com/watch?v=Yrch66gdjjk (accessed 28 March, 2014).

Although on revision…at that moment in time – on the event horizon of the internet, on the brink of the oblivion that is the fate of everything happening before the invention of the world wide web – when we had only just started littering the virtual and not just the wild as hitherto…they all seem so frighteningly real: Bono in his vinyl-on-vinyl fetish-fashion pant suit combo, Prince before he became a symbol, MTV video jockey Simone Engelen in all her un-photo-shopped denim clad glory and Staller and Koons' wedding video with the voiceover asking, *"Is it art or is it pornography?"*

The answer is yes.

While Bono's lyrics beg to let him "slide down the surface of things and ride on the waves that you bring," the visuals of the video suggest that this superficiality has a powerful gravitational pull of something much deeper from which you will not escape unscathed. Much like the gravitational pull of Cicciolina on the eyes of the world.

Although she seems entirely new and artificial in all her trashy plastic glory, she is entirely of, and connected to this old world. She is for real. Like the giant *Pacific Trash Vortex* is for real, with a pull and a power of its own.[14]

To illustrate this power, consider Robert Sullivan's travelogue from an afternoon spent climbing the compacted trash of the garbage hills of New Jersey:

> There had been rain the night before, so it wasn't long before I found a little leachate seep, a black ooze trickling down the slope of the hill, an espresso of refuse. In a few hours, this stream would find its way into the…groundwater of the Meadowlands; it would mingle with toxic streams… But in this moment, here at its birth…this little seep was pure pollution, a pristine stew of oil and grease, of cyanide and arsenic, of cadmium, chromium, copper, lead, nickel, silver, mercury, and zinc. I touched this fluid – my fingertip was a bluish caramel color – and it was warm and fresh.[15]

The list of piled up ingredients lends the quote a poetic potency, and pulls the experience of the "pure pollution" out of its ethical conundrum and into the aesthetic realm of the "pristine." Layered like the sludge of the landfills it describes, the lan-

---

14 National Geographic, "Great Pacific Garbage Patch (Pacific Trash Vortex)", encyclopedic entry, *National Geographic Education*, http://education.nationalgeographic.com/education/encyclopedia/great-pacific-garbage-patch/ (accessed 1 May, 2014).

15 Robert Sullivan, *The Meadowlands: Wilderness Adventures on the Edge of a City* (New York: Random House, 1998), 96–97, quoted in Jane Bennett, *Vibrant Matter: A Political Ecology of Things* (Durham: Duke University Press, 2010), 6.

guage highlights the difference between archiving and composting that is at the heart of the matter, or rather – that *is* the throbbing heart of the inert matter that surrounds us. Where the archive is passive, the compost is active, and moves with an intrinsic agency, a power beyond our control.

In her book *Vibrant Matter* Jane Bennett relates Sullivan's account to her own encounter with a pile of debris in a storm drain, one morning in Baltimore:

> Sullivan reminds us that a vital materiality can never really be thrown 'away,' for it continues its activities even as a discarded or unwanted commodity. For Sullivan that day, as for me on that June morning, thing-power rose from a pile of trash. Not Flower Power, or Black Power, or Girl Power, but Thing Power: the curious ability of inanimate things to animate, to produce effects dramatic and subtle.[16]

In similarly dramatic and subtle ways, the Trash Vortex is not only out there in the Pacific Ocean – it swims within us.

Not only in the literal sense: that the plastic trash is ground down to minuscule plastic plankton, that enters the food chain when it is eaten by the small fish that are in turn eaten by the big fish, that are in turn eaten by the giant Yellowfin tuna, that is turned into Maki rolls that are in turn eaten by us – until we are plasticized from the inside out.

In every sense: our language, our literature, our poetry, our songwriting is pervaded by this ever present vibrant plasticity. As is this letter.

This may sound like sci-fi to you, but this is the sci-fi we live in now, and we might as well learn to ride on the waves that it brings, if we don't want to sink.

Artist Kembra Pfahler suggests this strategy for navigating the plastic sea, in an interview with the *New York Times*:

> I am an availablist, so I like just wandering about different neighborhoods looking around at how people are living, sort of like a minimalist extreme vacation. I like antinaturalism, finding beauty in odd urban decay, so there is plenty of that if that's your hobby.[17]

---

16 Jane Bennett, *Vibrant Matter: A Political Ecology of Things* (Durham: Duke University Press, 2010), 6.

17 Io Tillett Wright, "The Lowdown on Kembra Pfahler," *The New York Times*, 20 June, 2012, http://tmagazine.blogs.nytimes.com/2012/06/20/the-lowdown-kembra-pfahler/ (accessed 28 March, 2014).

When asked what she is working on right now, Pfahler replies:

> What's been at the forefront of my thoughts is 'Future Feminism.' I look around and wonder what I'm doing, what we are doing as artists in the year 2012. I ask myself, 'Am I a feminist? Am I a woman of independence and high esteem? Am I getting sucked into the system of despair that tries to brainwash women into thinking they are this or that?' I want to perpetuate a positive paradigm of visibility for women, despite what feels like backsliding and a sort of crass alternative greed – the greed that makes us isolate, and think about art careers instead of art.[18]

The *Future Feminism* she refers to is a movement she instigated together with musician Antony Hegarty, who describes it as follows:

> It's not a group that thinks women should just crawl towards economic equality in the way we have been engaged in since the '60s. That can't be the climax of feminism. It's like gay rights, as if gay marriage is the end point, as if we just want to be included in these business-as-usual institutions. That's not the point of being queer, just as mitigated reproductive rights aren't the point of being a woman. We want to move this forward. Do something great…overturn all these failed male structures of thinking, all this aggression in decision-making…[19]

There is a lot of power in these simple statements, a self-empowering license to take this vital matter into your own hands, a way of surfing the plastic wave instead of being sucked into the plastic maelstrom. And there is a lot of enlightenment to be found in the tip, rising like a giant Kundalini Cobra up the butt of consumer society.

Now, as your mother, I will absolutely not tell you to go and get a Cobra up your butt!

But I will say this to you:

I'm Sorry!

---

18 Wright, "The Lowdown on Kembra Pfahler."

19 Tim Adams, "Antony Hegarty: We Need More Oestrogen-Based Thinking," *The Guardian*, 19 May, 2012, http://www.guardian.co.uk/music/2012/may/20/antony-hegarty-interview-meltdown-gender (accessed 30 March, 2014).

I'm sorry to be handing down the world to you in such a sordid state. I don't like thinking about the giant Trash Vortex any more than you do, and yet I keep feeding it, because it is insatiable.

Like a washed out Koons retrospective it is filled with last year's consumer goods: vacuum cleaners, valentines, deflated inflatables, forgotten memorabilia, discarded trinkets, cuddly toys, and baby fleece blankets.

These are inanimate objects, but they are also compassionate objects. And they are passionate…[20]

If you tune in, you can hear them humming, like that old Kiss song:

> I was made for lovin' you baby
> You were made for lovin' me
> And I can't get enough of you baby
> Can you get enough of me?[21]

But we just can't get enough, because we can't separate ourselves from the world, any more than we can separate our desires from our objects of desire: we not only love the world, we are loved by it. We not only live in the world, we are lived by it. We not only move in the world, we are moved by it.

I hope that you can find your own way and your own beauty in it, as I do. Because it is awesome. Literally.[22]

And if you have to become plastic, to find your place in this plastic world, girl, don't go for the Barbie.

Go for *the Cicciolina*.

You go girl!

Love,

Mom

---

20 More on compassionate objects can be found in Elaine Scarry's book *The Body in Pain: The Making and Unmaking of the World* (Oxford: Oxford University Press, 1985).

21 Kiss, "I was Made for Lovin' You," *Dynasty* (Casablanca, 1979).

22 The Oxford online dictionary defines awesome as follows:

1. Extremely impressive or daunting; inspiring great admiration, apprehension, or fear: 'the awesome power of the atomic bomb.'
2. (informal) Extremely good; excellent: 'the band is truly awesome!'

http://www.oxforddictionaries.com/us/definition/american_english/awesome (accessed 28 March, 2014).

MOTHER of REVOLUTION

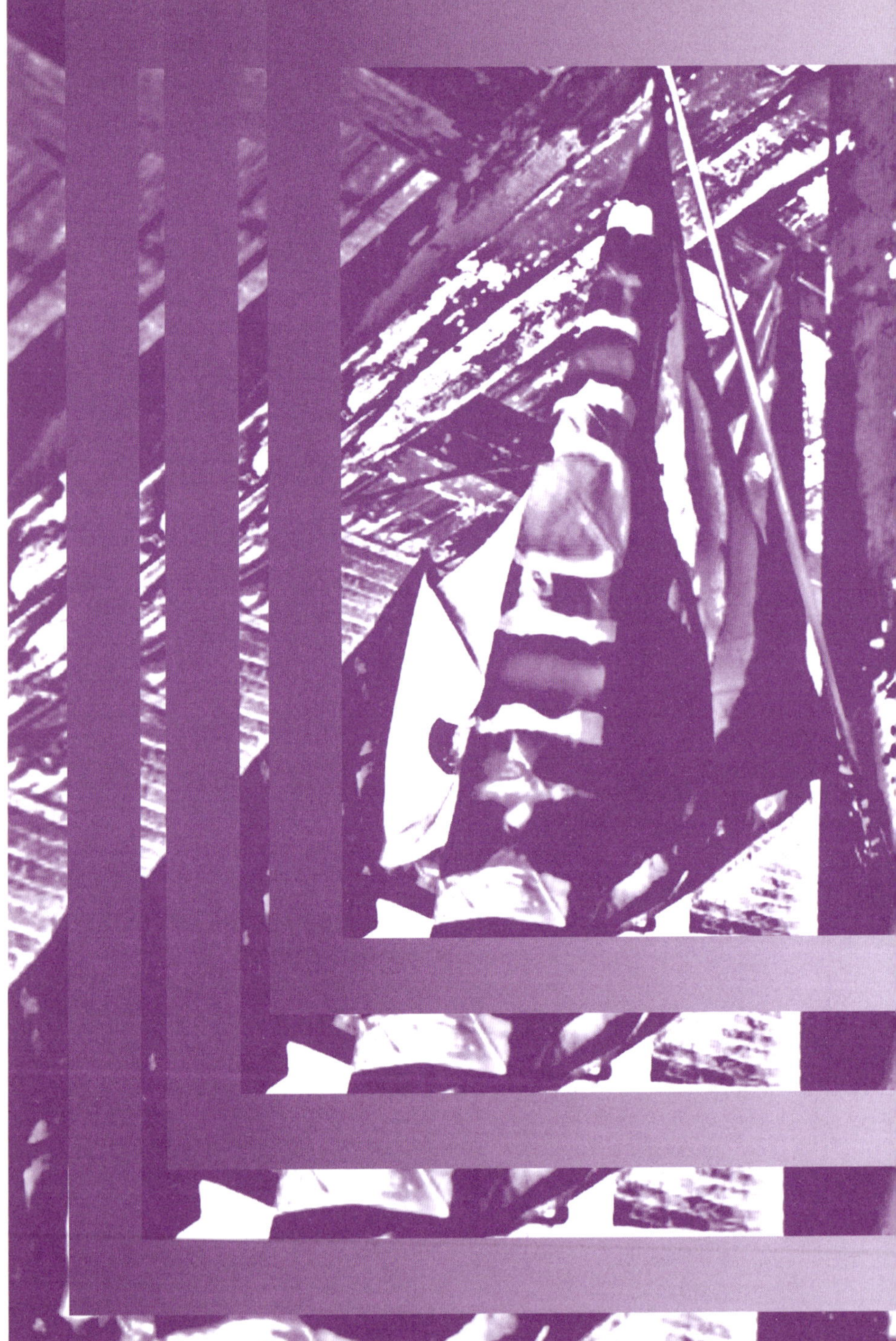

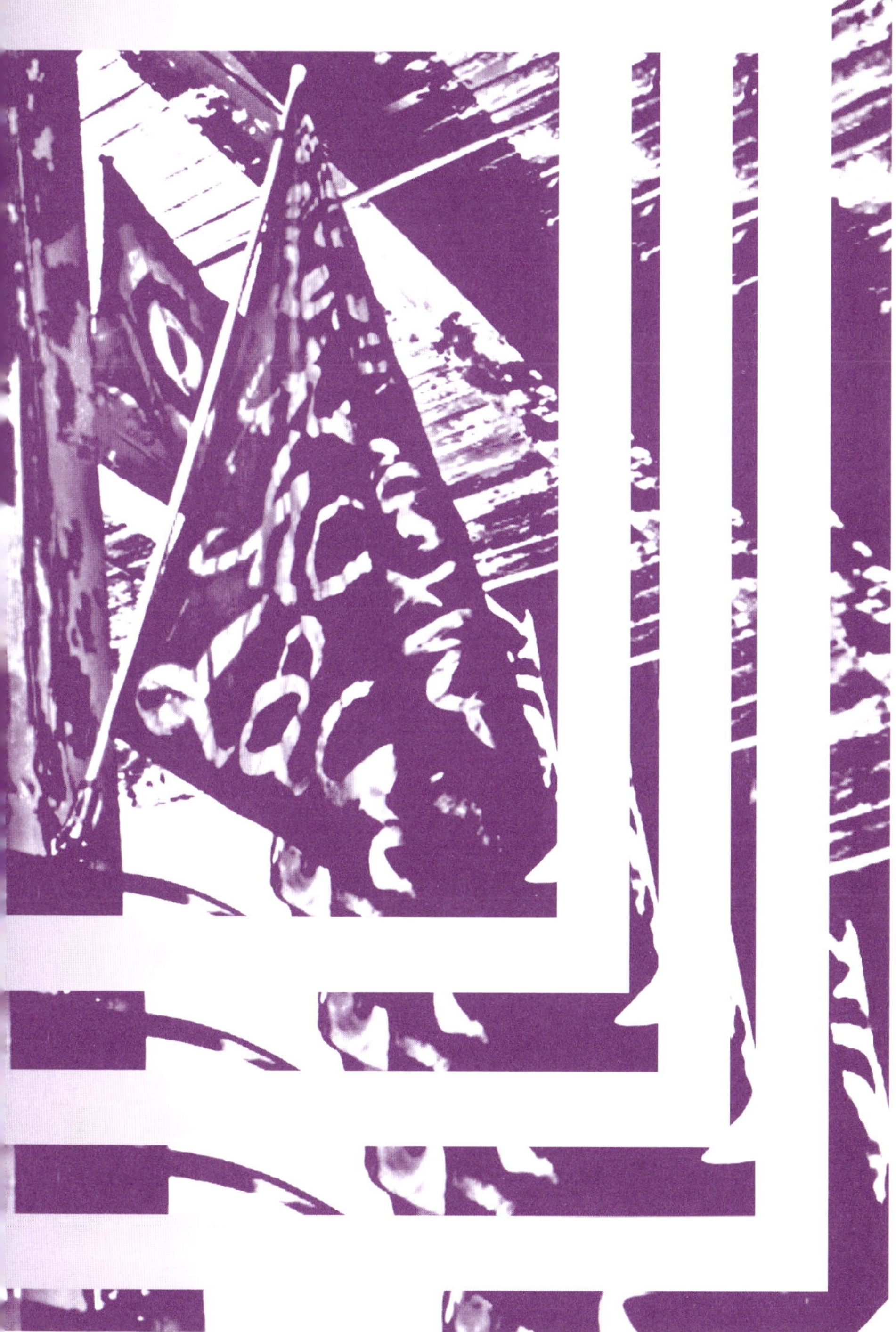

Dear,
Outside of the Museum of Contemporary Art, on the plaza, a great big neon sign spins around and around. Like a motel sign – from back in the day when motels actually had some kind of allure – only instead of "MOTEL" it reads "MOTHERS."

– Yes, like that, in motherfucking big, bold, luminous capitals!

> As the word 'MOTHERS' spins overhead, directly in front of the museum's main entrance, it becomes a glowing presence that is both celebratory and imposing. It had to be large [the artist] said, 'because mothers always have to be bigger than you are' and because 'it feels like mothers are the most important people in the world.'[1]

I visited the museum today, and I sat up on the top floor right by the windows in that little reading area, with the obligatory Mies van der Rohe Barcelona chairs, and some bookcases that look like they came from IKEA, but could almost pass as something from Design Within Reach.

In keeping with the theme of the exhibition on view – examining the role of the torn canvas as a signifier of the post traumatic stress of WWII – the shelves were filled with books about the traumatic birth of abstract expressionism. It was very macho – gut-wrenching, yet tasteful – but I enjoyed sitting there, resting for a minute, as it had started to snow outside and I was in no particular rush.

From this cozy comfort zone, I just couldn't take my eyes off that sign rotating, slowly, out there in the falling snow.

My head started spinning as I wondered:

Is this a MOTHER'S place according to the museum?

Out in the cold?

Up above the crowd?

Did they put us up there, just so we can't complain? To show us they actually care about MOTHERS, you know, the people in the museum?

---

1 Museum of Contemporary Art Chicago, "MCA Chicago Plaza Project: Martin Creed," *MCA Chicago*, August, 2012, http://www.mcachicago.org/exhibitions/now/2012/313 (accessed 28 March, 2014).

Through their glass facade they can see MOTHERS every day, out there in the real world.

Plenty of MOTHERS out there!

So why would we want MOTHERS *in* the museum? They already put us on a pedestal, to show how much they adore MOTHERS.

The word "MOTHERS" that is. The proverbial ones, not the actual ones.

The world revolves around "MOTHERS" as the word "MOTHERS" revolves on its pedestal, round and round. And round and round.

And as it revolves around and around—out there in the cold, on the museum plaza—the word evolves in my mind from a mantra to a curse: MOTHER, short for MOTHERFUCKER, which in turn becomes a sort of warning:

"There are some real MOTHERFUCKERS in here!" The museum seems to say.

Don't fuck with me!

I am not a MILF Motherfuckers! I'm a MOTHER yes, but not a proverbial one, a real one and as such I belong in the real world, but not in the real cold outside of the real museum!

So how does a MOTHER get bad enough to get inside of the museum? When are you a bad enough MOTHER?

Inside of the museum, there is a mad MOTHER on the loose. Her name is Niki. Darling Niki.[2]

Will you just look at the mess she made: Haphazardly arranged on an oblong wood panel a makeshift assemblage of various objects, among them a metal tractor seat, an axe, a shoe, and a toy gun are plastered together, as in literally plastered, covered in white plaster and then again drenched in rainbow colors pouring over the surface from a chicken wire contraption at the top end of the board where the piece was booby trapped with a battery of paint balloons, after which it was shot at with a .22 caliber rifle.

The seductive materiality combined with the shocking lusciousness of the color bleeding over the white plaster surface of her shooting paintings from the early 1960s, made them not only desirable haute commodities and art oddities—their creation also became social events for "the happy few", and well documented spectacles for the masses.

In Niki de Saint Phalle's universe, construction and destruction are conflated into one and the same action, and her revolver becomes the instrument of revolt and renaissance when the painting is *executed* in one big bang!

In her own words.

---

2 I wonder if Prince had Niki de Saint Phalle in mind when he wrote these lines:

She took me to her castle
and I just couldn't believe my eyes
She had so many devices
everything that money could buy

Prince and the Revolution, "Darling Nikki," *Purple Rain* (Warner Bros, 1983).

> I shot against men. All men. Big men, short men, my brother, fat men, society, my family, all men, daddy, I shot against myself, I shot against all men. I shot because it was fun, I shot for the extacy, I shot for the magik.[3]

Niki de Saint Phalle was born into Franco-American aristocracy. She married young to escape her philandering and incestuous father, and by twenty-one she was a mother as well as a celebrated photo model.

By twenty-two she was mad as hell and she was not gonna take it anymore!

Or, as she later explained: "Instead of becoming a terrorist, I became a terrorist in art!"[4]

After a nervous breakdown she decided to pursue her interest in painting. The body of work that she created on her lifelong path to recovery and, ultimately, death, oscillates between the pathetic and the revelatory, the therapeutic and the cathartic, the sublime and the kitsch.

Generously self-invested, mingling with the rich and famous, she grew from an avant-garde debutante into "the beauty who challenged the beast of male authority." She and her longtime companion and soulmate Tinguely were dubbed "The Bonnie and Clyde of the art world" and their explosive performance in the Nevada desert drew the biggest press corps the place had seen since underground nuclear tests at the same spot fifteen years earlier.[5]

Clad in a shooting uniform of her own design—a body-hugging futurist one-piece of the same vestal white as her soon to be deflowered canvases—footage from the time shows her finishing off her monumental works in front of an adoring high society crowd, including art world illuminati such as Robert Rauschenberg, Jasper Johns, and Ed Kienholz.[6]

Her Amazonian presence has a subversive beauty tinged with an undeniable flair for the fashionable—a *protest chic* that translates from the barricade to the dance floor—and her rebel yell is as eloquent as it is elegant:

> Ready! Take aim! Fire! Red, yellow, blue, the painting weeps, the painting is dead, I have killed the painting. It has been reborn. War with no victims![7]

---

3 1960geractuell, "Niki de Saint Phalle: Schiessbilder, 1961," *YouTube*, http://www.youtube.com/watch?v=jlP5xn0gyDk (accessed 2 April, 2014).

4 1960geractuell, "Niki de Saint Phalle: Schiessbilder, 1961."

5 I am not sure of the origin of the moniker "the Bonnie and Clyde of the art world," but among others it was used as the title for a film about the couple.

Niki de Saint Phalle and Jean Tinguely: The Bonnie and Clyde of Art, dir. Louise Faure and Anne Julien, 55 min., Dietrich Rodolphe for Zorn Production International (France, 2010).

6 1960geractuell, "Niki de Saint Phalle: Schiessbilder, 1961."

7 1960geractuell, "Niki de Saint Phalle: Schiessbilder, 1961."

Her early work is rife with these metaphors of (re)birth, with herself at the center as a destructive life-giver, collapsing the good and the bad mother into a good-enough-bad-enough-mother-of-a-mother.

But even for all her talk of births and rebirths, it wasn't until a few years later that Niki de Saint Phalle really took MOTHER to the MUSEUM.

Following the shooting paintings she began to explore various female archetypes, a period that culminated in a series of NANAs—voluptuous figures decorated with graphic patterns in a crass Crayola palette.

In 1966 she was invited to build a monumental sculpture, for the Moderna Museet in Stockholm, and she went to town: "I was going to build the greatest NANA of all, a great pagan goddess."[8]

But, instead of putting this goddess upon a pedestal, she laid her on her back!

Her pregnant belly protruded like a dome into the sky, her legs spread wide, displaying a giant cunt, opening up like a portal to the great unknown.

Niki de Saint Phalle continues:

> She was like a grand fertility goddess, receiving, absorbing, devouring, 100,000 visitors comfortably in her generosity and immensity. She was the greatest whore in the world![9]

Her name was *HON*, which means "she" in Swedish, and the rising birthrates in Stockholm that year were attributed to her.[10]

Unfortunately, I never saw *HON* as she was destroyed at the show's conclusion three months later, after a full and happy life.[11]

No, I didn't see *HON*, but I saw her little sister—although fashioned years later, by another artist, she was clearly related to Niki de Saint Phalle's hysterical vision—so let's call her *HUN*, as that means "she" in Danish:

---

8 André Blas: "Niki de Saint Phalle: Introspections and reflections," dir. André Blas, 35 min, *Vimeo*, 2003, http://vimeo.com/35057914 (accessed 28 April, 2014).

9 Blas, "Niki de Saint Phalle: Introspections and reflections."

10 Blas, "Niki de Saint Phalle: Introspections and reflections."

11 Niki de Saint Phalle's sculptural work, the NANAS and later *The Tarot Garden*, a megalomaniac sculpture park she completed toward the end of her life, and in part sponsored by launching her own perfume, is often interpreted as an invitation into play and childhood, but also as an invitation to encounter our greatest fears, and through these encounters, to find ourselves.

She tells about the creation of *The Tarot Garden*:

> I lived for years inside the protective mother. If I had not concretitisised [sic] my own dreams into sculpture, I might have become possessed by them, a victim of my own vision.

Blas, "Niki de Saint Phalle: Introspections and reflections."

The year was 1979, the international year of the child, and the mood was such it seemed logical that after liberating women, children would be next, and then we would liberate the men from the burden of their original patriarchal sin, and *then* we would ALL BE FREE!

(Yes, we can laugh about it now, but at the time it was awesome!)

But you have to start somewhere, so *we* started in the garden: we fenced off the plum tree at the bottom of it, and quixotically declared that in this area we would not mow the lawn, because the grass was allowed to "grow free" and no adults were allowed in unless granted permission.

In order to fully occupy our newly liberated territory, we decided we needed a cabin and a tree hut. Pragmatically, we now granted our dad, the patriarch, permission to come in and build us both, using repurposed wood from our old kitchen cabinets. The tree hut was really more of a viewing post – a platform up in the branches – from where we could survey the whole garden. In the ramshackle cabin we held our meetings and fabricated our own candles by melting down and recycling the burned down stubs of wax our parents would otherwise throw away. The fruits of our labor usually ended up in some shade of mauve, as purple, rust, and off-white candles were in that year.[12]

Most importantly, the candlelit cabin was where my best friend and I, both nine, together with our six-year-old sisters, recorded the aptly named *Sister Songs* on my battery-operated tape deck. Our songs were heavily influenced by the progressive *kid's rock* and *agit-pop* we were listening to at the time. They were also concerned with the same themes: injustice and liberation.

In tune with our new ideal of children's liberation, our words and actions were also inspired by our visit to the Louisiana Museum of Modern Art in Humlebæk, north of Copenhagen, where we and everyone we knew, went to see the "equally grandly conceived and equally flip 'Children are a People.'"[13]

In the fall of 1978, the exhibition had attracted an audience of more than 160,000 people – adults and children alike – with a vision that was as simple as it was profound; real art by real artists for real children!

Its highlights included a grass clad Volkswagen Beetle and a "flying contraption" – mounted high up under the ceiling and acces-

---

12 Could this be true? Did we really have our own bonfire at the bottom of our parents' garden? They were probably roaming close by with fire extinguishers on the ready, but that is not how it felt. It felt – and this may sound simultaneously radical and *laissez-faire* to contemporary ears – like they had some trust in us. Moreover, it felt like they had some trust in the world, and thus it was OK for us to roam in it. Within the freedom they granted it felt as if we owned the world – or at least our little corner of it. Perhaps we need a return to that *laissez-faire* parenting in order to let our kids become more self-possessed – instead of more *laissez-faire* economy, which just makes our children, and all the rest of us, more self-obsessed.

13 Pernille Stensgaard, *When Louisiana Stole the Picture*, trans. John Kendal (Copenhagen: Gyldendal, 2008), 195.

sible via a spindly wooden ladder, it consisted of a wooden plank with a sheepskin saddle and a pair of lever-operated taxidermy goose wings. What I remember most vividly, however, was a giant MOTHER – a pink papier-mâché torso lined with a polyurethane uterus. You could crawl inside and imagine being back in the womb.

The caption plastered across her plexiglass belly read: "Please take off your shoes." Unfortunately, by the time my family visited the exhibition, too many children had failed to heed to this advice and my sister and I were no longer invited to experience this amazing work as it was intended – from the inside.

Despite that disappointment, I still remember the preteen hype that had preempted our visit as the rumor spread like wildfire through the schoolyards of Copenhagen: "There is a MOTHER in the MUSEUM!"[14]

Disregarding the assumption that children don't "get" art – and therefore are not taken seriously as critical cultural producers – and given that she clearly has appeal to audiences of all ages – why is there still so little space for MOTHER in the contemporary art MUSEUM?

Perhaps the clue to this question is in another question, provocatively framed by Susan Suleiman: "What happens to the avant-garde when the mother laughs?"[15]

I think I actually have an answer to that question, and I will tell you, but first let me tell you about this image:

In 1982 Robert Mapplethorpe took a picture of Louise Bourgeois holding a big dick.

Bourgeois was 71 at the time, and she easily looks it. In fact, she looks ancient – like an *oer-mother* from the dawn of time.

The phallus tucked under her arm – like a baguette or an oversized evening clutch – is her own latex and plaster sculpture from 1968, *Filette*, meaning "little girl." It does not look anything like a little girl; it looks like a giant penis, but I guess she had her reasons.

Two enormous balls protrude from behind her right elbow and from here your gaze glides along the shaft, under her afghan fur clad arm toward the dickhead. Strangely, it is not the object itself that is obscene, but rather the way her hand gently squeezes it right below the glans as if pulling back its foreskin – a gesture that feels masturbatory while also referring to that thing men do better: standup peeing.

---

14 Unfortunately, apart from a single uncredited and untitled photo, I have not been able to find much information on this now anonymous HUN. The leads I do have, scans of photos and articles from the museums archives – including a vintage issue of *Louisiana Revy* dedicated to the exhibition – indicate that she was part of a larger "show within the show," called *Fata Morgana*, initiated by the artist Susanne Ussing and executed by a feminist art collective.

Sources: Facsimile of *Louisiana Revy August/October 1978* and Pernille Stensgaard, *When Louisiana Stole the Picture*.

15 Susan Suleiman, "Playing and Motherhood: or, How to Get the Most of the Avant-Garde," in *Representations of Motherhood*, ed. Donna Bassin, Margaret Honey, and Meryle Mahrer (New Haven: Yale University Press, 1994), quoted in Mignon Nixon, "Bad Enough Mother," in *OCTOBER, The Second Decade, 1986-1996* (Cambridge: MIT Press, 1997), 170.

So, in that sense her body language is territorial: *Don't fuck with this MOTHER!*

But it gets better: the *coup de grâce* of the image is the mischievous grin on the wrinkled face of that untamable shrew.

As Mignon Nixon describes it:

> In Mapplethorpe's photograph, Bourgeois made herself the very image of the bad enough mother: the mother who grins at the patriarchal overvaluation of the phallus, who parodies the metonymy of infant and penis, and in whose hand the phallus becomes penis, or in other words slips from its status as privileged signifier to become one more object of aggression and desire.[16]

Yes, Nixon is right, Bourgeois *is* a bad enough MOTHER, but in Mapplethorpe's photograph the old hag is also a laughing Medusa, shrugging it off like Cixous:

> Too bad for them if they fall apart upon discovering that women aren't men, or that the mother doesn't have one. But isn't this fear convenient for them? Wouldn't the worst be, isn't the worst, in truth, that women aren't castrated, that they have only to stop listening to the Sirens (for the Sirens were men) for history to change its meaning? You only have to look at the Medusa straight on to see her. And she's not deadly. She's beautiful and she's laughing.[17]

Yes, this old Medusa is beautiful when she is laughing!

It becomes her.

And I think this is the answer to our question: *What happens to the avant-garde when the mother laughs?*

It becomes her!

Love,

Mom

P.S. Writing this I burned the spaghetti. How the fuck did I burn the spaghetti? What kind of mother does that?

---

16 Mignon Nixon, "Bad Enough Mother," in *OCTOBER, The Second Decade, 1986–1996* (Cambridge: MIT Press, 1997), 171.

17 Hélène Cixous, "The Laugh of the Medusa," *Signs*, Volume 1, No.4 (Chicago: University of Chicago Press, 1976), 885.

MOTHER of REDEMPTION

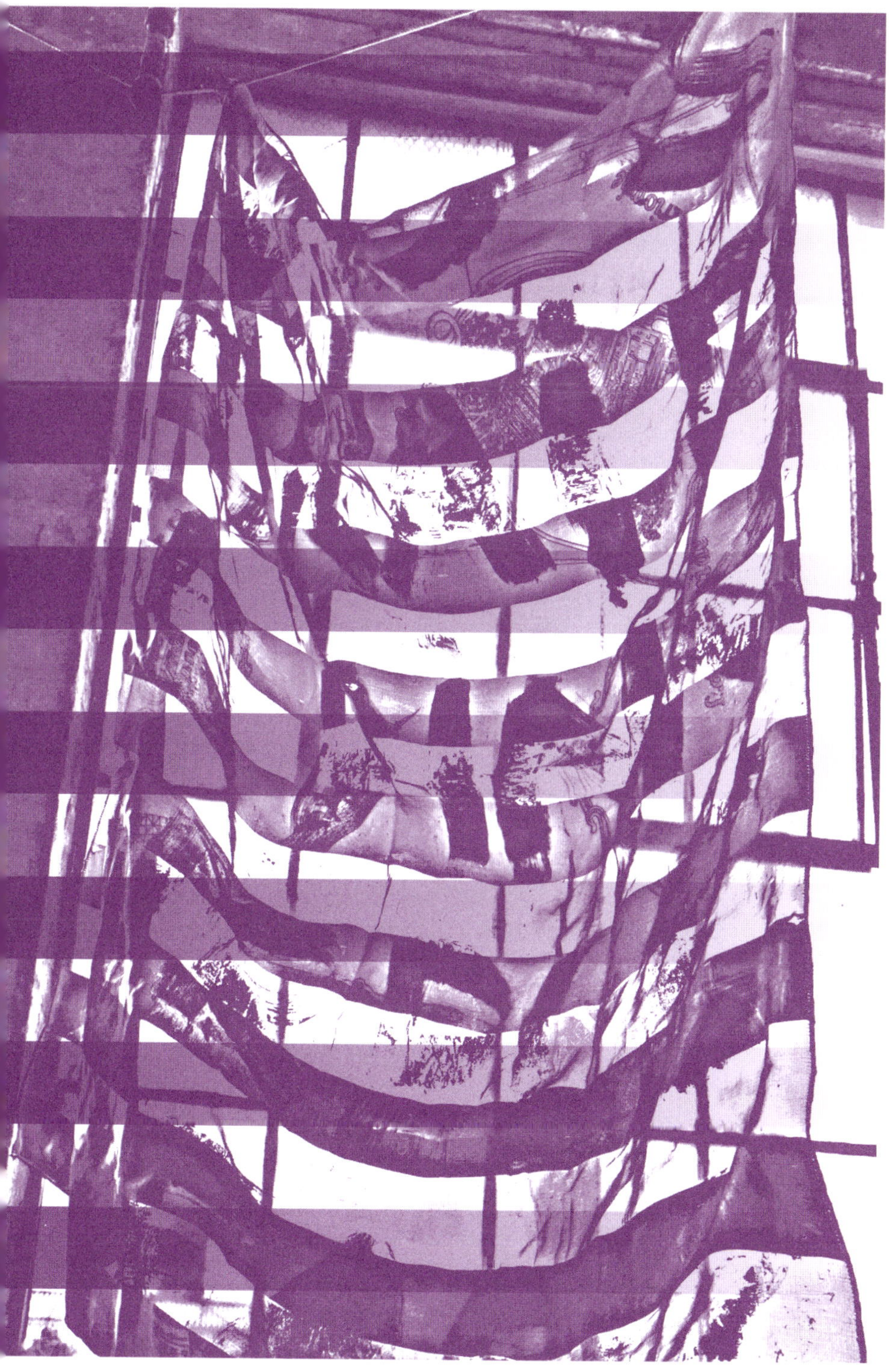

Hey Sis,
It's been a while since we've been writing letters to each other. Nobody seems to write them any more, or at least we don't. Not since we've become mothers. So let me write you a letter from one mother to another.

Of course you are not only a mother, you are also an academic, a scholar – like I aspire to be – so I will also write you a letter, unapologetically, from one scholar to another. Because luckily, as women we do not need to apologize for our academic ambition – not anymore!

I was just thinking of you again, back in the day, back in the garden and back in the cabin where we wrote our *Sister Songs*. Although nobody seems to be doing that anymore – nobody calls themselves *Sisters*, and nobody sings *Sister Songs* anymore. Still, I want to write you a letter from one sister to another: to write you a letter in the name of sister solidarity, which is another one of those things nobody needs or wants, (or dares to want) anymore.

Do you remember when I mentioned wanting to write about all this? I was trying to formulate a wish, along some vague lines of wishing to hand the feminist legacy that we have been handed by our (fore)mothers, over to my daughter.

You firmly and quickly pulled me out of the wishy-washy. In an email you sent me in response to my wishing-out loud, you wrote:

> Is feminist heritage a strict mother-daughter thing? Am I excluded from, or some sort of second grade citizen in the sisterhood, since I have no daughter? Is my lineage broken because my body produced boys not girls? What about my granddaughters, if I have any, can I pass my female heritage on to them, or do they belong 'more' to their maternal family, as used to be the case in the classic patriarchy? As I feel strongly about the legacy that was passed on to me, and still see feminism as a badge of honor, I am enraged by such a notion.
>
> Is it not important that we hand the feminist legacy down to our sons (and to the sons and daughters of the world whose mothers were not included in the emancipation that we and our foremothers have experienced), for their sake and for our daughters'

> sake? And could this perhaps be part of today's feminist legacy – that gender equality goes both ways, and that whilst we still have a lot of battles to battle to obtain equal rights and equal treatment, we also have to be ready to share the privileges that have been exclusive to women. Turning our sons into losers would be a sad victory.[1]

You have a point. Not in the least because our sons are as dear to us as our daughters. Yet, there is a specific female experience bound in great part to the female body that must be addressed, that we must not gloss over, that we need to own in order to share it, to get over it or to give it away, now. More so because that female specificity is so often defined by "lack" or "loss."

In our daily lives, in practice, but also in theory and in discourse – so in this letter I'll have a go at gendering that theoretical discourse. Although many female and feminist thinkers out there talk about gender, an overwhelming part of the conversation revolves around gender-as-performance. As though to suggest that if we could only stop *performing our femininity* and get over ourselves, behave ourselves, we could be "gender-neutral" – reasonable and not hysterical. But I don't want this letter just to be about gender-as-performance, but also, most importantly, what I will call *the gendered re-embodying of the interiority*.

While the theory of interiority is supposedly gender-neutral in praxis this "genderless" void is male by default, as most of the theoretical, philosophical, and psychological discourse about it is written by a chorus of male scholarly voices. It is into this chorus I want to bring my own female voice and experience, and I want to share it with you.

Specifically, I want to share some of my thoughts on how archives of female experience, psychological *and* physical, can be inserted into (and thereby expand) a discourse on the desired normalcy of the female.

But, before we get too theoretical, let's see how these archives could look in real life. Better yet, let's share the experience, let's participate – let's go get ourselves photographed by *Kussomaten*!

Kussomaten is a traveling photo booth, designed for women to take anonymous snapshots of their genitalia. Its cozy interior is somewhat reminiscent of a Victorian water closet: a comfy wooden chair with a U-shaped hole cut out of the seat is placed above a floor-mounted camera. The simple instructions that are printed out and mounted in the gilded, golden frame above the "throne," read as follows:

1 Rikke Baggesen, email correspondence with the author, 21 September, 2012.

> Wipe down the seat with the sanitizer provided.
> Pull down your pants/pull up your skirt.
> Sit back as far as you can on the seat.
> Check that your clothing is not covering the lens of the camera.
> Spread your legs as far as you can.
> Smile and take a picture.

I was a bit puzzled by this last instruction, until you reminded me that the word *labia* really means *lip–like, duh!*

I imagine our smiling genitalia would look like *Laughing Medusas* boldly asserting:

> they riveted us between two horrifying myths: between the Medusa and the abyss. That would be enough to set half the world laughing, except it's still going on. For the phallocentric sublation is with us, and it's militant, regenerating the old patterns, anchored in the dogma of castration. They haven't changed a thing: they've theorized their desire for reality! Let the priests tremble, we are going to show them our sexts![2]

Let half the world laugh and the other half tremble–the backstory that prompted *Kussomaten*, is otherwise serious enough: when the team behind *kvinde kend din krop*, a classic which every self-respecting Danish woman has in her book collection, started researching for their revised 2013 edition they surfed the internet for usable photographs of female genitalia. To their dismay, they didn't find any![3]

They initiated their photo booth archive out of the following considerations:

> Way too many of the photos of female genitalia, that can be found on the internet, are pornographic. The pornographic pussy lives up to certain, specific ideals: it is totally symmetrical, with ultra-small labia–and of course it is hairless.
>
> Many women think that they look wrong in this region, if they don't live up to the porno ideal. We would like to change that! We would like to build a collection of photographs, which show the multitude of pussies. They can be symmetrical, asymmetrical,

2 Cixous, "The Laugh of the Medusa," 885.

3 Various authors, *Kvinde Kend Din Krop – En Håndbog*, 5th ed. (Copenhagen: Tiderne Skifter, 2013).

Kvinde Kend Din Krop is the Danish equivalent to the American *Our Bodies Ourselves* (1970). Its first edition from 1975 is one of the bestselling Danish books ever. 2013 saw the release of its fifth, thoroughly revised, edition.

> have large or small labia and of course they can have varying covering of hair.[4]

Since its debut on International Women's Day March 8th, in 2011 at the Goethe Institute in Copenhagen, *Kussomaten* has toured various cultural, social, and medical venues in Denmark, including a provincial old people's home, a student club at the medical faculty of the University of Copenhagen, the Women's Museum in Aarhus, and the Roskilde Festival.[5]

In the media storm that followed (naturally), the group behind *Kussomaten* have kept their cool, maintaining that – whatever other impulse may prompt viewers to take a look at the pictures – the purpose of the archive is informative, providing a database of what a "normal" cunt looks like, and guess what: "happiness is knowing what is normal, and the normal has wide boundaries."[6]

Every time a new photo is added to the database (which counted 158 contributions on the opening night), the boundaries of normalcy are widened accordingly – nobody is turned down, nobody is edited out.

Gazing over the full, frontal *nakedness* of hundreds of vulvae in *Kussomaten*'s online gallery is an unusual experience – you may want to avert your eyes, but the female genitalia on the screen remain unflinchingly present and undeniably *normal*.

Unsurprisingly, the main point of critique of these images is not that they are morally offensive (after all, in 21st century Denmark, admitting to be morally offended would be to admit defeat). No, instead the images were accused of being…unappetizing!

Now, this is where I want to drop my pants in gratitude!

Although the above response was written on a respectable debate website, and by a sympathetic enough gentleman who claims to "love pussy," he is still reaffirming the dogma: a vulva's sole *raison d'être* is to be just that. Appetizing. By extorting this reaction, *Kussomaten* has succeeded in validating its own existence; namely to provide an alternative to the pornographic image that is the prevailing, if not exclusive, image of female genitalia on the internet today.

Moreover, with its participatory nature, *Kussomaten* has framed the discourse on "normalcy" in a multilateral way.

In *The Body and the Archive* Allan Sekula writes:

> Michel Foucault has argued, quite crucially, that it is a mistake to describe the new regulatory sciences directed at the body in the early nineteenth century

4 *Kvinde Kend Din Krop*, http://kvindekenddinkrop.dk/ (accessed 27 March, 2014).

5 Denmark's biggest music festival.

6 I am quoting the slogan of Danish sexologists and sex-education pioneers Anne and Steen Hegeler, whose sex advice column ran weekly in *Ekstra Bladet* (a major Danish tabloid paper) through the '60s and '70s.

> as exercises in a wholly negative, repressive power. Rather, social power operates by virtue of a positive therapeutic or reformative channeling of the body.[7]

Unlike Sekula's examples—the convicted criminals of Bertillon's photographic police records or Galton's ethnic specimens that made up his composite portraits of racial characteristics—the women who contribute to *Kussomaten's* digital archive do so on a fully voluntary basis. But moreover: by participating in the archive they are also defining it and its definition of normalcy. In contrast to Bertillon's and Galton's archives, normalcy is thus not defined and contained from outside, nor subsequently proposed to be preserved, either by quarantine of unwanted elements after their deviation (Bertillon), or by selective breeding to avoid future deviations (Galton). Nor is it an attempt to typecast the "average pussy" via the social mathematics of Quetelet, whose composite character "the average man" was introduced in his 1835 treatise *Sur l'homme*. In it he argues that large aggregates of social data reveal a regularity that can only be taken as evidence of determinate social laws.

In Sekula's words, "this regularity had political and moral as well as epistemological implications." He quotes Quetelet saying:

> The greater the number of individuals observed, the more do individual peculiarities, whether physical or moral, become effaced, and leave in a prominent point of view the general facts, by virtue of which society exists and is preserved.[8]

By refusing to efface individual peculiarities but choosing to emphasize or, in perhaps an antiquated feminist lingo, to *embrace* the differences, *Kussomaten* demonstrates that the normal indeed has wide and flexible boundaries.

In doing so, it approximates the shaping of discourse described by Foucault in *The Archeology of Discourse*:

> Behind the visible façade of the system, one posits the rich uncertainty of disorder; and beneath the thin surface of discourse, the whole mass of a largely silent development (*devenir*): a 'pre-systematic' that is not of the order of the system; a 'pre-discursive' that belongs to an essential silence. Discourse and system produce each other—and conjointly—only at the crest of this immense reserve. What are being analyzed here are

7 Allan Sekula, "The Body and the Archive," *October*, 39 (Cambridge: MIT Press, 1986), 7.

8 Adolphe Quetelet, *A Treatise of Man and the Development of His Faculties*, trans R. Knox (Edinbourgh: Chambers, 1842), 96, as quoted in Sekula, "The Body and The Archive," 6.

> certainly not the terminal states of discourse, they are the 'pre-terminal regularities' in relation to which the ultimate state, far from constituting the birthplace of a system, is defined by its variants.[9]

In a similar way, *Kussomaten's* archive, in its ultimate state, is defined by its variants. Yet this archive also uncovers and addresses the *pre-discursive silence* in its genderedness.

In what can best be described as *philosophy in motion*, in a recent lecture Mika Hannula illustrated how the reflective creative self situates *itself* in the crux between art and life known as practice, arguing how spatial and social imagination make and shape the act of giving content to a localized concept.[10]

As he points out in his essay "Teaching Discourse":

> Discourses are not sitting on a shelf, they are actualized and situated. This implies our responsibility to participate. Rather than seek to pin down and conquer them, the task is to find ways to take part in the shaping and making of these discourses. It is not about having it right, but about getting into the groove.[11]

Following that logic, *Kussomaten* employs the participatory responsibility by inviting its users (on both sides of the lens) to get into the groove and participate in the making and shaping of discourse about the desired "normativity" of the female body(parts).

I am using the gender-neutral term "users" here, because while the photo project collects snapshots of female genitalia only, *Kussomaten* is not a project made by women for women, but *by women for everybody*—because the discourse it provokes is shaped by men and women alike and as such both groups are its audience.

(So not only our daughters, but also our sons, our fathers, mothers, grandparents, lovers, and their lovers. Everybody is invited to (re)view the collective's body of evidence.)

Kussomaten was never intended as an art project, and I suspect its initiators would prefer for it to operate outside the framework of contemporary art. Nevertheless, I argue that *Kussomaten* successfully implements social practice strategies through its participatory, reflective nature and opens itself up to be interpreted as a successful example of social sculpture within the realm of relational aesthetics.

---

9 Michel Foucault, *The Archeology of Knowledge And The Discourse on Language* (New York: Tavistock Publications Limited, 1972), 76.

10 Mika Hannula, "Mind Mapping: School of the Art Institute of Chicago," *Vimeo*, http://vimeo.com/channels/522660/66763409 (accessed 28 March, 2014).

11 Mika Hannula, "Teaching Discourse (Reflection Strong, Not Theory Light)," in *Learning Mind: Experience into Art*, ed. Mary Jane Jacob & Jacquelynn Baas (Oakland: University Of California Press, 2010), 107.

In this context the term social sculpture should be interpreted quite literally, as *Kussomaten* aims to shape the social field into a collective broad-mindedness and a more accepting (self)image of the women who inhabit it. Through its inclusiveness, *Kussomaten* channels what Sekula described as "social power operat[ing] by virtue of a positive therapeutic or reformative channeling of the body," and challenges our narrow definitions of the female body's desirable normalcy.

In other words: *Kussomaten's* particular way of giving content (photographs) to a localized concept (the normal female body) sparks the social imagination and provokes us to reconsider the in- and exclusiveness of its definitions.

To return to Foucault for a moment, I am reminded of this interview with Stephen Riggins, in which Foucault states:

> I am not interested in the academic status of what I am doing because my problem is my own transformation… This transformation of one's self by one's knowledge, one's practice is, I think, something rather close to the aesthetic experience. Why should a painter work if he is not transformed by his own painting?[12]

As we transform the archive of *Kussomaten* by adding our own snapshot, we not only help define and broaden the definition of "normalcy" to the outside world, but also toward ourselves.

The transgression of baring your privates in public is counterbalanced by the project's anonymity making the line you cross not one between the private and the public, but between the private and the *social* domains: thus the project invites a transgressive movement from an exclusive position toward an inclusive, collective awareness.

I could well imagine this move to be more transformative for some than others, but I feel that we would all be transformed by declaring:

"I am normal, and don't I know it!"

Such knowing ownership of your own body and its specific gendered interiority – not as spectacle but as experience(d) – is also the theme of *If 6 was 9* by Eija-Liisa Ahtila, which she herself describes as follows:

> *If 6 was 9* is a video installation and short film about teenage girls and sexuality. It is based on research and real events, but the story itself and the dialogues are a fictional combination of various elements.[13]

---

12 Michel Foucault, "An interview by Stephen Riggins," in *Ethics: Subjectivity and Truth. The Essential Works of Michel Foucault, 1954–1984*, Volume One, ed. J. Faubion, trans. Robert Hurley (Middlesex: Penguin, Allen Lane, 1997), 131.

13 Eija-Liisa Ahtila, *Fantasized Persons and Taped Conversations* (Helsinki: Kiasma Museum of Contemporary Art and Tate London, 2002), 60.

As a group portrait the work is therefore not "socio-realistic," but rather a composite-image (much like Galton's) of a demographic group or a generation of girls or women: an archive of female voices, partaking in a gendered discourse.

Consider this monologue delivered by "Elsa":

> Here I sit with my legs apart, like a little girl who hasn't learned anything about sex, who has no idea that a woman must hide her private parts and lust. In fact I'm 38 years old, I have a woman's breast and labia that opens beautifully when aroused, and a very feminine way to disguise aggression.[14]

In the video, Elsa blends in effortlessly with young girls less than half her age. Her blonde bobbed hair, her white button-down shirt and her short dress, reminiscent of a school uniform, are in tune with the piano prodigy she once was – but oddly dissonant with the vulgar directness with which she vents her frustration at the male dominance she faced as a grown-up:

> I ended up playing the piano and I was damn good at it. But I wasn't satisfied. My man left me when I wanted more sex. I wanted full pay for my work and the same recognition, which pushes men forward. I wanted all sorts of things. There was no end to it. They told me to be nice and that you have to earn it. But I had lost my belief. I thought high-school was over – and both in bed and in life I can get top grades just by doing things that are important to me.[15]

Upon viewing and reviewing the piece several times, Elsa has come to stand out to me as the main protagonist. There is an obvious point of identification, given my own advanced age, but let us not forget that this piece was made in 1996, when Ahtila herself was in fact thirty-six years old. And, I think that through revealing her age, Elsa also hands us the key to the title *If 6 was 9*.

If we examine the dialogue more closely – the consistent use of the past tense and the tone, which is almost reminiscing – it sounds like these voices are carrying across a generational divide.

---

14 The quotes from "Elsa," as well as from "Anne" and "Tiina" in the following are excerpts from the dialogue from Eija-Liisa Ahtila's video work *If 6 was 9*, as transcribed in Eija-Liisa Ahtila, *Fantasized Persons and Taped Conversations*, 70–71.

15 Ahtila, *Fantasized Persons and Taped Conversations*, 70–71.

Listen, for instance, to "Anne's" sexual adventures:

> Guys thought I was a God's gift to them. Everybody wanted to be with me. Shy ones came to me stammering, trying to say something. Losers just stared and blushed as I noticed them. Older guys wanted me to notice their new bike or car. Even if they were with other girls, they stared at me behind their backs. I'm not boasting. That's just how it was. That's why girls didn't like me much. Flat-breasted bookworms wondered if I had too big a mouth – and artificial lashes… Tough girls called me a whore. And sapling feminists thought I was just stupid. Really?[16]

Really? Well, really, I could imagine a teenage girl *doing* the things described here, but recollecting them and summarizing them in this manner seems odd for somebody who is at the *beginning* of her sexual career. I mean, really, how many teens would describe their contemporaries as "flat-breasted bookworms" and "sapling feminists?" Really?

It occurred to me that perhaps the characters in Ahtila's *Kammerspiel* are in fact *mutton dressed as lamb*, old women's voices disguised as young girls, because even more unpalatable than the young girl's desire, is the mature woman's lust.

(If we pause for a second to consider the pornographic pussy as described by the initiators of *Kussomaten* earlier in this letter, it is in fact a description of a sexually immature young girl's hairless labia – an infantilized ideal.)

As Ahtila explains:

> [*If 6 was 9*] shows an ongoing metamorphosis from childhood to adulthood. The girls want to possess, to embrace it with their arms, legs, cheeks, tits and arses. Their hopes, memories and thoughts, and events in their lives form a non-chronological narrative fabric, and the installation space becomes a 'body' of separate parts, each moving at a different pace and rhythm.[17]

In a sequence toward the end of the video, "Tiina" (whose voiceover describes the twenty-four best places in Helsinki to make love outdoors) is making collages. Using a pair of scissors, she cuts up porno magazines, which have been a reference to sexual maturity throughout the video – collaging the dismembered body-parts so as to cover up black and white portraits of innocent-looking young girls.

---

16 Ahtila, *Fantasized Persons and Taped Conversations*, 70–71.

17 Ahtila, *Fantasized Persons and Taped Conversations*, 60.

Her actions seem to hint – perhaps in contrast to what we are led to believe by her words – that the teens in the story are not *revealing* anything with their confessions, but rather *covering*.

The portraits used are in fact the casting portraits Eija-Liisa Ahtila made of the young girls featured in the video, as a preparation for the work, yet here she reduces them to props.[18]

The sequence administers an elegant formal layering: through the collage work within the video frame, a model of the work is literally inserted within the work by reference to the "body of separate parts" from her description of the work. Likewise, by introducing her casting portraits into the work, she underscores its non-chronology and its intricate layers of fact and fiction.

Eija-Liisa Ahtila's "non-chronological ongoing narrative fabric" lets the dialogue flow both ways across the generational divide – allowing the girl and the woman, the face and the voice, behold and mirror each other, reflecting the very *normal* desire they both share. There is a mutual fascination amidst the reversal of roles, between the promiscuous teenage girl – so often perceived as easy sexual *prey* – and the mature woman deserted by her husband for being sexually *predatory*: if you tried walking in my shoes. If I were you. If you were me. If 6 was 9.

As Cixous said to Foucault of Marguerite Duras:

> she is fascinated, she is absolutely caught up by something – or in someone – so absolutely enigmatic that all else in the world just falls away.[…]But what fascinates her, as we gradually discover – and, I think, she herself discovers, has us discover – is a mixture of eroticism bound up with female flesh (it really functions through what can be so overwhelming and beautiful in something indefinable in woman) and death. […] As if death enveloped life, beauty, with the terrible tenderness of love. As if death loved life.[19]

This mutual, almost morbid, fascination between Girl and Woman is perhaps also what prompts Taru Elfving to pose the question "Who is the Girl?" and answer it herself, beautifully:

> Due to her peculiar place in representation the Girl is easily passed unnoticed. I circled around the Girl as if she was a black hole, focusing instead on time

---

18 The *Casting Portraits* are presented in the catalogue as autonomous work, and have also been presented as such in gallery shows at Galleri Wallner in Copehagen and other places, according to the included CV.

Ahtila, *Fantasized Persons and Taped Conversations*, 72-75 and 242-244.

19 Hélène Cixous: "On Marguerite Duras, with Michel Foucault (1975)" in *White Ink, Interviews on Sex, Text and Politics* (New York: Columbia University Press, 2008), 160.

> and space as potentially radical aspects that challenge linear narrative in Eija-Liisa Ahtila's video installation works. Then she suddenly emerged as a crystallization of all the questions I had been asking, but defying any attempts to define or locate her. Questions of difference, subjectivity, time and space, all were sucked into a whirl that is the girl.[20]

In her vivid pictorial language, describing the Girl as a black hole or a vortex, a maelstrom of interiority, Elfving's quote reverberates with this awesome (as in literally awesome, as in beautiful-and-terrifying-to-behold) literary image that emerges, as we return to Cixous:

> And it's a kind of very black sun, with this woman in the center – the one who saps all the desires in all the books. In text after text there's an engulfing (*ça s'engouffrer*), a gulf, an abyss. It's the body of a woman that doesn't know itself, but that knows something there, in the darkness, that knows darkness, that knows death. She's there, she's embodied and then once again there's this inside-out sun since all its rays are male and they come to graft themselves onto this abyss that she is, shine towards her.[21]

(And then suddenly, in my mind's eye, an image of the imploded black hole sun appears, turning itself, once again, inside out and resembling…an egg! An egg being fertilized, and I snap, art-historically speaking, back out of it again and voilà: here we have not the average, but the *ultimate cunt*, as immortalized in Courbet's *L'Origine du monde*.)

These very deep and somewhat donut-shaped descriptions of the Girl, that correspond with the concaveness of her sexual organ, are in sharp contrast to Gilles Deleuze and Felix Guattari's description of the Girl as:

> an abstract line, a line of flight. Thus girls do not belong to an age group, sex, order or kingdom: they slip in everywhere, between orders, acts, ages, sexes.[22]

---

20 Taru Elfving, "The Girl," in *Fantasized Persons and Taped Conversations*, ed. Eija-Liisa Ahtila (Helsinki: Kiasma Museum of Contemporary Art and Tate Modern, London, 2002), 210.

21 Hélène Cixous, "On Marguerite Duras, with Michel Foucault" (1975), 160.

22 Gilles Deleuze and Felix Guattari, *A Thousand Plateaus: Capitalism & Schizophrenia* (London: The Athlone Press, 1988), 277, quoted in Taru Elfving, "The Girl," 210.

This may sound lyrically liberating, but their abstraction of the Girl is problematic and ultimately misogynistic: as we all know, lines do not have interiors!

In an attempt to explain themselves, they argue:

> The question is ultimately that of the body – the body they steal from us in order to fabricate opposable organisms. This body is stolen first from the girl: […] The girl's becoming is stolen first, in order to impose a history, or prehistory, upon her.[23]

Elfving's counter argument is that:

> Deleuze and Guattari refuse to consider the Girl in her embodied specificity, although they first place that very body at the heart of the question. Thus overlooking the specificity of embodied subjectivity runs the risk of positioning the Girl again as an empty, blank playground for different forces. One can ask, if the Girl's body is stolen again, but for a slightly different purpose, by Deleuze and Guattari?[24]

I will argue, that the women participating in *Kussomaten's* photo projects, as well as the women and girls who are given a voice in Ahtila's video work, challenge this theft. Through their emphasis on the psychological and physical *inclusively normal interiority* of the female, these two very different archives each formulate an assertive: *"We are stealing it back!"*

Please don't tell me that in your metamorphosis from girl to women to becoming mother, you have not often wanted to "possess the world, to embrace it with your arms, legs, cheeks, tits and arse?" To possess and embrace the world with these, but also with these in it?

This we need to do: reclaim the female body, not as spectacle but as experience(d), to claim our interior as well as exterior space in this world. We need to reclaim our bodies, our spaces, and our voices, in order to pass it all down to our daughters, our sons, and everybody else.

Free your ass and your mind will follow!

Love,

L

---

23 Deleuze and Guattari, *A Thousand Plateaus: Capitalism & Schizophrenia*, 276.

24 Taru Elfving, "The Girl," 213.

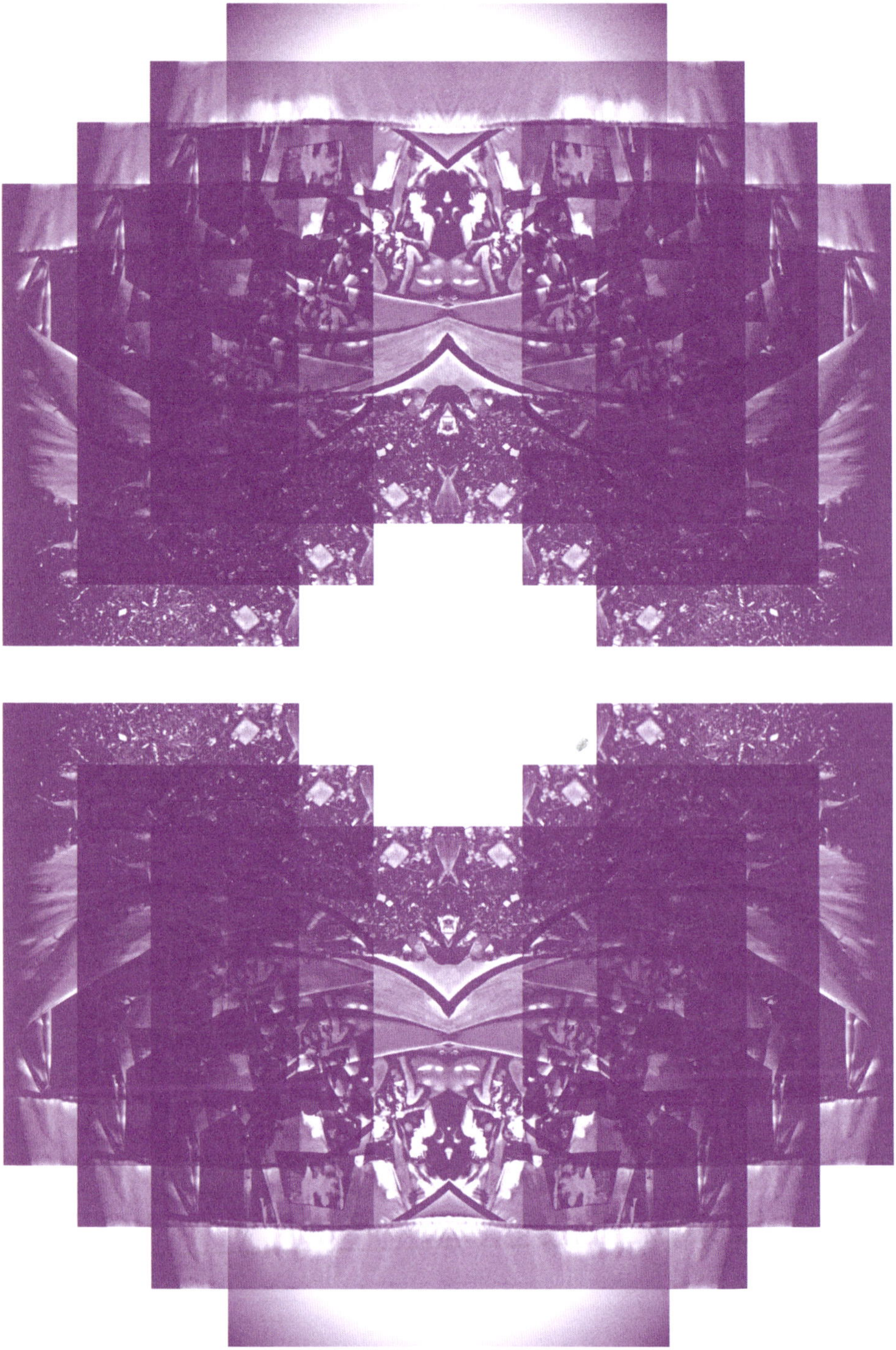

MOTHER of REPARATION

Dear,

We need to talk about rape.

We need to talk about rape, dear, and rape culture.

And we need to talk about repair.

Rape is a four-letter word that follows us around wherever we go in this rape culture. It is spray-painted onto the walls of desolate underpasses and pedestrian tunnels of our minds, or in dripping blood red capitals on banners and signs waved outside of abortion clinics. It hangs over our heads in gloomy thought bubbles when we go out on a date. It is implied in text messages with "Let me know when you arrive" and "If you don't hear from me by X o'clock, please call…" There is now even an app to remind us, that wherever we go, we might get raped.[1]

First off, let me say that I hope that you will never ever get raped, and that no one you know will ever get raped, and that nobody they know will ever get raped. If we could only prevent all rapes from ever happening to anyone, it would make me very happy.

But it can happen.

So if you do get raped, I hope your rapist will repent, will say sorry and mean it, and not go and do it with your best friend just after, or that other girl who is, by all accounts more experienced than you (with rape too, or so they say). And I hope that you will be a little bit drunk, but not so drunk you don't know what is happening to you. I hope your rapist doesn't boast about it or post pictures of it somewhere on the internet. I hope that if that happens, people will know that you are not the one that should be ashamed of yourself.

If something like this should happen to you, I hope you can walk out of there and put it behind you. I hope you don't get pregnant from it. But if you do, and if you choose to go on with the pregnancy, I hope you do so by choice and that you realize that a choice like

---

1 The Kitestring app, copyrighted in 2014, is an SMS service. You can access via their website, by providing them with your emergency contacts and following three simple prompts:

1. Going Out? Whether you're meeting up with a stranger or just taking a midnight stroll, give us a heads up.
2. Check in via SMS. We'll check up on you with a simple text message. Reply to let us know you're okay.
3. Stay connected. If you don't check in, we'll send your emergency contacts a customizable alert message.

Kitestring, "Kitestring. Safety with strings attached," *kitestring.io*, 2014, https://www.kitestring.io (accessed 21 April, 2014).

that implies both hope and forgiveness. I hope you understand that forgiveness does not have to include your rapist, but that it may. I hope that if you should choose to terminate the pregnancy, you will do so by choice – and I hope that you won't have to argue with some bureaucrat about whether or not you were legitimately raped. I hope that if you get pregnant, you get pregnant in a state where you won't have to be assaulted again with an ultrasound probe, in order to establish your pregnancy before terminating it, should you wish to do so.

If you must get raped, I hope you suffer little additional violence. I hope your body won't be penetrated with foreign objects (broken bottles, metal rods, whatever is at hand). I hope you are not threatened or hurt with a weapon. I hope you are not left outside to die, in the snow, if it happens in the winter and it's cold outside, or thrown out of a car in some ditch, too drunk to walk home. I hope you survive. Most of all, I hope you survive.

I hope you survive and that you will know that it wasn't your fault. I hope that you will allow yourself to survive and repair yourself, because I cannot keep you under my roof forever, and you wouldn't want that anyway. But I hope that you know that you can always come back,

> No matter what or who you've been
> No matter when or where you've seen
> Or the knives seem to lacerate your brain
> I've had my share
> I'll help you with the pain
> You're not alone[2]

As you can tell, I am not ready for this conversation. As your mother, I don't know if I ever will be. My head is spinning, and I can't think straight. That's what happens when the word "rape" is mentioned. We go into this tailspin and the walls come tumbling down as shame, guilt, anger, and terror mix up into this toxic event, which is THE WORST THING THAT CAN EVER HAPPEN TO YOU! That's what rape culture has taught us; that is what rape culture is all about.

A friend of mine once told me: "Sometimes I think of all the things I didn't do when I was young, because I was afraid of being raped. And then one day I thought: maybe being raped is not the worst thing that can happen to you?"

As she said it, the realization that being raped might not be the worst thing that could happen seemed to her like a revelation, an option she had never considered. She was by no means trivializing it, and neither was she joking. She was in no way suggesting

---

2 David Bowie, "Rock 'n' Roll Suicide," *The Rise and Fall of Ziggy Stardust and the Spiders from Mars* (RCA, 1972).

that rape is a joking matter, nor am I: rape is not a joke. If you think it is a joke, you should read this poem called "Rape Joke."[3]

But, perhaps the joke about rape – the joke that is on us – is a lie? Maybe the lie is that rape is irreparable and that it is the worst thing that can happen to you? Perhaps the joke about rape is that living in constant fear of being raped is the worst thing that can happen to you?

And that, I fear, is what is happening to all of us, all the time. I suppose that would be funny, if it wasn't so sad.

Of course there are things you can do, to avoid getting raped: you can wear Anti-Rape Wear, for example. Yes, it exists!

Anti-Rape Wear is an Indiegogo crowdsourcing campaign started in October, 2013, a fundraiser to begin production on reinforced underwear "designed to present a substantial barrier to sexual assault," offering the user "wearable protection when things go wrong."[4]

Apart from our obvious inability to predict when "things go wrong" (otherwise I guess Ana Mendieta could just have worn her parachute underwear that day, or Frida Kahlo her air bag corset) which brings us to the impracticality of having to wear this modern day chastity belt 24/7, if you believe "it is better to be safe than sorry;" there are a couple of obvious flaws in AR Wear's promotional material.

First off, a rape victim is not always young. She is not always white. She is not always pretty. She is not always a she. Likewise your rapist is not always (in fact rarely) a "stranger." Nor is he always a he.

Secondly, sexual assault is not always limited to, nor does it have to involve the genital area. Something the burka acknowledges – but maybe AR Wear will launch a balaclava model for spring/summer?

Additionally, the very notion of anti-rape wear in unsubtle ways puts the burden of blame on the potential victim. As Amanda Hess remarked on *Slate*:

> While we're working on that whole rape culture thing, AR Wear will help women move freely about the world with the confidence that only a reinforced skeletal structure around her vagina can provide.[5]

But, you may say, we live in a rape culture? Yes, we live in a rape culture. A rape culture that is perpetuated not only by rapists.

---

3 Patricia Lockwood, "Rape Joke," *The Awl*, 25 July, 2013, http://www.theawl.com/2013/07/rape-joke-patricia-lockwood (accessed 28 March, 2014).

4 AR Wear, "AR Wear – Confidence and Protection that can be Worn," *Indiegogo*, 13 October, 2013, http://www.indiegogo.com/projects/ar-wear-confidence-protection-that-can-be-worn (accessed March 30, 2014).

5 Amanda Hess, "The Comfortable, Elegant Chastity Belt for the Modern Rape Victim," *Slate*, 4 November, 2013, http://www.slate.com/blogs/xx_factor/2013/11/04/ar_wear_these_anti_rape_shorts_update_the_chastity_belt_for_the_rape_culture.html (accessed 28 March, 2014).

Although the general assumption is that "rape culture" is a game the perpetrators (men) play with the victims (women), some nuance must be added to this picture.

You see: rape culture has an ugly twin. (Can it get any uglier, you ask? But I didn't say uglier, I said ugly. They are both pretty ugly.) Her name is purity culture. (They are co-joined at the hip.) According to purity culture, female sexuality is considered fragile and delicate—appreciated for a chasteness or purity that decreases with wear and tear—and can be damaged beyond repair.

In this frame of mind, rape is an analogy to a basic profit/deficit analysis; if something is "valuable" (like say, chastity or innocence) it can be "taken" or "stolen" and if neither works out it can be "spoiled" or even "ruined." According to Angela Davis:

> In the United States and other capitalist countries, rape laws as a rule were framed originally for the protection of men of the upper classes, whose daughters and wives might be assaulted.[6]

That means that if your purity is infringed upon, you are broken, shamed; your name should not be mentioned with the affiliated crime. Although victims are named publicly with other crimes, rape victims often remain anonymous—as though their assault is something to be ashamed of. One isn't ashamed of a robbery or hijacking, but rape is different. You are shamed by rape. Otherwise, why would we not speak your name?

In contrast to this purity ideal for women, general consensus has it that male sexuality is of a sturdy, use-it-or-lose-it kind. Boys and men are expected to be able to "pull themselves together" and repair themselves after adversity (be it physical violence or otherwise). This ability is somehow central to the social construction of male identity; by overcoming adversity boys become men.

(Which bizarrely is perhaps exactly the reason why infant male circumcision is still not only an accepted but revered practice in many parts of the world, including the US. Although arguably it has little to no medical benefits and carries considerable risks, the physical and psychological scarring that it entails, guarantees thick-skinned manhood.)

The rewards, on the upside, are bountiful:

> Heaven loves ya
> The clouds part for ya
> Nothing stands in your way

6 Angela Davis, *Women, Race & Class* (New York: Vintage Books, 1981), quoted in Virginie Despentes, *King Kong Theory* (New York: The Feminist Press, 2010), 29.

When you're a boy
Clothes always fit ya
Life is a pop of the cherry
When you're a boy[7]

It should be clear from this, that the cherry is not yours to pop, but somebody else's to covet.

(You don't have the cherry, you are the cherry.)

Let's consider the cherry, before we move on: contrary to what you might have learned, there is no physical barrier that guards your virginity. There is no "hymen" to be broken, no "membrane" to penetrate. Instead there is the *Vaginal Corona*:

> Often known by the established term 'hymen,' the vaginal corona is the subject of many myths and misunderstandings. The most important of these is the notion that a person's vaginal opening is covered by a membrane that ruptures with, or is 'broken' by, vaginal sex. This is incorrect […] The vaginal corona is located 1–2 centimeters just inside the vaginal opening, not deep inside the vagina. Every corona looks different – just like ear lobes, noses and labia – and differs in size, color and shape. It consists of thin folds of mucous tissue, which may be tightly or more loosely folded. It is slightly pink, almost transparent, but if it's thicker it may look a little paler or whitish. It may resemble the petals of a rose or other flower, it may be carnation-shaped, or it may look like a jigsaw piece or a half-moon. In the vast majority of cases, it is elastic and stretchy.[8]

So the "cherry" doesn't exist physically, only symbolically. It is mythical, which is why it is so painfully hard to get rid of. Although most females actually do not bleed when they loose their virginity, the pain that is often associated with "The First Time" is usually the result of negative expectations – that the sexual encounter is supposed to equal assault in some form to the female.

But outside of the myth of physical virginity, for everyone who is initiated into a life of sexual activity, that initiation is hopefully a pleasant one – followed by other pleasant sexual encounters.

---

7 David Bowie, "Boys Keep Swinging," *Lodger* (RCA, 1979). Released as a single in the UK on the 27th of April, 1979. Due to a controversial video, which features Bowie in drag, RCA decided against releasing it as a single in the US, choosing "Look Back in Anger" instead.

8 Anna Knöfel Magnussen, "My Corona: The Anatomy Formerly Known as the Hymen & the Myths That Surround It," *Scarleteen*, (undated), http://www.scarleteen.com//article/bodies/my_corona_the_anatomy_formerly_known_as_the_hymen_the_myths_that_surround_it (accessed 28 March, 2014).

Rape is not pleasant. In fact some will argue that rape is not even a sexual encounter, but instead an act of violence, employing a sexual organ as one might a blunt instrument. Rape is a crime.

Not a perfect crime, mind you. The perfect rape does not exist. Rape is messy. It is dumb. It is blunt. But that does not mean – should not have to mean – that repair is not possible, that you are broken, that you will never get over it.

If you had been battered with a blunt instrument, your primary concern would be to heal yourself; you would expect your surroundings to give you the help, care and support you need to do so. You may also seek to get the offender prosecuted, but that alone is not a remedy.

I am not suggesting you shouldn't press charges if you feel fit to do so. Just bear in mind that you may not feel able (or willing) to do so. To begin with, pressing charges might force you to relive a traumatic experience again, while also being a traumatic experience in itself. It might victimize you further, and it is OK if you don't want to submit yourself to that.

Additionally, putting someone else in prison may not set you free. While in some cases this may seem adequate compensation (as well as in some cases, offer some protection against the return of the rapist), it is still a focus on the rapist, and by extension (via the idea of compensation) – a focus on the business side of things.

But whether you decide to press charges or not, someone else cannot set you free – only you can do that! Paradoxically, this freedom can be acquired, not necessarily by taking full responsibilities for your own actions, but by denying responsibility for somebody else's.

This argument is employed by William Blake in his poem "Vision of the Daughters of Albion": Oothon, having being raped by Bromion and therefore rejected by her beloved Theothormon, boldly asserts that she can never, no way, be spoilt, ruined, or sullied by actions imposed upon her. Actions she had no wish or desire for nor willful engagement with will be no cause for her moral turpitude. She is in fact rejecting that whole blame-the-victim thing about where she was and what she was wearing at such an ungodly hour, laying the burden of blame solely on her perpetrator, where it belongs. Meaning that she did not have to forgive herself.[9]

I am reminded of a woman – a social worker turned fellow painter – whose kids I used to babysit.

Her name, incidentally, was Vibeke, which in old German means "little woman" and that's what she was, petite, with the astonished, almost angelic, open face of a child. In that '70s feminist way that can make dungarees sexier than lingerie, she was by all accounts a natural woman if ever I met one.

---

9 William Blake, "Visions of the Daughters of Albion" (1793), *Digital Poet's Society*, http://users.compaqnet.be/cn127848/blake/collected/chap-20.html (accessed March 30, 2014).

You may ask, is it important? Is it important what her name was and if she was beautiful? Yes and no. It is important that a woman who owns her sexuality is a beautiful thing. It is not important that her petite frame matched her name, but it is kind of poetic.

At twice my age she was forever young but old enough to be my mother, and so she often gave me motherly advice on top of my babysitting wages. Why she did this I do not know, but I remember she once said to me that despite my age I knew something about love – about what people would do for love and how they might hurt each other with love.[10]

---

10 She was alluding to my boyfriend at the time: a boy I loved but wanted to leave and was habitually leaving to be with others. Then I would call him, remorsefully, and say I was sorry. Every time he would say: "If you leave me I will kill myself!" and then I would say: "Please don't! I could never forgive myself! I will never do it again!" And then we would kiss and make out. He was the one I ran to after yet another break up, after I met that man in the park one early morning. I was actually trying to stay broken up that time, because we so habitually hurt each other, but after this episode he was the one and only friend I could turn to and I was so freaked I couldn't tell if I had been let off easy…

> If I was your one and only friend
> Would you run to me when somebody hurt you?
> Even if that somebody mean was me?
> Baby, sometime I trip on how happy we would be…Please!

But, here is what happened: I was on my way home from my cousin's house on an early summer morning after having stayed over, so as not to cycle home after dark. We had been sitting up all night, smoking or whatever and I was feeling kind of mellow, so I decided to take a shortcut through the park, wheeling my bike at the hand. That morning I was donning my self-styled version of anti-rape wear: a thrift-store swim suit, worn as a body stocking, with, over it, a pair of jeans so tight they would have to be surgically removed, and a leather jacket. A man was sitting on a bench and he waved at me and told me how beautiful I looked, and started following me. Not in a creepy way at first, just walking next to me and striking up a conversation and he seemed friendly and he said (this is embarrassing, but, anyway…), he said he was a photographer and he wanted to take pictures of me, make me famous, he would come and pick me up in his little red Corvette, because I was so pretty. He wrote down his number for me, so I could call his agency. I was flattered of course, although I very well knew that I wasn't model material at all, and stuffed the note in my pocket. Then all of a sudden he started crying and telling me that he was gay, but he couldn't come out, which was why he was cruising the park in the early mornings, because he couldn't tell his family or anybody else about it – but I seemed like a good person, which is why he was telling me. I put an arm around him for solace, when suddenly he grabbed both my wrists, and said he wanted me to give him head and pretend I was a boy (I think he must have been in the wrong park, but right there and then I knew I was.) I refused, pulling back; I said I couldn't do that and he said he was sorry and then he started crying again, but he still wouldn't let go! Then he said he wanted me to stand behind him and put my fingers up his ass. I refused again, I said, I'm sorry (Why did I say that? Why did I have to apologize?). I said, I can't do that, and then he said he was sorry again (You're sorry??!? You bet your sorry ass!), but could I please stay? Would I hold him while he jerked off? I figured I could neither fight nor flee him at this point – so I just stood there, in the park in the early hours of a summer morning, behind him with my arms around his waist while he jerked off (was I holding his hand or was he holding mine and does it matter?), pretending I was a boy, or not myself anyway. And then I went home.

> Chev brakes are snarling as you stumble across the road
> But the day breaks instead so you hurry home
> Don't let the sun blast your shadow
> Don't let the milk float ride your mind
> You're so natural–religiously unkind…

Upon returning home I washed my hands for a good long time. I tried to console myself that I had managed to haggle my way out a tricky situation. (Which is kind of how I feel about it now, so many years later: while it was an unpleasant experience, it could have been so much worse.) But then I panicked! I suddenly realized that during our conversation I had told him where I lived. I tried calling the number he had given me from a pay phone, as I didn't have a phone myself, and found out that it was for a dentist out in the suburbs. That's what really creeped me out because it meant that way before our conversation went off the rails as far as I was concerned, he knew what he was doing; he was lying to me.

One time Vibeke told me about a trip to Greece – some twenty or so years before – when she and a friend went there to celebrate their newfound sexual freedom, and the pill. She told me how they hitchhiked their way around Greece, sleeping with so many men on their way: old ones, young ones, big ones, and small ones – and how beautiful they were. Their body hair, their odor, how they somehow seemed to be made out of the same fabric of the landscape – its rugged and archaic beauty in their core and in their pores. One memory she described was of a bacchanalia that had taken place in a cave, and in the Plato's cave of my mind I could see their shadows dancing. There had been six men with them in the cave. Afterwards they hitchhiked their way to the next village.

At the time, the implications of their reverse sex tourism didn't really hit home with me. This was in the early '90s and we were not so obsessed with political correctness, but all the more so with bodily fluids:

"But," I asked, "what if you were raped?"

At this she paused, shrugged and said: "Oh, but we were!"

Not casually and certainly not wistfully – this was not a woman who enjoyed sexual domination, but just as a matter of fact: "Of course we were."

Under the circumstances, it seemed like collateral, damage, yes – but not irreparable damage. And in her words, in the context of our age difference, and her intuitive knowledge of what was going on between me and my boyfriend at the time, I think she was also passing a secret on to me – that maybe the worst thing that can happen to you, is not being raped, maybe the worst thing that can happen to you is to live in fear of getting raped?

So I will pass it on to you, and you can decide.

Now that I'm older – more than twice the age I used to be, or about the same age Vibeke must have been when she told me her story – I imagine that perhaps in the way she was acknowledged

---

There was a killer loose in the city that summer, several girls had been found dead with no clues whatsoever, and I suddenly felt so…nauseous. Like I was going to be sick. So I went to the police. To my surprise, they took it very seriously: at the station an officer took my testimony. He also took the note with the false number on it and sent it to a graphologist. The same officer came to my apartment the next day and said that the note did not look like it was written by a psychopath, so they couldn't really do anything else. And really, what could they do? They already had enough dead girls to worry about. But not me. That's when I called my ex-boyfriend and told him the whole thing. I decided to get out of the city for a couple of days, in case Mr. Creepy came back to look for me, and I asked my ex if I could come visit, because where else would I go? I mean, I could hardly go back to my parents and tell them about the creep in the park, now could I? (Of course I could, but little did I know! So I'm just telling you now, so that you know.) He said, yes of course you can come, and I did, and then we kissed and made out. And he said if I ever left him after this he would kill himself. It was the last time we broke up. Except when we finally broke up when I decided, for other reasons, that it was time to love him and leave him. For good, as it turned out. He didn't of course, kill himself. I still love him for that.

Lyrics quoted: Prince, "If I Was Your Girlfriend," *Sign "O" the Times* (Paisley Park, 1987).

David Bowie "Rock 'n' Roll Suicide," *The Rise and Fall of Ziggy Stardust and the Spiders from Mars* (RCA, 1972).

being raped, without suffering the consequences you are supposed to suffer when you have been raped – the guilt, the shame, the remorse, and everything else – she was perhaps employing the logic of Oothon.

Or maybe she reckoned that the risk of a violent encounter (rape) was worth running in pursuit of a sexual encounter (sex). Asserting again, that sexual actions against you without your consent are in fact not sexual, but violent actions involving sexual organs.

In *King Kong Theory*, Virginie Despentes gives a harrowing account of her own rape and its aftermath in the essay "She's So Depraved, You Can't Rape Her." She also delivers a remedy in the form of a voice, making the unspeakable speakable. In her case, this voice was Camille Paglia's. After reading Paglia's essay in the magazine *Spin*, Despentes experienced that:

> […] nothing was ever compartmentalized, sealed off as it was before. Thinking of rape in a different way for the first time. Until then the subject had been taboo. Rape is a minefield where no one dares to enter other than to say 'how awful' or 'poor girls.' For the first time, someone was valuing the ability to get over it, instead of lying down obligingly in the anthology of trauma. Someone was devaluing rape, its impact and consequences. This did not invalidate any part of what happened, or efface anything we learned that night.[11]

Amazingly, Paglia does this not by naming, blaming, or (slut) shaming, but by "inviting girls to look at rape as a risk worth taking if you want to leave the house."

(And I am writing this letter to you because one day you will want to leave the house.)

According to Despentes:

> [Paglia] was the first to represent rape as something other than absolute unspeakable horror, that which must never happen. She made it into a political circumstance, something we have to learn to cope with. Paglia changed everything: it was no longer a matter of denial or collapse, but of dealing with it.[12]

Fifteen years later, Paglia elaborates to Despentes in an interview:

---

11 Virginie Despentes, *King Kong Theory* (New York: Feminist Press, 2010), 39.

12 Despentes, *King Kong Theory*, 40.

> On campus in the '60s, the girls were shut into their dormitories at 10pm, whereas the guys did whatever they liked. We asked, 'Why should we be treated differently?' and they explained, 'Because the world is dangerous and you might get raped,' and we replied, 'Well, we want the right to risk being raped.'[13]

Somebody who has, publically, not only exercised the right to take that risk, but also, provocatively, claimed it victoriously, is artist Tracey Emin.

In *Why I Never Became a Dancer* from 1995 she recalls her first (of many) sexual encounters, and her farewell both to the innocence of childhood and to her hometown of Margate. In the voiceover for the amateurishly shaky 8mm footage of a typical southern English seaside arcade she describes sex as a welcome distraction from the overall ennui of her teenage years, and as an empowering experience. As she puts it:

> It didn't matter that I was young – thirteen, fourteen… It didn't matter that they were men of eighteen, nineteen…twenty-five, twenty-six… it never crossed my mind to ask them what the attraction was. I knew. Sex is what it was. And it could be good. Really something! I remember the first time someone asked me to grab their balls, I remember the power it gave me.[14]

Any modern feminist(ing) blogger will be quick to point out that a girl of fourteen cannot (legally or otherwise) give her consent to sexual encounters with men twice her age, and that Emin was therefore raped, yet Emin refuses to be victimized (again) in this way. She insists: "There were no rules or morals or judgements. I just did what I wanted to do."

Later in the video Emin recalls how an army of former lovers ganged up against her in an act of public slut shaming. When, at fifteen she moves on from sex to dancing, it feels like she is defying gravity, like her soul is truly free. She decides to enter into the Margate Disco Dancing Competition, which represents not only a chance of expressing her self, but also a social climbing and a ticket out:

> London! The Empire Leicester Square Ballroom! Dancing for TV! Big prizes! The British Disco Dance Championship of 1978!

---

13 Despentes, *King Kong Theory*, 40.

14 Tracey Emin, "Why I Never Became a Dancer," Video, 1995, *YouTube*, http://www.youtube.com/watch?v=2e1SU17plhw (accessed 28 March, 2014).

> And, as I started to dance, People started to clap, I was going to win! And then I'd be out of here, nothing could stop me!
>
> …And then *they* started: Slag! Slag! Slag!

Humiliated, she fled the stage, the ballroom…

> I'm leaving this place! I'm getting outta here! I'm better than all of them! I'm free![15]

…and Margate, never to look back. Until now.

At the end of the video she gives a shout-out to those boys: "Shane, Eddy, Tony, Doug, Richard, this one is for you!"

The video culminates triumphantly with a shot of Emin dancing to the uplifting beat of Sylvester's "(You Make Me Feel) Mighty Real." The camera swirling around the actress is the infatuated eye of a universal dance partner, and she's loving it back…

There is no revenge like living well!

Yes, we all know that Tracey Emin has done very well for herself, thank you very much! But the magic of this six-and-a-half minute wonder is not in her driving home that point. Rather it is in acknowledging that we cannot regret what made us. Regret is for the details, for the little things – if we want to propel ourselves forward it is through despair and repair.

Emin was never afraid to hang out the dirty laundry. Her most famous piece, *My Bed* – for which she was shortlisted for the Turner Prize in 1999, to much sniggering applause from the British tabloids – consists of nothing much but. In all its embarrassing, unmade glory, the bed itself was presented in the state Emin claimed to have left it after staying bedridden for several days with suicidal depression due to relationship problems. In and around the bed are strewn the debris of solitude and intimate relationships: bottles, condoms, newspapers, cigarette butts, candy wrappers, cuddly toys, and panties soiled with menstrual blood. I imagine a certain nest odor emanates from that piece, repugnant and inviting at the same time.[16]

Where I would most like to rest my weary head, however, is inside the blue dome of *Everyone I Have Ever Slept With, 1963–1995*. As the

---

15 Emin, "Why I Never Became a Dancer."

16 According to Reuters, Saachi has put "My Bed" up for auction at Sotheby's to go on sale in July of 2014. As one of the most important works of the YBA generation and of British postwar art, it is estimated to sell for between 800,000 and 1.2 million pound sterling ($1.34–2.02 million).

Michael Roddy, "British Artist Tracey Emin's 'My Bed' Heads for Auction," *Reuters*, 28 May, 2014, http://www.reuters.com/article/2014/05/28/us-art-britain-emin-idUSKBN0E813H20140528 (accessed 30 May, 2014).

title suggests it is a tell-all, in the shape of a modestly sized camping tent. The canopy opens itself up as a motherly embrace in which we can curl up and forgive ourselves; Tracey doesn't judge and she doesn't mind.

Oh no love! You're not alone
You're watching yourself but you're too unfair
You got your head all tangled up
But if I could only make you care
Oh no love! you're not alone
No matter what or who you've been
No matter when or where you've seen
And the knives seem to lacerate your brain
I've had my share,
I'll help you with the pain
You're not alone…[17]

I was lucky enough to experience the piece myself in Emin's first museum survey *10 Years Tracey Emin* at the Stedelijk Museum in Amsterdam in 2002, before it got lost in the Momart warehouse fire in 2004 – along with some hundred more YBA works from the Saatchi Collection. Emin famously refused to reproduce the work because, "I can't recreate that feeling again, it's impossible," despite allegedly being offered the full insurance sum of one million pound sterling in return.

(That, to me, is mighty real!)

Poking inside the humble abode, I read – in lovingly hand stitched patchwork – the names of Shane, Eddy, Tony, Dough, Richard as well as every Harry, Mark, and John that Tracey Emin has ever slept with, but not only in the sexual sense; she also included drinking buddies, friends, and family members – like her grandmother – as well as two unnamed, numbered foetuses. But most importantly:

"With myself, always myself, never forgetting."

Love,

Mom

17 David Bowie, "Rock 'n' Roll Suicide."

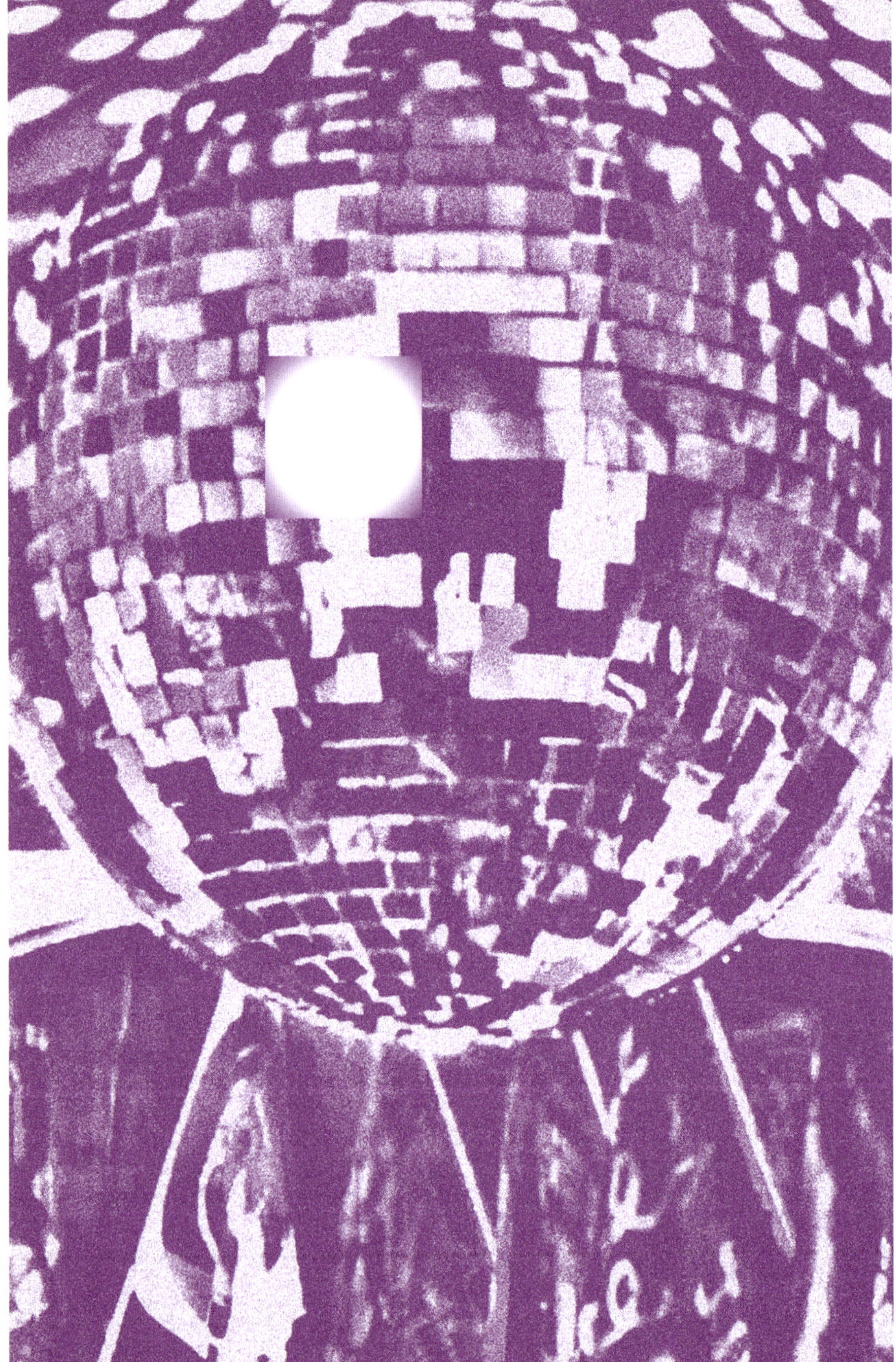

MOTHER of DEMOLITION

Dear Sis,

Yes, it's me again!

You know that song by The Smiths? The one where Morrissey sings:

> Burn down the disco
> Hang the blessed DJ
> Because the music they constantly play
> It says nothing to me about my life
> Burn down the disco
> Hang the blessed DJ
>
> HANG THE DJ, HANG THE DJ, HANG THE DJ[1]

But did you know that it actually happened? Not like that of course, they didn't hang the DJ. Instead the DJ burned down the disco.

On July 12th, 1979 the two worst teams in the American League – the Chicago White Sox and the Detroit Tigers – were scheduled for a double header in Chicago's Comiskey Park . Not expecting a big turnout on their double bill, White Sox owner Bill Veeck and his son Mike needed a stunt that could fill the stadium.

Following their own advice that, "you can draw more people with a losing team plus bread and circuses than with a losing team and a long, still silence," Mike Veeck, as the White Sox's Promotions Manager, approached rock DJ Steve Dahl, who was touring local bars with a routine that included breaking disco records over his head dressed in a surplus army uniform and helmet.

Dahl's personal vendetta against disco had begun when the station WDAI changed to an all-disco format and fired him on Christmas Eve. Not long after, he was picked up by rival album-rock station Loop 98, where he found a platform for his anti-disco crusade. Dahl recalls:

> Every day I would play a disco record, drag the needle across it, you know, and scratch it and then blow it up! But I tapped into something! There was an undercurrent of hatred for disco.[2]

1 The Smiths, "Panic," single (Rough Trade Records, 1986).

2 Steve Dahl, "ESPN: Disco Demolition Night at Comiskey Park in Chicago 1979," *YouTube*, http://www.youtube.com/watch?v=I1CP1751wJA (accessed 30 March, 2014).

Dahl was game, and promoted "Disco Demolition Night" on air, announcing his plan to blow up a crate of disco records between games and promising a mere 98 cents admission price to anyone willing to donate a disco record for destruction.

On the night of the event, turnout exceeded expectations; while the box of donated records filled up quickly, people continued to pour in, carrying their uncollected records into the bleachers until the stadium was filled to capacity with 52,000 visitors.

Another 20,000 or so clamored outside the ballpark. Not content to remain there, many tried to gain access to the stadium – leaping turnstiles, and climbing over fences or through open windows. With enough security on hand for an estimated crowd of 35,000, Mike Veeck sent what guards were available to the gates to quell the gatecrashers, leaving the field unattended. In their absence the crowd started tossing their vinyl albums onto the field where the game was still going on.

One player recalls how the records would slice through the air like Frisbees, and plough into the field: "It wasn't just one, it was many. Oh, God almighty, I've never seen anything so dangerous in my life."[3]

At intermission, Dahl took to the field proclaiming: "This is now officially the world's largest anti-disco rally!"[4]

He circled the stadium in a Jeep together with Lorelei – the seductive model and "face" of Loop 98 – then grabbed the mic and lead the audience in a chant of his mantra "Disco Sucks!" followed by his Rod Steward-inspired anthem "Do You Think I'm Disco?"

After that, he ignited the crate, causing an explosion that sent shards of disco records flying everywhere and tore a large hole in the outfield grass.

While the teams were warming up and getting ready for the second game, a few spectators leapt from their seats and ran onto the field. As the audience sensed that security was not strong enough to hold back the tide, more and more people poured out of the stands and started going berserk on the field. Some climbed up the foul posts, while others set records on fire or started to rip up the grass. The batting cage was destroyed and one witness later recalled: "I'm pretty sure I saw two people having sex behind third base." Meanwhile the players barricaded themselves in the field house.[5]

After forty minutes of mayhem, and several futile attempts to call tho crowd to order, the Chicago police arrived in full riot gear. To the applause of the outnumbered baseball fans in the stadium, the disco demolition posse was escorted off the field, which was

3 Paul Dickson, *Bill Veeck: Baseball's Greatest Maverick* (New York: Walker Publishing Co., 2012), 315.

4 Steve Dahl, "ESPN: Disco Demolition Night at Comiskey Park in Chicago 1979," *YouTube*.

5 Barry Rozner, "ESPN: Disco Demolition Night at Comiskey Park in Chicago 1979," *YouTube*.

left pockmarked and covered in debris; the second game was at first postponed, but later given to the Detroit Tigers, on the grounds that the home team is always responsible for ensuring a playable field.

The day after the event, Steve Dahl appeared on air during his usual morning slot. Although admitting that maybe things got out of hand, when asked if he would do it again, he answered: “Sure, with a few more security guards!”

Mocking the indignant headlines in the local papers, that this was a crime against baseball, Dahl chose to completely ignore other critical voices who suggested his attack on disco could be interpreted, not as a dude prank aimed a popular music genre, but as another battle in a deep-seated cultural war.

In *Rolling Stone*, music critic Dave Marsh was one of the first to deem the event an expression of bigotry, calling it: “Your most paranoid fantasy about where the ethnic cleansing of the rock radio could ultimately lead.”

Marsh pointed out:

> White males, eighteen to thirty-four are the most likely to see disco as the product of homosexuals, blacks, and Latinos, and therefore they’re the most likely to respond to appeals to wipe out such threats to their security. It goes almost without saying that such appeals are racist and sexist, but broadcasting has never been an especially civil-libertarian medium.[6]

And really, isn’t it quite the coincidence for a music genre associated with homosexuals, with blacks, with Latinos, with femininity, with queerness, with everything that is not white and male, to be ridiculed in a baseball stadium with the chant *“Disco sucks!”*

Given the racial and sexual profile of his fan base, Dahl probably didn’t feel the need to justify himself, although in an interview on *The Tomorrow Show*, he does admit: “It’s actually not so much the music that I hate, it’s the culture!”[7]

Twenty-five years later, when the event was commemorated and Dahl was asked in a interview if “the night that disco died,” signaled the end of disco as the predominant music genre in the US, he would recall it with a wistful gloating:

---

6 Tony Sclafani, “When ‘Disco Sucks!’ echoed around the world,” *NBCNews*, 10 July, 2009, quotes Dave Marsh, *Rolling Stone Magazine*, “The Flip Side of ‘79,” December, 1979, http://www.today.com/id/31832616/ns/today-today_entertainment/t/when-disco-sucks-echoed-around-world/ (accessed 2 April, 2014).

7 Steve Dahl and Tom Snyder, “Tomorrow Show with Tom Snyder, August 13, 1979,” *YouTube*, http://www.youtube.com/watch?v=8aU3WIUxLj4 (accessed 28 March, 2014).

In a double interview with Meatloaf, you see Dahl inhaling helium in order to do a pitch perfect imitation of the Bee Gees’ “Staying Alive,” with his own lyrics: *Well you can tell by the way I use my wok/ I’m a Chinese cook…*

> The Bee Gees actually later flamed me for killing disco, which I took as a victory for me, I took that as a win![8]

In the meantime, over in our little corner of the world, we had no idea that disco had died – we were just getting into it![9]

But why am I telling you all this?

(Besides the fact that you share my love for all things disco, and its utopian promise; that out there, somewhere, in there is a great big poly-amorous pile where we can all just *Oooooooooh, love to love you, Baby.*)

Perhaps at this point, it is time to diverge down the side alley of personal experience: coming of age as a female painter in the boys club that is (still!) the art world mainstream, I was often applauded for "painting like a man" while being chided for my subject matter which was "too feminine." Although my autobiographical work was generally considered "hot" when I was a party girl, it was quickly labeled "not" as my life – and hence my subject matter – steered toward the chartered waters of family affairs.

Entering academia in the United States, I found myself once more stereotypically typecast, but now as the cisgendered, heterosexual, mother/housewife – you know that poor oppressed woman, who services her husband and children, with no chance of ever *liberating* herself (or anybody else, for that matter!) – here I have to say with Morrissey: "it says nothing to me about my life…"[10]

And even, if and when this stereotype does, in fact, offer me some insight, it doesn't offer itself as an instrument of libera-

---

8 Steve Dahl, "ESPN: Disco Demolition Night at Comiskey Park in Chicago 1979," *YouTube*.

9 Perhaps Disco Demolition Night, rather than being the death of disco, marks the point where the history of disco diverges on both sides of the Atlantic. American disco really seems to grind to a halt, with radio stations dropping it from their programming and the closure of the increasingly decadent *Studio54* in February, 1980.

Meanwhile the Eurodisco beat goes on, merging with New Wave into the sound of New Order – the Disco Monsters that ate Salford – whose monster hit "Blue Monday" incorporates the click track from Donna Summer's "Our Love" into an angry, industrial, uplifting and danceable *j'accuse*). From here on in this wave washed over Europe, morphing into the rave and techno of the nineties club kids, and finally meets its counterpart that had survived as an undertow in the American mainstream, on the dance floors of Rotterdam and Detroit, Chicago, and Berlin.

"Blue Monday," was described by the BBC Radio 2, "Sold on Song" feature thus: "The track is widely regarded as a crucial link between seventies disco and the dance/house boom that took off at the end of the eighties."

BBC Radio 2 "Sold on Song – 'Blue Monday'" (April, 2005), *BBC.co.uk*, http://www.bbc.co.uk/radio2/soldonsong/songlibrary/indepth/bluemonday.shtml (accessed 2 April, 2014).

According to Bernard Sumner.

> "Blue Monday" was influenced by four songs: the arrangement came from "Dirty Talk," by Klein + M.B.O.; the signature bassline with octaves came from Sylvester's disco classic, "You Make Me Feel (Mighty Real)"; the beat came from "Our Love," by Donna Summer; and the long keyboard pad on the intro and outro was sampled from the Kraftwerk song "Uranium," from the Radio-Activity album.

New Order Discography, "New Order: Singles: Blue Monday," *Niagara.edu*, http://www.niagara.edu/neworder/singles/bm.html (accessed April 2, 2014)

10 The Smiths, "Panic."

tion – as all it really wants to do with me, is to further fix a set of expectations for motherly behavior in and outside of the home.

Whereas in Comiskey Park, a queer subculture was singled out and hated upon by Dahl's "anti-disco army," you would almost get the impression that the world of art and academia share a set of anti-mothering sentiments along similar lines – complete with *hating the culture!*

From the outside, it is often argued that academia is a position of privilege – an ivory tower – that has little bearing on or affinity with the lived reality of "real" mothers. Meanwhile the conversation on mothering within the world of art and academia is often stunted by the argument that the art space is the free space – the queer space – where one should not comply to expectations of the mainstream, which is rife with imagery that promotes motherhood as destiny.

In my experience, the queer academic conversation has little use or need for the mother, other than as the (m)other, an unexamined and un-nuanced embodiment of the gender-normativity it wishes to define itself against. Either way, as a mothering female – artist or academic – you are required to check your motherhood at the door. Or in a queer colloquialism, you are expected to "cover."

Perhaps this reluctance toward Mother joining the academic conversation on gender stems from the feminist aversion of motherhood as *destiny*? While I agree that motherhood is, in a sense, a point of no return – you cannot, after all, "un-mother" yourself – I do not agree that it is an end point.

Beginning with the old feminist premise of the female as "the second sex,"[11] and lesbianism as a third,[12] I suggest that motherhood is a fourth… and hell, who knows? Maybe menopause is a fifth and so on… Because if we can accept motherhood as one sex among many, we can perhaps relieve the inevitable burden of motherhood perceived as a stagnant destination. Perhaps we can instead introduce it into a conversation opened up by queer theory, in which categories of gender are more fluid, moving and bleeding into each other.

To have a true plurality of discourse, we need a conversation, not of motherhood as "myth" or "destiny" but as lived reality, inside (as well as outside) the "hallowed halls" of art and aca-

---

11 As Simone de Beauvoir baptized it with *The Second Sex* (1949) (New York: Random House, 2010).

12 As Monique Wittig suggests in *The Straight Mind* (1978), where she states:

> …it would be incorrect to say that lesbians associate, make love, live with women, for 'woman' has meaning only in heterosexual systems of thought and heterosexual economic systems. Lesbians are not women.

Monique Wittig, "The Straight Mind," in the *Straight Mind and Other Essays* (Boston: Beacon Press, 1992) 32.

demia. And not only as context – as hurdles to overcome – but also, and most importantly, as content.

It therefore bothers me when a feminist panel on motherhood and art – like one I recently attended (and, I might add, thoroughly enjoyed) – ends up in a debate on practical issues of childcare while climbing the career ladder of tenure track positions, or how to substitute or intensify time spent in the studio. Although those are important and acutely felt problems when navigating the day-to-day, it doesn't substantially change the fact that few people still want to hear what we have to say as *Mothers*.[13]

What I am asking for here, I guess, is for mothers to occupy spaces and conversations within art and academia, to claim a voice, many voices, to speak within and against the canon, to reflect on the complexities of mothering and motherhood within that context.

One of the rare (and therefore precious) motherly *and* scholarly voices, speaking to this today is Julia Kristeva's. In her essay "Motherhood Today" she lays her finger on the tender spot:

> What we lack is a reflection on maternal passion. After Freud and with Lacan, psychoanalysis has largely been preoccupied with the 'paternal function' – its need, its failures, its substitutes and so on and so forth. Philosophers and psychoanalysts seem less inspired by the 'maternal function,' perhaps because it is not a function but more precisely, a passion. The term 'a good enough mother', coined by Winnicott, who took this theme further than Freud, nevertheless runs the risk of playing down the passionate violence of the maternal experience.

After (com)passionately laying down the implications of ignoring this maternal passion and its potential for sublimation, creativity, and (yes!) humor, in a small but dense gem of an essay, she concludes:

> by turning all our attention on the biological and social aspects of motherhood as well as on sexual freedom and equality, we have become the first civilization which *lacks a discourse on the complexity of motherhood*. My dream is that the arguments I'm trying to develop here will help to remedy this lack, that they will stimulate mothers and those who accompany them (gynecologists, obstetricians, mid-wives, psychologists, analysts) to sharpen our understanding of this

13 Tracers, "Tracers take on Feminism: Conversations about Motherhood, LGBTQ and Race," panel talk at Threewalls, Chicago, 14 February, 2014, *YouTube*, https://www.youtube.com/watch?v=CqGNvXLgUpg (accessed 2 April, 2014).

> passion, pregnant with madness and sublimity. This is what motherhood lacks today.[14]

I agree, and I would like to add artists, academics and philosophers to her list of "mothers and those who accompany them." I believe we need a new theory of motherhood, a philosophy of motherhood. A place to speak from, where we are not expected to "cover" or check our motherhood at the door (as disco records to be blown up, to the amusement of the crowd), but where the mothering experience is a valid point from which to speak. And moreover, where mothering is regarded as a position of expertise, and not just a position of privilege – a career mom's entitled "having it all."

I call it *Mothernism*, and I am venting this idea in a letter to you because I know you are facing similar frustrations maneuvering your own academic career, albeit from a different perspective. These different perspectives are crucial. In order to have a conversation about motherhood, we also need to recognize each (m)other as an individual – who sometimes does and sometimes doesn't fit within the stereotypes by which we are typecast – but always with singular perspectives, that offer nuances to the (re) definition of those stereotypes.

We can time-manage until we are blue in the face, but we won't change the conversation until we come up with a new set of ideas, of content, as to what this conversation about mothering, art, and discourse could be about. Not simply as a kind of administrative role that one must juggle on a professional field, but also the meaning of communicating a legacy to future generations, or the philosophical immensity entailed by being an autonomous adult carrying an emerging sovereign consciousness within her body.

All that and more. Like for instance how the nurturing nature of the mother is seemingly at odds with the idiom of the singular (masculine) genius on which the mythology of the ivory tower of art and academia is built. Which perhaps is why she is met with so much animosity right here on his home turf? (Just a thought!)

Cyril Connolly's misogynist one-liner: "there is no more solemn enemy to good art than the pram in the hallway," becomes a self-fulfilling prophecy when a conversation about mothering is not considered bon-ton in these institutions, but his biting sarcasm reminds us of Klein's *Envy and Gratitude*:

> The envious and destructive attitude towards the breast underlies destructive criticism, which is often described as 'biting' and 'pernicious.' It is

14 Julia Kristeva, "Motherhood Today" (2005), *kristeva.fr*, http://www.kristeva.fr/motherhood.html (accessed 3 May, 2014).

> particularly creativeness which become the object of such attacks.[15]

Or maybe it just reminds us that bigotry never goes out of style?[16]

(That, of course, would be the worst fashion statement ever!)

Perhaps we cannot reverse this trending bigotry overnight, but as they say: *if you've got it, flaunt it!*

Perhaps by flaunting our motherhood in the face of academia with the same stubborn resistance as indicated by great slogans such as, "We're Here and We're Queer!" or "Say it Loud, I'm Black and I'm Proud!" we can begin to force an acknowledgment of (the existence and position of) the (m)other, as the Mother – but also the acknowledgment that you might one day find yourself in the (m)other's position. Gloria Gaynor, whose disco anthem "I Will Survive" testifies to the resilience of the genre, once observed:

> Disco never got credit for being the first music ever to transcend all nationalities, race, creed, color and age groups… It was common ground for everyone.[17]

In her opinion, one reason that disco is still relevant, is that it delivered on an egalitarian ideal that early rock'n'roll only promised.

I do not wish to suggest that motherhood is "common ground for everyone," nor that it needs to be. What I will say, though, is that higher art and academic education will never deliver on its own egalitarian ideal until it ceases to ignore the Mother, and invites her to partake in the creation of art and academic discussion, as Mothers who speak to and on behalf of Mothers (*and* others,) both inside and outside of the Ivory Tower.

Until that day, my dear sister, when we get to sit at the academic table as Mothers and not (m)others, I will say:

When the music that they constantly play, in the provincial towns where you jog 'round, says nothing to you about your life, please don't hang the DJ.

Dance to your own tune.

Love,

L

---

15 Melanie Klein, "Envy and Gratitude," in *Envy and Gratitude, and other works 1946–1963* (New York: Simon & Schuster, 1975), 202.

16 See for example: Nick Clark, "What's the biggest problem with women artists? None of them can actually paint, says Georg Baselitz," *The Independent*, 6 February, 2013 (2013!), http://www.independent.co.uk/arts-entertainment/art/news/whats-the-biggest-problem-with-women-artists-none-of-them-can-actually-paint-says-georg-baselitz-8484019.html (accessed 30 March, 2014).

17 Tony Sclafani, "When 'Disco Sucks!' echoed around the world," *NBCNews.com*, 10 July, 2009, http://www.today.com/id/31832616/ns/today-today_entertainment/t/when-disco-sucks-echoed-around-world/ (accessed April 2, 2014).

P.S. Morrissey, who opened this letter, once answered the question "Do you like disco music?" with: "It doesn't really exist as far as I am concerned. Not even to a minuscule degree."[18]

So, to Morrissey, I will say this: *I know that you are human and you need to be loved, just like everybody else does…and I still love you, only slightly, only slightly less than I used to, my love.*[19]

Especially after that pun you made on the case of Anders Breivik and his right-wing-extremist-delusion-of-grandeur inspired massacre on Norwegian youth at a socialist summer camp. Don't you remember? That you said to your Polish concert audience, "That's nothing compared to what's going on at McDonald's and Kentucky Fried Shit every day!"[20]

I hope you were only joking when you said that!

Because I can't deal with that! I can't deal with that kind of wounded working class hero pride, that dude attitude, that makes it OK to blow up other people's music, or their books, or their children, because the world won't listen!

---

18 "Morrissey In Quotes," *Facebook*, http://www.facebook.com/pages/Morrissey-In-Quotes/354253683427 (accessed 28 March, 2014).

19 This quote is not really a quote at all, but a mash-up bastard of two of my favorite Morrissey lyrics, namely The Smiths, "How Soon is Now" and their "Stop Me If You've Think You've Heard This One Before." Because, for all he has said and done, Morrissey still wrote a trove of the finest pop treasures in music history—hands down!

20 Megan Conway, "Morrissey's 15 Most Outrageous Quotes," *Rolling Stone Magazine*, 16 March, 2013, http://www.rollingstone.com/music/news/morrisseys-15-most-outrageous-quotes-20130306 (accessed March 28, 2014).

MOTHER of RECONSTRUCTION

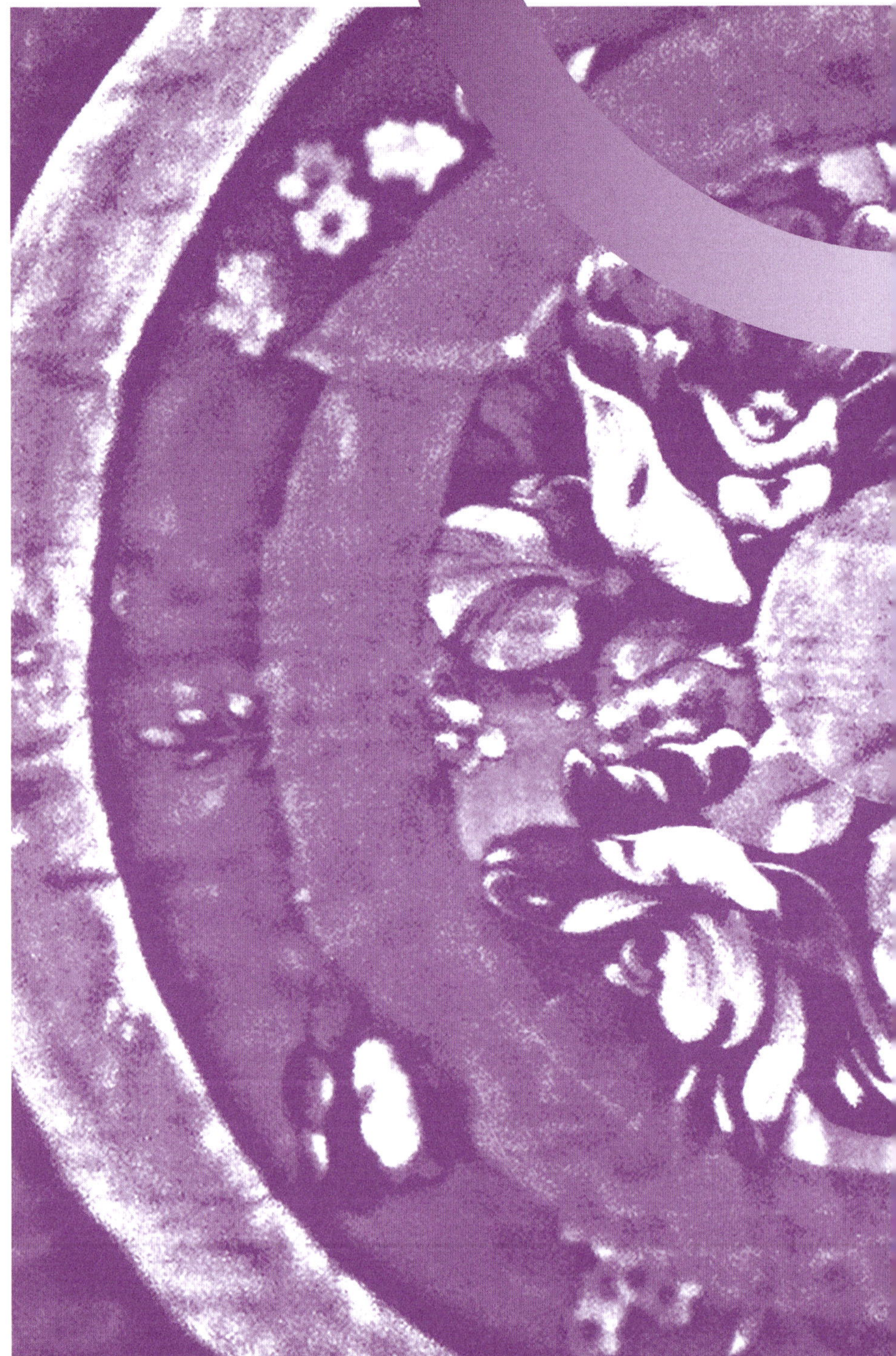

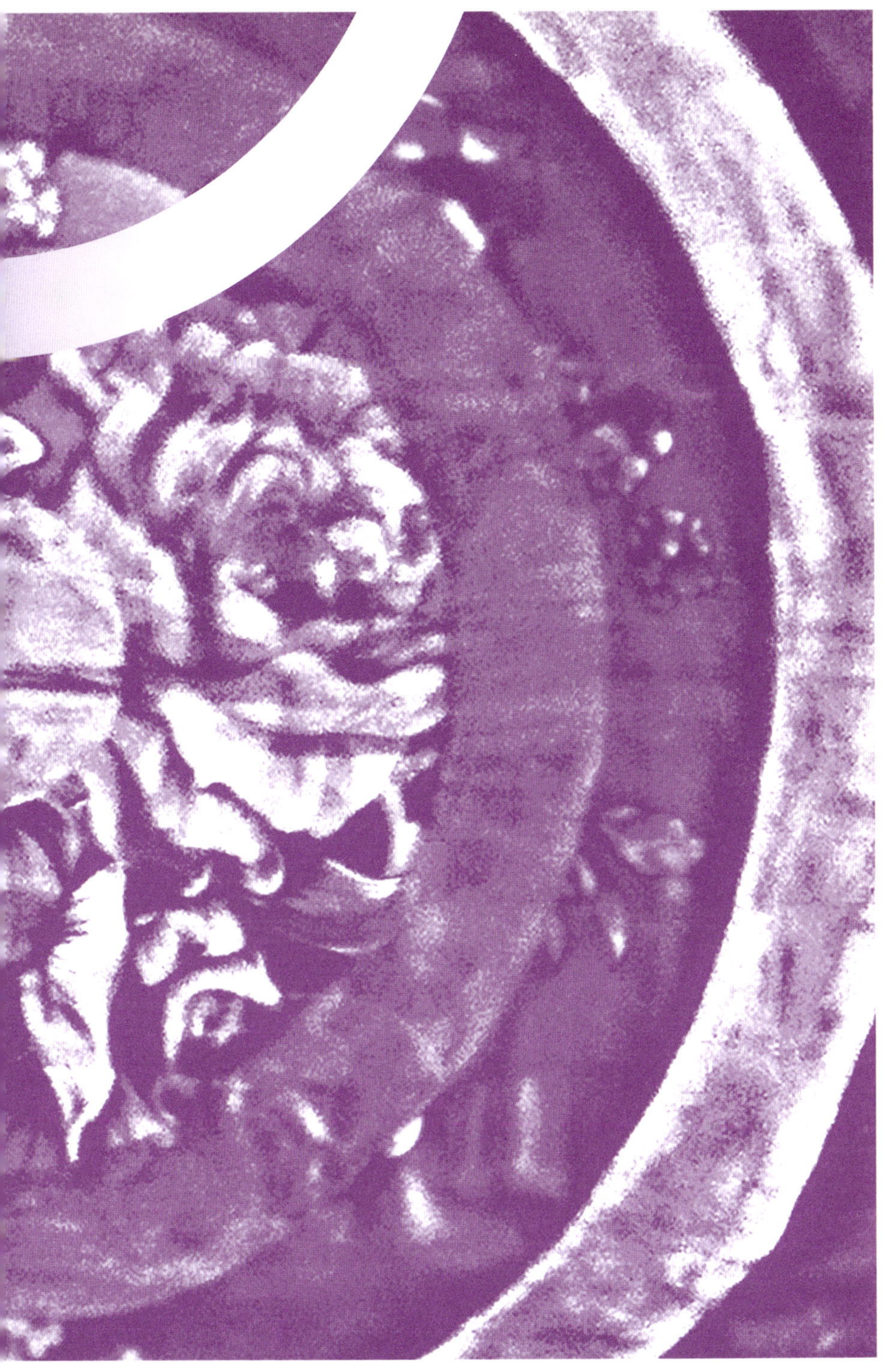

Dear Mom,[1]
It is about time I wrote you a letter too, so this I will write as a mother's daughter.

Nowhere do we carry our maternal heritage more prominently than on our chests, and nowhere is it mapped out and scrutinized more thoroughly than in our annual mammograms.

I have your small breasts. Not the kind of mammalian glands to turn heads when walking down the streets, or for prepubescent boys to fantasize about – but very productive, nevertheless!

It wasn't until my third day of motherhood – when the let-down reflex set in and endowed me with a pair of tenderly engorged milk jugs – that I curiously noticed visitors to the post-natal ward greeting my bosom first and my face second. By then, however, I already had more important things on my mind.

Feeding didn't come easily nor did it feel natural in the beginning. Or, it did feel natural – in the way that I imagine walking for the first time feels natural – triumphant and frustrating at the same time. Frustrating, mainly because I got so little encouragement. The nurses in the maternity ward handed me a sample pack of powdered formula milk – sponsored by a big company with a pair of nesting birds on their logo – while telling me I had already "done enough" and that breastfeeding usually was a lost cause after a caesarian. Since my newborn was in the prenatal ward in an incubator, I had to yell at them at 3am to wheel in that breast pump – right now! I still remember sitting up in my bed, sweating, bleeding, cursing, crying (because I longed for my baby SO MUCH!)…and…lactating…

A baby-fist-sized portion of yellowish colostrum was expressed – the perfect amount to fill my newborn baby's baby-fist-sized stomach.

(Enough to make me the perfect mother!)

The pump collected the milk in a brown bottle which I decorated with hearts like a love letter, and sent by bottle messenger to my son. When they finally let me have and hold him, the savage tenderness of real carnal motherhood came over me as he latched on and suckled.

I allowed this sensation to knock me out completely and purge me of the doubts I had had throughout pregnancy about my fitness as a mother, and also of the failure I perceived in his birth by emergency

1 My spellcheck suggested "Dear Mom and Dad," but since this letter is one of many on the topic of "Mothernism," or the "mother-shaped hole in contemporary art and discourse," I will stick to "Dear Mom." Dear. Mom.

c-section. I felt up to the task. In fact, the task at hand felt as natural, and blissful as walking (another thing I longed for at that moment in time).

Oh nurture. Oh nature. Bliss. I can do this!

But to suddenly have breasts that attracted attention felt very odd. Because of their new function, and because I couldn't just leave my motherhood at home – whenever I left the bubble of our home, they came with.

Six weeks after his birth, I decided to take him for a walk to our local park. I had just had my postnatal checkup, and although I was feeling skeptical when the gynecologist bade me farewell with: "See you back in two years!" I was happy with his compliments as to how beautifully my scar was healing. I no longer felt like I had been run over by a train, or that the wind blew right through my mid-section when I ventured outside, so I set off confidently, walking toward the park in good spirits.

The park was about a mile from our house. It was big and very quiet, with an early autumnal chill in the air. A couple of weeks earlier it would have been bustling, but now with school back in session, and parents at work, the park was nearly empty. I enjoyed walking around there – just my baby and I – but I got tired after a while, as walking was a recently reacquired skill. My scar felt heavy and my baby started to stir, getting cranky in his pram. I found a bench on a corner of an empty playground, opened my very practical blouse and my maternity bra, and let him latch on to my breast.

Oh nurture. Oh nature. Bliss. I can do this!

A woman spotted us from across the (very big) playground. She opened the metal gate and marched toward us, but instead of greeting me, she walked behind the bench where we sat. She popped her head over my shoulder and addressed my baby (her face less than a hand away from his): "Are you getting enough to eat?" She then walked around the bench again stopping right in front of where I sat, looking down at me from about an arm's length away. My playground bully took a chatty lock-kneed position, arms crossed, head slightly tilted, and started interrogating me: she had heard of people who would still breastfeed their three-year-old toddlers! What did I think of that? I tried to protest that my baby was only six weeks old, but she must have felt that our conversation had come to an end, as she abruptly turned around and walked away. My eyes followed her as she left the same way she came in, closing the gate behind her.

I didn't know if I should laugh or cry, so I just sat there, stunned.

Had I been in Pittsburgh about a decade later, I could have called *The Milk Truck*. As the name suggests, it is an ice cream truck converted into a mobile breastfeeding unit, offering space and moral support for mothers to breastfeed in public. The initiator of the project, artist Jill Miller, describes her very collaborative social sculpture project, which she conceived for the 2011 Pittsburgh Biennial at the Warhol Museum, as follows:

> *The Milk Truck* is a combination of guerilla theater, activism, and a little slapstick humor. Yes, we have a truck with a giant boob on the roof. There's a reason for making *The Milk Truck* – to create a mobile breastfeeding unit that allows mothers to feed their babies in places where they have been discouraged – restaurants, shopping malls, public spaces, etc. Babies should be able to eat anywhere. And everywhere.[2]

As part of the Feminist Art Project's 2014 CAA panel *The M Word*, an all-day series of talks on art and motherhood, Miller explained that the idea for the truck came to her when she found herself in Pittsburgh with a hungry infant. Having recently arrived from San Francisco's Mission District, with its live-and-let-live attitude toward public expression of affection, she did not think twice about nursing (discreetly) in public; however she was quickly and firmly called to (public) order by shopkeepers, restaurant owners and others, who would inform her that they did not allow this kind of (public) display on their premises.[3]

Although in her panel presentation she stressed that she would not describe herself as a "lactivist" – instead believing that breastfeeding is an individual choice – she lamented the lack of respect and support for women, should they wish to nurse. The defiance with which Miller backed up this grievance, is apparent from *The Milk Truck* blog's FAQ's:

> [Q:] Are you concerned that you may offend people with that obnoxious boob on the top of the truck?
> [A:] I'm concerned that we offend hungry babies every day by not letting them eat when they need to.
> [Q:] Are you a bunch of angry moms looking for vengeance?
> [A:] Right. And you know the saying: vengeance is best served in public with a giant boob on top. Come on![4]

I know you may feel that such a public display of frustration is a little in-your-face and perhaps typical of a generation who has come of age with unprecedented self-exposure via various social

2 Jill Miller, "The Milk Truck," http://www.themilktruck.org/Info.html (accessed 28 March, 2014).

3 TPAF/The Feminist Art Project, *The M Word*, Panel: "Mothers/Artists/Children," CAA (College Art Association of America) Chicago, 15 February, 2014, https://feministartproject.rutgers.edu/calendar/view/3347/ (accessed April 6, 2014).

4 Jill Miller, "The Milk Truck."

media, but bear in mind that we are also a generation of women – your daughters – who were not raised to be silent in assemblies.

A complaint commonly aired when people take offense at nursing mothers, is that it is unappetizing (or, you know, gross) and exhibitionistic. This is usually followed by a remark about it being unaesthetic – because most new mothers don't hold up to the standards of beauty we set today!

In other words: it is OK for Angelina Jolie to nurse her newborn on the cover of *W Magazine*[5] or for Gisele Bündchen to tweet an image of herself "multitasking while getting ready for a photo shoot," breastfeeding her one-year-old, surrounded by a busy makeup team grooming her hair and nails.[6]

TIME magazine's cover story "Are You Mom Enough" and its accompanying image of a mother breastfeeding her three-year-old caused a stir, more due to the infant's age, than to its provocatively framed headline.[7]

More run-of-the-mill mothers risk censorship if they themselves post similar photos on social media (where female nipples in the name of prudence should as a bare minimum be dressed in a tassel!). But this censorship also translates back and forth between the digital and the public realm: public shaming was the fate of a mother in Staffordshire, UK, when photographed by an anonymous internet-troll. He saw her feeding her infant on a front door step, and seized the opportunity to post her picture on Facebook with the caption: "I know the sun is out and all that but there is no need to let your kid feast on your nipple in town!! TRAMP!"[8]

Her (perfectly appropriate) response was to organize a mass-breastfeed in protest – because as we know by now, vengeance is best served in public with a giant boob on top – damn right!

Plain face-to face rejection befell a Texas mom who asked to use a fitting room – at Victoria's Secret of all places – to quietly nurse her infant after having spent $150 at the store, but was told by a store employee to go and sit at the mall plaza outside. A spokesperson for Victoria's Secret later apologized by asserting that

---

5 Christopher Bagley, "Brad Pitt's Personal Photos of Angelina Jolie," *W Magazine*, November, 2008, http://www.wmagazine.com/people/celebrities/2008/11/brad_pitt_angelina_jolie/ (accessed 26 March, 2014).

6 Nardine Saad, "Gisele Bundchen, supermodel mom, shares breastfeeding photo," *Los Angeles Times*, December 10, 2013, http://www.latimes.com/entertainment/gossip/la-et-mg-gisele-bundchen-breastfeeding-daughter-multitasking-20131210,0,1219750.story (accessed 28 March, 2014).

7 Kate Pickert, "Are You Mom Enough?" *TIME*, 21 May, 2012, http://content.time.com/time/covers/0,16641,20120521,00.html (accessed 2 April, 2014).

(I sure hope the park-ranger-lady got herself a copy, so she can wave it under babies' noses, next time she goes policing the playground!)

8 Mumsnet.com, "TRAMP?" *Facebook Timeline Photos*, 10 March, 2014, https://www.facebook.com/photo.php?fbid=10152255954544025 (accessed 3 April, 2014).

this was not company policy and by rewarding the aggrieved mother a Victoria's Secret gift card with a value of, you guessed it, $150.[9]

Since these are just a few examples of the double standards mothers are supposed to adhere to, maybe our whole generation (and not only Victoria's Secret), ought to be reminded that breasts have a function outside of the commercial realm?

You would have to be blind not to notice the amount of cleavage occupying public space: billboards, store fronts, bus-stops, strip bars, music videos, TV, movies, video games, social media, magazines…breasts are everywhere and they are everybody's business. Through this massive marketing our breasts are fetishized to the point where they've become all but synonymous with the female body. We sometimes have to remind ourselves *women are not breasts, they have breasts*.

But as much as our culture adores breasts, it also fears them. An example of this is the diligence with which recent generations of women are being screened for breast cancer, and the million-dollar-industry that screening and its associated "awareness" has become.

We should be well aware by now, thanks to the War on Cancer (which moves in the same not so mysterious ways as the War on Terror, namely by spreading fear and paranoia in turn validating persistent and invasive screening of our most intimate spheres) that we as women are essentially wearing our womanhood (much like, we are told, suicide bombers their manhood) as ticking time bombs on our chests. An explosive mix of nurture and nature.

But, as Eve Kosofsky Sedgwick points out in her essay "You're So Paranoid, You Probably Think This Essay Is About You," the paranoid position is not so much misinformed, as it is apprehensive.[10]

A while back, the story broke about Angelina Jolie's prophylactic intervention with her genetic destiny (a BRCA1 gene mutation and an estimated 87% chance of breast cancer, and a 50% chance of ovarian cancer), in the shape of a preventive double mastectomy and breast reconstruction.[11]

How should we read her public disclosure of this very private decision?

Given Angelina's public persona and its particular punch, it almost feels like she had been typecast for the part; a "Glamazon"

9 Amy Graff, "Victoria's Secret Employee Denies Mom the Right to Breastfeed," *The Mommy Files*, SFGate, 23 January, 2014, http://blog.sfgate.com/sfmoms/2014/01/23/victorias-secret-employee-denies-mom-the-right-to-breast-feed/ (accessed 28 March, 2014).

10 Eve Kosofsky Sedgwick, "Paranoid Reading and Reparative Reading, or, You're So Paranoid, You Probably think This Essay Is About You," in *Touching, Feeling: Affect, Pedagogy, Performativity* (Durham: Duke University Press, 2003).

11 I am quoting Angelina Jolie's own op-ed piece from *The New York Times*, in which she refers to her family history and the testing informing her choice. She does not indicate a time frame for these probability estimates, so I am assuming that the risk is calculated for a lifetime.

Angelina Jolie, "My Medical Choice," *The New York Times*, 14 May, 2013, http://www.nytimes.com/2013/05/14/opinion/my-medical-choice.html (accessed 28 March, 2014).

in the frontline of the War on Cancer—even Britain's Foreign Secretary William Hague told *Sky News* that "She's a very brave lady."

People magazine quoted Dr. Oz:

> When a young, sexy woman electively, because of the remarkable advancements in technology, allows some of her most sensuous parts to be removed in order to save her life so she can be here for her kids, that's a seismic shift.[12]

Making her decision a Promethean act of defiance toward her biological destiny.

In their *TIME* magazine cover story "The Angelina Effect," Jeffrey Kluger and Alice Park are a little more nuanced.

> The seeming straightforwardness of Jolie's case masks a murkier reality, one that involves science, policy and probabilities, not to mention Americans'—indeed everyone's tendency to observe what the famous do and then conclude that we should do the same.[13]

They continue:

> A growing number of women who discover cancer in one breast are electing to have both breasts removed protectively, even without evidence that they are at genetic risk of having the disease spread. That kind of overreaction, [Brawley argues], reflects 'the Pinking of America,' the high-profile campaigns to raise awareness about the risk of breast cancer.[14]

It's hard to feel that we are overreacting when confronted with personal testimony or indeed a diagnosis: the circumstances, the evidence and her maternal history all considered, Angelina's choice may have been my own.

Given our own family history, you are understandably all about the cure; between losing your sister to breast cancer and a breast of your own, the advances in medical treatment that have come about in your lifetime must seem like a godsend!

---

12 Michelle Tauber, "Angelina Jolie: I Made a Strong Choice," *People Magazine*, 27 May, 2013,http://www.people.com/people/archive/article/0,,20705013,00.html (accessed 30 March, 2014).

13 Jeffrey Klouger and Alice Park, "The Angelina Effect: Her Preventive Mastectomy Raises Important Issues about Genes, Health and Risk," *TIME Magazine*, 27 May, 2013, http://content.time.com/time/magazine/article/0,9171,2143559,00.html (accessed 2 April, 2014).

14 Klouger and Park, "The Angelina Effect: Her Preventive Mastectomy Raises Important Issues about Genes, Health and Risk."

Collectively, as a society, we are also all about the cure; we walk for the cure, we run for the cure, we shop for the cure, we even trash for the cure.

(I kid you not – we have pink garbage trucks roaming the back alleys of Chicago, where I now live!)

Genetically connected and generationally separated, there are sentiments we share, and others we don't. But I think you would have shared my baffled amusement when, just after moving to the US, I walked in to my local Walgreens, and saw the storewide promotion: *"Watermelons for the Cure"* benefitting the Susan G. Komen Breast Cancer Foundation.

I bought one, partly because I didn't want to be "against the Cure," but also because it was in the early days of my life in the States, when even the most mundane purchase had a tinge of souvenir shopping, and I felt that this would be a good story for you folks back home.

Of course the visual pun didn't escape me as I cut open the fruit into two ample D-cup sized halves, and exposed the pink flesh riddled with black seeds, each one sizable enough to cause concern on any routine mammogram – you know when you've been pinked!

The picture gets less rosy when the revenue from all that "pinking" of America gives the Susan G. Komen Foundation the leverage to lobby in (party) political debates.

Like when they announced their plan in 2012 to withdraw funding to Planned Parenthood – one of the primary mammogram providers in the US – a decision that was reversed, only after a major public outcry. Or, when it surfaced that a lump sum of Komen's revenue goes toward lawsuits against smaller cancer patient interest groups for using the color pink or the word "cure" in their fundraising material.[15]

Like that other war, the War on Cancer has become so entrenched we don't seem to mind the collateral anymore. The amputation of healthy limbs, for example.

When our breasts loose their main function as a source of nourishment and comfort for infants, they become an appendix whose symbolic value grows exponentially and form can be perfected, in a perverse reversal of the modernist ideal. As such, Angelina's sculpting, not of the body beautiful (she already had a beautiful body, in case we need reminding), but of the body immortal, symbolically collapses the aesthetical and the ethical, genotype and phenotype, the prophylactic and the political choice, to fit the collective mantra of *Better Safe Than Sorry!*

---

15 According to Laura Bassett:

> So far, Komen has identified and filed legal trademark oppositions against more than a hundred of these Mom and Pop charities, including Kites for a Cure, Par for The Cure, Surfing for a Cure and Cupcakes for a Cure – and many of the organizations are too small and underfunded to hold their ground. [...] According to Komen's financial statements, such costs add up to almost a million dollars a year in donor funds.

Laura Bassett, "Susan G. Komen Foundation Elbows Out Charities Over Use Of The Word 'Cure,'" *Huffington Post*, 7 December, 2010, http://www.huffingtonpost.com/2010/12/07/komen-foundation-charities-cure_n_793176.html (accessed 30 March, 2014).

(Alas, we can be both.)

The artful Hollywood breast is ultimately useless, except as a distraction from this fact, but maybe that's good enough?

Unfortunately the statistics suggest that our diligent annual screening of "low risk" (read: average) woman from age forty does nothing to bring down breast cancer mortality.

A recent article in *The New York Times* states:

> One of the largest and most meticulous studies of mammography ever done, involving 90,000 women and lasting a quarter-century, has added powerful new doubts about the value of the screening test for women of any age.
>
> It found that the death rates from breast cancer and from all causes were the same in women who got mammograms and those who did not. And the screening had harms: one in five cancers found with mammography and treated was not a threat to the woman's health and did not need treatment such as chemotherapy, surgery or radiation.[16]

To add injury to insult, the study also suggests that these massive preventive screenings were not only useless at reducing the number of cancer deaths, but that a serious side effect from the screenings – along with false positives and needle biopsies – was a significant over diagnosis of cancer and precancerous conditions, such as ductal carcinoma in situ, which might never have grown to be a threat to the carrier's health, but once detected was nevertheless treated with surgery, radiation, chemotherapy, or a combination thereof.

The study concluded that the death rate remained the same in both groups of 45,000 women, while subjects in the mammogram group had a 1:500 chance of receiving unnecessary treatment.

(While it would be incorrect in this case to employ the old proverb, "the cure worked, but the patient died," perhaps it would be right to suggest that the Cure (and its associated *awareness*) works in part by creating an army of "cancer-survivors," who might otherwise never have become patients?)

But, if "carpet-bombing"-style mammogram screening has no positive effect on preventing cancer deaths, what does?

Not surprisingly, as you taught me a long time ago: literally taking our breast (health) in our own hands!

---

16 Gina Kolata, "Vast Study Casts Doubts on Value of Mammograms," *The New York Times*, 11 February, 2014, http://www.nytimes.com/2014/02/12/health/study-adds-new-doubts-about-value-of-mammograms.html (accessed 28 March, 2014).

Regular self-exam is still the most reliable method for early (enough) detection of tumors.[17]

According to the National Cancer Institute's website, the main risk factor for developing breast cancer is the hormone estrogen, which is a component of both postmenopausal drug replacement therapy as well as (some) anti-conception drugs, but is also produced naturally in the female body:

> [Estrogen] helps the body develop and maintain female sex characteristics. Being exposed to estrogen over a long time may increase the risk of breast cancer.[18]

(So being a woman seriously increases your chances of developing breast cancer…who knew!!?!)

Short of preventative surgery, a nonsmoking, active lifestyle with limited alcohol consumption is recommended, and then of course there is – you've guessed it…breastfeeding! The longer the better, actually, as estrogen levels are lowered as long as the feeding continues. The slogan "breast is best" (both for children and mothers as it turns out) has been circulating the doctor's office for a while, and breastfeeding is on the rise.[19]

But, despite its obvious benefits to public health, it is still hard to find political backing for breastfeeding – particularly in the US, which is one of *only six countries in the world*, not to have paid maternity leave.[20]

I think we all recognize that style of home economics.

Given the current climate, maybe we still need reminding that (public) breastfeeding can be a blissful experience, albeit one requiring boldness and encouragement. So thank you, Mom, for leading by example and hands-on encouragement!

Let this letter be my way of paying your example forward, and let me end it with some anecdotal evidence that nursing in public is not always frowned upon, or even noticed:

One day I decided to take my baby daughter to the museum.

---

17 Rony Caryn Rabin, "A Fresh Case for Breast Self-Exams," *The New York Times*, 17 February, 2014, http://well.blogs.nytimes.com/2014/02/17/a-fresh-case-for-breast-self-exams/ (accessed 2 April, 2014).

18 National Cancer Institute, "Breast Cancer Prevention," http://www.cancer.gov/cancertopics/pdq/prevention/breast/Patient/page3 (accessed 2 April, 2014).

19 Recent numbers suggest that while 76.5% of American babies are breastfed at some point of their life (usually the beginning!) only 49.0% are breastfed at 6 months (16.4% exclusively) and 27.0% at 12 months.

National Center for Chronic Disease Prevention and Health Promotion, "Breast Feeding report card," http://www.cdc.gov/breastfeeding/pdf/2013breastfeedingreportcard.pdf (accessed 28 March, 2014).

20 Dave Gilson, "Overworked America: 12 Charts That Will Make Your Blood Boil," *Mother Jones*, July/August, 2011, http://www.motherjones.com/politics/2011/06/speedup-americans-working-harder-charts (accessed 30 March, 2014).

After walking around the exhibits, I went to the café because I was hungry and thirsty and so was she. I found a quiet corner by the window, where we could sit by ourselves.

I figured that if there was one place where it would be OK to feed my baby in public, this must be it: after all, the museum is one of the only places where we publicly display images of nursing mothers and suckling babies. Because it was a Contemporary Art Museum, however, there weren't many of those on display – even where pictures of nursing are considered art (and not pornography), they are rarely considered contemporary.

But anyway – I wasn't trying to put MOTHER in the museum, just to mother in the museum. (And not in the public bathroom, please.) And the best part: nobody noticed, and nobody minded!

They just went about their normal business of eating lunch, just like my baby and I.

As I settled into my little corner of the museum café, my mind drifted to half a year earlier when I had been here in the same space, at the Queen's annual reception awarding grants to a selected group of young painters. As it was the 100th anniversary of the grant, the Queen had invited all living grantees (myself among them), to shake all of our hands once more. When my turn came, she admired my huge belly and joked conspiratorially about the joys of being a working mom.

On that day, the now-quiet space had been crowded with everybody who was anybody in my particular scene at that time, and the room buzzed with enthusiasm. It was a week or so before my solo show at the gallery that had represented me for years, but I wasn't yet aware that this would be my last one there. After the show was taken down, my gallerist told me that it would probably better for both of us, if we stopped working together. He told me that we had grown apart.

Now carrying my second child in my arms instead of my belly, I was out of a job, and not really the working mother I had been. But it was early days, so I could still pretend that I was on (unpaid) maternity leave, and I felt optimistic – some might say foolhardy – as I made a silent promise to myself and my daughter: that this mother would return to the museum as an artist.

I wore the scarf you gave me so that I could nurse my winter baby privately in public places. The scarf was intarsia woven, woolly and very big, with a graphic pattern that read: *aesthetic terrorists unite!*

I opened my very practical maternity blouse and my maternity bra and pulled out my bosoms, about ready to explode. I nestled my daughter snugly against my chest underneath the scarf and absorbed the quiet of the museum.

Oh nurture. Oh nature. Bliss. I can do this.

Love,

L.

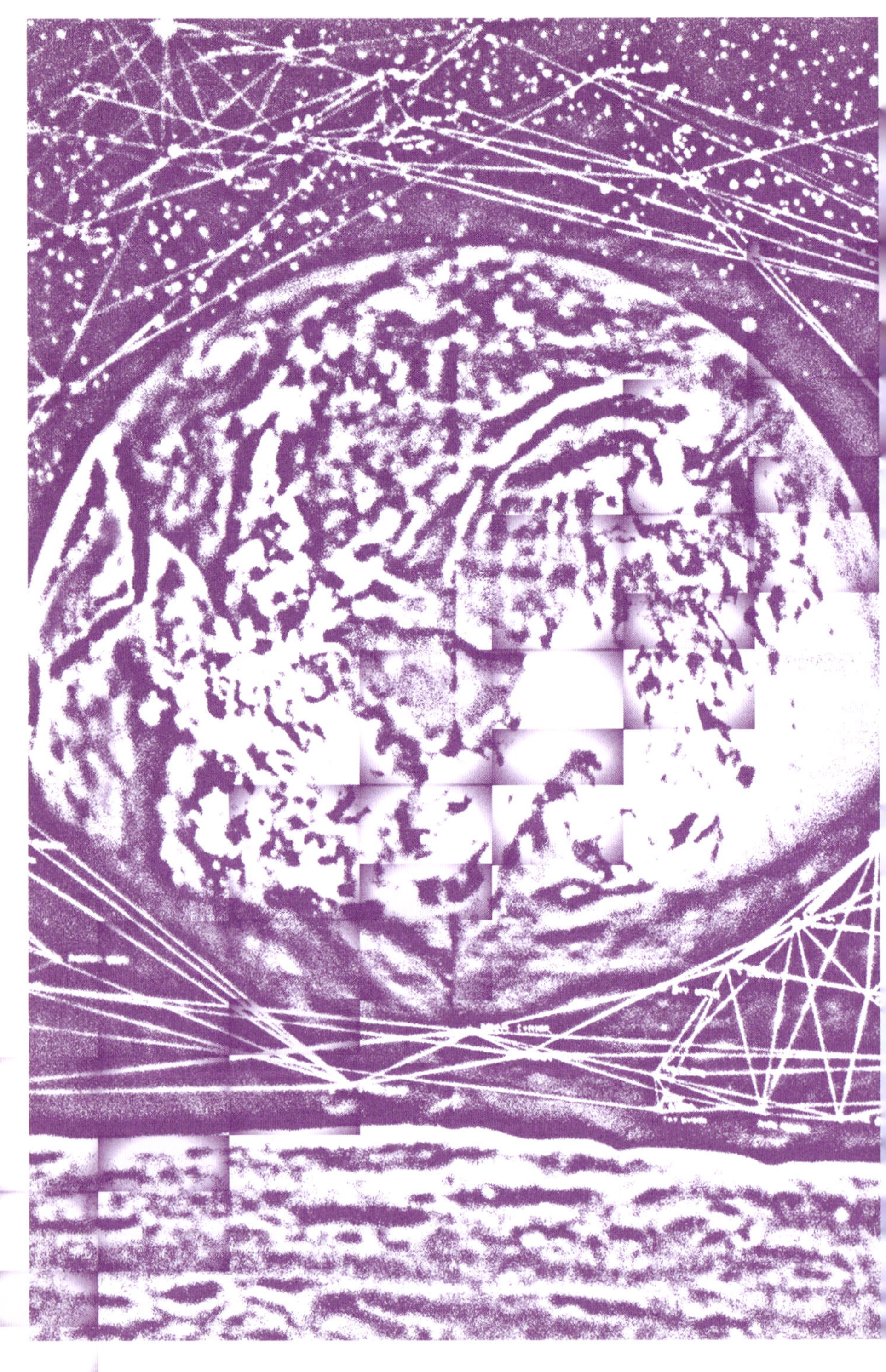

MOTHER of ABSTRACTION

Dear,
Draw a circle. Draw another circle inside it. Draw a dot in the middle. In, further in. You have a target. An egg. A pregnancy. An abstraction.

I want to tell you a story about abstraction.

But let's start with the egg.

Clarice Lispector asks: "What kind of love is as blind as an egg cell?"[1]

I was basking in that maternally blind love the other day during my yoga practice, visualizing an impregnation. Like one of those movies you will watch in sex-ed class; a microscopic view zooming in on millions and millions of little tadpole spermatozoids racing toward the expectant egg cell like a venereal Survival of the Fittest, getting closer and closer, until the lucky winner gets to dive in, head first…

But that's not quite how it happens. In reality, the impregnation of an egg cell is not the work of one fit little bastard's superior tail fin. Rather, the fertilization of an egg is a collaborative project in which the egg is marinated in all that lively willing and able spunk, until by some enzymatic osmosis the membrane protecting the egg becomes porous, and she is READY!

This "marinating" – called the pre-conception attraction complex – preempts the fusion of egg and sperm cell, and is a process that can take up to several hours. The flocking sperm shed their acrosome (outside shell), prodding the membrane of the egg cell, while provoking a chemical change in her outer "coat" until it merges with the membrane of one (and only one) sperm cell allowing their DNA to mingle in one cell: the zygote.

This is not just a matter of the "passive" egg cell waiting to be fertilized by the "active" sperm, and it is therefore not correct to say that the sperm "penetrates" the egg. Instead, they melt together when ready. Incapable of differentiating between forced entry or courtship, that bilateral readiness of egg and sperm is as dumb as it is deaf and blind; still it has an inherent intelligence.

Maybe you can imagine a school of spermatozoids swarming around the egg in inherently intelligent patterns, readying the egg, which in turn ripens into an intelligent readiness?

---

1 Clarice Lispector, *The Passion According to G.H.* (Minneapolis: University of Minnesota Press, 1988), 11.

Think of it, by way of murmuration: how a flock of starlings, converging to fly south in the winter accumulate in bigger and bigger flocks gathering the force of millions of birds, all moving together like a single organism ebbing and flowing across the sky as if breathing. So enormous is that protean organism its weight occasionally breaks branches of trees where it rests. But when the flock moves, oh how it moves – like a shimmering black sun, an amorphous pattern with a singular intelligence. An intelligence, not of the individual bird, but of the pattern itself.[2]

The ingenious slime mold moves in similar, intelligent, ways: previously considered a fungus, the slime is in fact neither plant nor animal, only it behaves occasionally like both. This soil-dwelling amoeba – living most of its life as a brainless unassuming single-cell organism – will, in times of scarcity, congregate and move as a single body. A body that can grow up to several feet long, traversing huge distances, before it settles down and transforms again; this time taking the form of a blooming flower called a "fruiting body."

The fruiting body contains millions of spores in its popsicle-shaped head. When the time, temperature, and humidity, is right, the head explodes – releasing all of its spores into the atmosphere. While the cells that formed the stem die, spores are transported – by the wind, a passing insect, or an animal – to new places, where they start the process again as single cell organisms: gathering, moving, ripening, disseminating.[3]

In a similar way you can imagine new ideas emerge, not as singular strokes of genius, but in response to the readiness of the collective; the singular mind being ripened in the marinade of the collective, until it is good and ready to conceive of an idea. So it was that at the beginning of the 20th century, the collective mind was good and ready to conceive of abstraction.

A specific abstraction, that is – the one that has been defined by and associated with modernist painting for the last century.

Clement Greenberg, regarded by many as the ob/gyn – if not the father – of this particular abstraction, delivers with surgical precision and cuts away with any sentimentality – linking abstract painting to the scientific method and with it, the essence of Modernism:

---

2 In Denmark, this phenomenon is called *Sort Sol* meaning "black sun" and every year bird spotters from all over the country will gather in the marshlands of Jutland to watch the murmuration. My grandfather would take me by the hand and walk me out to the edge of a slope overlooking a little fjord by their house where the birds gathered at dusk. He was not a man of many words, but I never interpreted his silence as being inarticulate. Rather, communicating a secular reverence also manifest in an interest in astronomy and the quantum theories of Niels Bohr. Yes, I was only nine or ten at the time, but I got the message!

3 Rebecca Jacobsen, "Slime Molds: No Brains, No Feet, No Problem," *Science Thursday, PBS News Hour*, 5 April, 2012, http://www.pbs.org/newshour/rundown/2012/04/the-sublime-slime-mold.html (accessed 3 April, 2014)

> The essence of Modernism lies, as I see it, in the use of characteristic methods of a discipline to criticize the discipline itself, not in order to subvert it but in order to entrench it more firmly in its area of competence […] At first glance the arts might seem to have been in a situation like religion's. Having been denied by the Enlightenment all tasks they could take seriously, they looked as though they were going to be assimilated to entertainment pure and simple, and entertainment itself looked as though it were going to be assimilated, like religion, to therapy. The arts could save themselves from this leveling down only by demonstrating that the kind of experience they provided was valuable in its own right and not to be obtained from any other kind of activity […] Because flatness was the only condition painting shared with no other art, Modernist painting oriented itself to flatness as it did to nothing else […] That visual art should confine itself exclusively to what is given in visual experience, and make no reference to anything given in any other order of experience, is a notion whose only justification lies in scientific consistency […] From the point of view of art in itself, its convergence with science happens to be a mere accident, and neither art nor science really gives or assures the other of anything more than it ever did. What their convergence does show, however, is the profound degree to which Modernist art belongs to the same specific cultural tendency as modern science, and this is of the highest significance as a historical fact.[4]

No confusing the baby with the bathwater here!

By disassociating Modernist art from religion and the spiritual realm – a realm he argues has been reduced to entertainment and (shudder) therapy (!) – and aligning visual art instead with the scientific method, Greenberg lifts abstract painting (and his own subjective preference hereof) into a purely objective realm, as pure and tentatively objective as the scientific method itself.

In his postscript from 1978, Greenberg nevertheless feels the need to rectify a basic misunderstanding:

> 'Pure' art was a useful illusion, but this doesn't make it any the less an illusion. Nor does the possibility of its continuing usefulness make it any the less an illusion.[5]

4 Clement Greenberg, "Modernist Painting" (1960), *Clement Greenberg* (undated), http://www.sharecom.ca/greenberg/modernism.html (accessed, April 3, 2014).

5 Greenberg, "Modernist Painting."

In spite of this disclaimer, and rather than deny a lineage of modern painting, Greenberg retraces the history of art, in order to conclude modern abstract painting a vantage point from where visual art can be observed as a self contained system – contained within its own flatness –the petri dish of modernism if you wish.

But, by disassociating visual art with anything outside of its own (flat) realm, perhaps after all, Greenberg is throwing the baby out with the bathwater.

The scientific method didn't spawn overnight, nor did the birth of abstraction just happen in one place and at one time. It evolved through shifts in a collective, disparate paradigm. Not all-together-now, but gradually and suddenly, simultaneously, at the nexus of modernity – in the early 20th century metropolis – but also, interestingly, at its periphery. So that when you dig down in search of the origin, the genius, the father of abstraction, you might instead find the mother: as early as 1906 – several years before Kandinsky, Mondrian and Malevich painted what is normally regarded the pioneer works of modern abstract painting – a woman in Sweden developed a singular vision: a new – abstract – pictorial language derived from her occult practice. A practice she herself considered scientific but is considered a party game at best and hogwash at worst, by today's scientific community: Spiritualism.

Hilma af Klint was born in Sweden in 1862 to a family of Naval officers. A sensitive and prodigal child, she was susceptible to extrasensory experiences and became seriously involved with spiritualism at the age of seventeen. Otherwise, her main interests were mathematics, botany, and portrait painting, which she began studying at an early age. In 1882 she entered the Royal Academy in Stockholm and upon graduation, she was awarded a studio together with two of her female colleagues.

The studio building also housed one of Stockholm's most prestigious art galleries of the time, exhibiting contemporaries like Edvard Munch and the visionary, albeit delusive, Ernst Josephson, who was widely discussed in the spiritualist circles she frequented.

Despite this exposure, her portrait, flower, and landscape paintings – which she successfully exhibited and sold throughout her life – are skillfully and traditionally academic, showing little influence from the major breaking art movements of the time. If anything they demonstrate her keen interest in botany and the scientific classification hereof. Her personal library – apart from a Bible – consists mainly of botanical works – as well as translations of spiritualist and theosophical publications, including texts by Madame Blavatsky and Rudolf Steiner, whom she admired.

Other than her keen interest in the esoteric, there is nothing unusual about her biography—except perhaps that as a female academic and professional, she was a novelty in the provincial backwaters of Stockholm at the time. She never married or had any children. Nor did she travel outside of Sweden until late in life, due to her limited knowledge of foreign languages, and an obligation to care for her widowed and ailing mother.

But where she was unable to go in her body, her mind travelled all the further and, in 1896, together with four women artists, Hilma af Klint formed the spiritualist group The Friday Group (or The Five as they called themselves).

In tightly scheduled séances The Five received instructions from supernatural beings called The Sublime, who urged them to produce automatic drawings under their spiritual guidance.

Scared by the example of Josephson, whose work with automatic drawings caused him to become mentally ill (while admittedly creating beautifully and mystically liberated work in the process), some members of the group were hesitant to follow this approach. In one of her many notebooks, Hilma dryly remarks: "My friends have disowned my mediumistic work, because they saw more dangers than benefits in it."[6]

Hilma however persevered and—being the most gifted or perhaps daring—became the group's leader and main medium, receiving and interpreting messages from her (mostly male) spirit guides: Amaliel, Ananda, Gregor, and Georg.

A note in The Friday Group's séance book for November 7th, 1906 reads:

> You H [Hilma] when you are to interpret the color hearing and seeing tones: try to tune your mind into harmony and pray: 'O Thou, give me the picture of inner clarity. Teach me to listen and receive in humility the glorious message that Thee in Thy dignity deign to send to the children of the earth…'
>
> Amaliel draws a sketch, which H then paints. The goal is to represent a seed from which evolution develops under rain and tempest, lightning, and storm. Then heavy grey clouds are coming from above.[7]

In 1904 the sublime Amaliel gave Hilma a great task: she must devote one year exclusively to the painting of a message to mankind. She fulfilled her promise from May 1907 to April 1908, producing

---

6 Note by Hilma af Klimt, quoted by Pascal Russeau in "Premonitory Abstraction—Mediumism, Automatic Writing, and Anticipation in the Work of Hilma af Klint" in *Hilma af Klint: A Pioneer of Abstraction* (Stockholm Moderna Museet and Hatje Cantz, 2013), 175.

7 Note by Hilma af Klint, quoted by Åke Fant in "The Case of the Artist Hilma af Klint," in *The Spiritual in Art: Abstract Painting 1890-1985* (New York: Abbeville Publishers and Los Angeles County Museum of Art, 1986), 157.

the series *The Ten Largest (De tio största)*, about which she writes in her journal on September 27th, 1907:

> Ten paradisaically beautiful paintings were to be executed; the paintings were to be in colors that would be educational and they would reveal my feelings to me in an economical way…It was the meaning of the leaders to give the world a glimpse of four parts in the life of man. They are *called childhood, youth, manhood, and old age*.[8]

When her idol Rudolf Steiner visited Stockholm as general secretary to the German Theosophical Society the following year, she invited him to her studio.

I have only seen one picture (dated around 1895) of Hilma af Klint in this studio. She is photographed in the long skirt and high collared shirt typical of the time, reclining in a chair. Her hand is supporting her head in a pensive pose, while her elbow rests on a nearby worktable next to a vase holding a single flower. The tulip (for that's what it is) is contorted into a Jugendstil arabesque, growing toward the light that pours in from windows outside the picture onto her left side, illuminating half of her face, tilted ever so slightly upwards. Her (blue or gray?) eyes meet the viewer's (mine), with a very pale gaze that appears to look through, or slightly behind me. With her mousy hair and typical Scandinavian features, including our straight brow, thin lips and cleft chin, she looks positively bland, yet positively bold – almost defiant – or am I making this up? Regardless, it speaks to her boldness that she persuaded Steiner, who was by then at the height of his fame – a touring rock star and Renaissance man of the new century – to come to her.

I am trying to imagine their studio visit: Hilma af Klint is forty-six at this point, Rudolf Steiner a year older. Did they speak the same language or did they need an interpreter? Was she hoping to meet him as an equal, or as the student does a master? Was she even secretly hoping for a romantic connection, a spiritual union, made in heaven? Did she line up all ten heavenly canvasses next to each other or did she pull them out one by one? The paintings were much larger than she was, each measuring about eleven by eight feet. Did he help her, or did he just watch? Was he sitting, standing, or walking toward the canvasses to admire them up close? Was she nervous? What was she expecting?

From what sources I found, I sense that the studio visit was not the meeting of minds that Hilma af Klint hoped it would be. She was asking advice in interpreting the message in her paintings, which

8 Fant, *The Spiritual in Art: Abstract Painting 1890–1985*, 157.

she herself, painfully, did not understand. They had apparently not "revealed her feelings to her in an economical way" as she had predicted in her diary. Steiner declined to analyze them for her, and expressed skepticism at her spiritualist approach, further predicting that her work will not be understood for another fifty years.

(A man walks into a woman's studio. He looks around. He doesn't get it. He says: "I don't get it." He says: "if I don't get it, nobody will get it." He leaves. How often has that happened in art history?)

The studio visit marked the beginning of a four-year hiatus from her work, partly induced by the worsening of her mother's condition, but perhaps also brought on by Steiner's rejection. About twenty years later, when upon her mother's death af Klint travels to Steiner's *First Gotheanum* in Dornach, Switzerland, to spend long periods studying anthroposophy and attending lectures, a five-year break in her otherwise incessant production occurs.[9]

Each meeting with Steiner seems to bring about deep bouts of self-doubt in af Klint, and a reconsidering of her whole oeuvre, yet she remains a devotee until her death. But perhaps there is more at stake than the fear of being a misguided mentee, or an unrequited admirer?

Perhaps Steiner's skepticism touches a raw nerve in her – a fear of being "ousted," or stripped of her credibility as a medium, and her access to a creative vein as a result? It is likely that Hilma af Klint found herself in a double bind at that point of her life and career. Both the Scandinavian art scene as well as the Rosencreuzean and Theosophist circles she frequented harbored some deeply misogynist "theories" about the mental and creative abilities of men and women. [10]

Accordingly, female mediums were favored in spiritualist circles, because they were considered more receptive to messages from the spiritual realm. Their perceived "inability to conceive of original

---

9 Ylva Hillström, "Biography," in *Hilma af Klint – A Pioneer of Abstraction*, ed. Iris Müller-Westermann and Jo Widoff (Stockholm: Moderna Museet and Hatje Cantz, 2013), 278–279.

10 Those ideas resonated with dominant theories of the scientific community at the turn of the 20th century. Darwin's *On the Origin of Species* had only just been published in 1859, and although his evolutionary theory was gaining ground, the science of genetics was still in its infancy. Meanwhile, the prenatal field of epigenetics – the theory that an individual being develops by successful differentiation of an unstructured zygote – was entirely novel. Although Aristotle came close when he described how "some animals come into being from the union of the male and the female," the theory had since been abandoned by the scientific community in favor of preformationism – the idea that the growth of living beings during pregnancy was merely an increase in the volume of parts already present in the egg (according to the ovists), or in the sperm (in the case of spermists). Since the Enlightenment, when in 1794 Dutch microbiologist Nicholaes Hartsoeker observed spermatozoa under his magnifying glass and saw tiny homunculus squirming inside, the spermists considered themselves victorious. Interestingly, in human sperm he allegedly observed a soul.

Jane Maienschein, "Epigenesis and Preformationism," in *The Stanford Encyclopedia of Philosophy* (Spring 2012 Edition), ed. Edward N. Zalta, http://plato.stanford.edu/entries/epigenesis/ (accessed 28 March, 2014).

thought," rendered them vestal vessels in which the masculine principle (spirit/intellect) would fertilize the female (matter/sensation).[11]

(Not the first or the last time that art has sided with (pseudo) science to "prove" that the seat of female fertility, our womb, makes us unsuitable as creators, producers, or anything other than reproducers.)

The Scandinavian artistic avant-garde, spearheaded by Edvard Munch and the writer August Strindberg—who both also dabbled in spiritual practices—would wallow in visions of insatiable female vampires sucking the (creative and sexual) life force out of men.

We know af Klint must have seen Edvard Munch's work when he exhibited some of his most groundbreaking paintings in Stockholm in 1894, *The Kiss*, *The Scream*, and an early *Frieze of Life* among them. Perhaps (knowingly or unknowingly) she was dared and challenged by the scope of this work?

If we look at the *Paintings for the Temple* she produced more than ten years later, including the series *The Ten Largest*, they certainly share a similar vision and ambition, even in terms of format. They are surprisingly sensuous, broody and even steamy: Figurative paintings depict naked bodies swirling in and around each other in a cosmic, erotic ballet. Abstract compositions throb with primordial forms reminiscent of flowers and snails and, yes, labia and uteri, and even primitive stylized renderings of cell structures merging and multiplying as though by impregnation.

For somebody with the declared intention of living "vestal and ascetic in the service of the Lord," her paintings erupt with a titillating energy, although the challenge of representing the male physiology at times seems to have baffled the sexual novice.[12]

Perhaps unconsciously, her paintings express a longing to merge with the sublime in both a spiritual *and* carnal way, as though by the very act of painting, af Klint explores an eroticized inner universe.

As interpreted by Pascal Rousseau:

> The winged uterus, a symbol of terrestrial desire sublimated as celestial passion, is an emblem of the spiritualization of the flesh, but also an image antidote to the possible hysterization of the passion for the supernatural.[13]

---

11 Pascal Rousseau, "Premonitory Abstraction—Mediumism, Automatic Writing, and Anticipation in the Work of Hilma af Klint" in *Hilma af Klint—a Pioneer of Abstraction* (Stockholm Moderna Museet and Hatje Cantz, 2013), 163.

12 "Vestal and ascetic in the service of the Lord" (Author's translation) is the inscription on the painting *Primordial Chaos, No. 9, Group I, The WU/Rose Series (1906–1907)*, Cat. 26, in *Hilma af Klint—A Pioneer of Abstraction* (Stockholm Moderna Museet and Hatje Cantz, 2013), 25.

13 Pascal Rousseau, "Premonitory Abstraction—Mediumism, Automatic Writing, and Anticipation in the Work of Hilma af Klint," 169–170.

Meanwhile, on a couch in Austria, this libidinous inner female territory was being colonized and named: *hysteria*.

Psychotherapy, as a new science, wanted to establish itself squarely within the scientific method and within the canon of medical history. Consequently, at the turn of the century the Spiritualist community was attacked from more sides:

> Medicine and, and in particular experimental psychology, which fought against invasion by 'psychic studies' seized on this uncertainty and diagnosed the supernatural powers of 'mediums' as indicative of a form of psychiatric disorder. The correlation was soon made between madness and spiritism as Henry Maudsley argued that the abnormal powers of certain mediumistic subjects were related to a disorder in the functioning of the brain, which was immediately associated with hysterical symptoms (recalling the powerful determinism given by the etymology hysteria/uterus).[14]

What's a woman to do?

Hilma af Klint continued to work under spiritual guidance for the rest of her life, producing a massive body of work that remained in her studio and was never exhibited during her lifetime.

After her death in 1944, her estate – including her 125 notebooks on her occult and artistic practices – was entrusted to her nephew with the explicit stipulation that her output of more than one thousand occult paintings must not be shown publicly until twenty years after her death, as the world was not yet ready for her message.[15]

The first time a selection of these works were presented to a larger audience was at the Los Angeles County Museum of Art in 1986, as part of the exhibition *The Spiritual in Art, Abstract Painting, 1890–1985*. The main ambition of the grand survey was to demonstrate that:

> the genesis and development of abstract art were inextricably linked to spiritual ideas current in Europe in the late nineteenth and early twentieth centuries.[16]

By the mid-'80s abstraction had long since "come of age," inserting itself into the mainstream and disassociating itself (with the help of Clement Greenberg, among others) from any mysticism aside from the male mystique of artistic genius. Not the kind of

14 Rousseau, "Premonitory Abstraction–Mediumism, Automatic Writing, and Anticipation in the Work of Hilma af Klint," 169.

15 Ylva Hillström, "Biography," 279.

16 Maurice Tuchman, "Hidden Meanings in Abstract Art," in *The Spiritual in Art: Abstract Painting 1890–1985* (New York: Abbeville Publishers and Los Angeles County Museum of Art, 1986), 17.

genius to seek impregnation by the sublime, it had freed itself from references to anything outside of itself…it had become self referential, really.[17]

But before then, back in Hilma af Klint's studio, abstraction was not a goal in itself—not really a goal at all—but a means: a means of connecting with the other and the outside. The outside of the realm of the singular human mind, perhaps?

As Wassily Kandinsky described it a few years later, with a fitting metaphor:

> The great epoch of the Spiritual which is already beginning, or, in embryonic form, began already yesterday…provides and will provide the soil of in which a kind of monumental work must come to fruition.[18]

I am reminded of another studio visit, which has since acquired mystical status within the canon of abstract expressionism and art history of the 20th century; in 1953, Clement Greenberg brought two of his closest friends, Morris Louis and Kenneth Noland, with him to visit Helen Frankenthaler and to admire her monumental *Mountains and the Sea*. Upon her return from Nova Scotia in 1952, the twenty-three year old Frankenthaler had secured a seven by ten foot piece of raw unprimed cotton duck canvas to her studio floor and created a painting fresh from the memories, which were by her own account "embedded not only in her mind but in her wrists as well."[19]

By pouring thinly diluted oil paints straight onto the canvas, the color, like the memory, embedded itself within the canvas, like dyed cloth, creating the illusion—the fluidity, lightness and translucency—of a giant watercolor. The scale and the method of the painting overtly references Jackson Pollock—who supremely ruled Greenberg's (and with it New York's art-) world at the time—but is devoid of his

17 Originally an apocryphal story, it has since been canonized by art history: under the code name "Long Leash," the CIA employed its press division, the Propaganda Assets Inventory, to sponsor the popularization of Abstract Expressionism (among other American art forms, such as Bebop Jazz and the writers of the Beat Generation), through highly secretive organized chains of sponsorships, spin-doctoring and publicity. As the errand of the CIA was not primarily that of art criticism, but rather defeating the Russian/Chinese power axis and its associated communist ideology, Abstract Expressionism was therefore promoted as a beacon of unique improvisational individualism, that could only thrive in the "free world." Not only was Abstract Expressionism a triumph of the singular genius over the collective, it was also touted as America's first self-generated art movement and as such became a poster-child of its inborn, democratic success.

Frances Stonor Saunders, "Modern art was CIA 'weapon,'" *The Independent*, 22 October, 1995, http://www.independent.co.uk/news/world/modern-art-was-cia-weapon-1578808.html (accessed 28 March, 2014).

18 Wassily Kandinsky's words from 1910–11 are quoted in Earl A. Power's foreword to *The Spiritual in Abstract Painting, 1890–1985* (New York: Abbeville Publishers and Los Angeles County Museum of Art, 1986), 11.

19 Michael McNay, "Helen Frankenthaler Obituary," *The Guardian*, 28 December, 2011, http://www.theguardian.com/artanddesign/2011/dec/28/helen-frankenthaler (accessed 28 March, 2014).

angsty search for the sublime. Instead she self-assuredly trusts this "sublime" to already rest within her own memory—and her body itself.

Frankenthaler never really makes the cut in Greenberg's sovereignly masculine canon—a fact that is perhaps attributable to a romantic interest gone sour—regardless, the meeting leaves an unshakeable impression on both Noland and Louis, who was later quoted saying that Frankenthaler's painting was "the bridge between Pollock and what is possible."[20]

In fact, what we are witnessing here in Frankenthaler's studio is the seminal moment of color field painting as both Noland and Louis adopt her technique, and from it each create new bodies of work.

(Two men who want to paint like a woman, how often has *that* happened in art history?)

Although both Hilma af Klint and Helen Frankenthaler would probably rather not be labeled as "female" painters—not to mention "feminist" painters—I see similarities in the approach they take to their medium, and the way they both invade macho territory via the back door. Like Joan of Arc before them, to acquire the fire of a "devil may care" attitude, it helps to adopt a "the devil made me do it" defense—whether the "devil" manifests itself in the form of "guardian angels," "spirit guides," or "embedded memories."

Although this idea of being "chosen" or "guided" could be interpreted as self-indulgent, or even narcissistic, it is not the kind of narcissism we know (and ~~love~~); around the same time Hilma af Klint was painting under "sublime" guidance, her contemporary Lou Andreas-Salomé, emerged as one of the first female psychoanalysts. As a close friend and colleague of Sigmund Freud, she developed a theory of narcissism in parallel with him, while diverging in crucial ways. According to Carolee Schneemann:

> When [Andreas-Salomé] worked with Freud she created a theory of narcissism that doesn't have to do with self-involvement or self display. Her theory has to do with losing the self in its identification with what it perceives. So it's a very painterly theory of narcissism. A narcissism that's not a narcissist, but a process of deeply identifying with perceptual forms. For me, that's a very painterly kind of narcissism, but it's not the one that's bantered about regarding certain kinds of woman's activisms that are explicitly erotic or physical.[21]

20 McNay, "Helen Frankenthaler Obituary."

21 Priscilla Frank, "Carolee Schneemann, Feminist Performance Pioneer, Talks 'Olympia,' Deodorant And Selfies," *Huffington Post*, December 11, 2013, http://www.huffingtonpost.com/2013/12/11/carolee-schneemann_n_4415261.html (accessed 28 March, 2014).

Can we perhaps characterize af Klint's and Frankenthaler's involvement with the "sublime" as similar to this painterly narcissism – a process of deeply identifying with perceptual forms?

In her essay, "The Art and Healing Oeuvre," in which she compares the work of Hilma af Klint to the work of Emma Kunz and Agnes Martin, Bracha Ettinger links this "unselfish, painterly narcissism" to an investment in the archaic m/other, as prerequisite for artistic creation:

> The investment in the archaic m/other as self-object is narcissistic but this is a 'neither pathological nor obnoxious' narcissistic investment, necessary for the development of psychic life and for artistic creativity. Thus, the libidinal investment is, from the beginning, a contact with the other and the outside…[22]

By answering this siren's call from the other and the outside, resonating within, both Hilma af Klint and Helen Frankenthaler access an abstraction that is not simply masturbatory and self referential, but pouring through them from elsewhere, *connecting with an intelligence, not of the singular mind, but of the pattern itself*.

Perhaps this "elsewhere" accessed is the psychological space Bracha Ettinger calls *The Matrixial Borderspace*, a shared (pre-natal) space in which I and non-I co-emerge. In this (feminized) space, the creative impulse is not originating from you, but flowing through you, resonating with, and connecting you to – your first (prenatal) encounter, with the other and the outside – your m/other's voice.

According to Ettinger:

> The womb and the prenatal phase are the references to the real to which the imaginary Matrix corresponds. But as a concept, the Matrix is no more – but no less – related to the womb than the Phallus is related to the penis. That is, Matrix is a symbolic concept.[23]

More so, because:

> The Matrix is not the opposite of the Phallus; it is rather a supplementary perspective. It grants a different meaning. It draws a different field of desire.[24]

---

22 Bracha Ettinger, "The art-and-healing Oeuvre: Metramorphic Relinquishment of the Soul-Spirit to the Spirit of the Cosmos," in *3 Times Abstraction; New Methods of Drawing by Hilma af Klint, Emma Kunz, and Agnes Martin*, ed. Catherine de Zegher and Hendel Teicher (New York: The Drawing Center, 2005).

23 Bracha Ettinger, "Woman-Other-Thing: A Matrixial Touch" in *Matrix-Borderlines*, ed. David Elliott and Pamela Ferris (Oxford: MOMA Oxford, 1993), 12.

24 Bracha Ettinger, "The Matrixial Borderspace" (Minneapolis, University of Minnesota Press, 2006), 1.

This different field of desire, manifests as a melting with, a bleeding of the territorial boundaries between the inside and the outside, the subject and the object, the I and the non-I, which in fact, as Ettinger describes it, co-emerge, come into existence, simultaneously as an investment in the archaic m/other.

This contact with the other and the outside, is perhaps also what Melanie Klein grants us (re)access to in her essay "Envy and Gratitude," by reminding us that we once roamed a *different field of desire*. In her description of the infant's relation to the good breast we see a (similar) reversal – or overlapping – of interior and exterior space:

> The good breast is taken in and becomes part of the ego, and the infant who was first inside the mother now has the mother inside himself.[25]

This "mother inside himself" is a source of nourishment deeper than the purely physical:

> We find in the analysis of our patients that the breast in its good aspect is the prototype of maternal goodness, inexhaustible patience and generosity *as well as creativity*.[26]

The good breast is thus the gift that keeps on giving. Once you have accessed its reparative cornucopia your creativity allows self repair, but can also trigger the fear of loss:

> If the identification with a good and life giving internalized object can be maintained this becomes an impetus towards creativeness. Though superficially this may manifest itself as a coveting of the prestige, wealth and power which others have attained, its actual aim is creativeness. The capacity to give and preserve life is felt as the greatest gift and therefore creativeness becomes the deepest source of envy.[27]

I can readily imagine creativeness to be a deeper source of envy, both to Hilma af Klint in her day as well as Frankenthaler in hers, as female painters were rarely (if at all) granted access

---

25 Melanie Klein, *Envy and Gratitude and Other Works, 1946–1963* (New York: Simon and Schuster, 1975), 179.

26 Klein, *Envy and Gratitude and Other Works*, 1946–1963, 180.

27 Klein, *Envy and Gratitude and Other Works*, 1946–1963, 202.

to the creative canon – but even today the idea of creativity, is (still!) linked to a specific masculine mystique – a certain "phallic sublimation."

Of course if you say envy, you have to say penis, thus again evoking the link between phallus and creativity, but I think these three female psychoanalysts, Salomé, Klein, and Ettinger are out in a bigger errand here, namely reversing the gender of the creative impulse.

Or, perhaps not exactly reversing it, but blurring, and expanding it. Perhaps what we are looking at here via the works of these two female pioneers of abstract painting – contrary to what Greenberg will have us believe, or for that matter what Freud and Lacan will have us believe (with their Phallic object separated from the fabric of the world via the Phallic gaze) – is not a self contained system confined to and defined by the thing itself, but linked with the no-Thing behind it; the no-Thing with which it co-emerges: *the pattern itself*.

Now I realize this can be a little hard to get your head around.

Getting your head around the Phallus – which is really just a penis with an overinflated ego – of course is easy! (It can even be enjoyable, if consensual and to your taste!) But getting your head around the Matrix – the non-Phallus – that's hard…

But say Freud is right that penis envy indeed exists, and Melanie Klein is right that envy and gratitude are intrinsically linked, penis gratitude could also exist – not as the "opposite" of penis envy – but as a different, endlessly abstract field of desire?

The bridge between yourself and what is possible, perhaps?

Like the realization when looking at ourselves in the mirror, that there is no distance between us and the mirror, that we are our reflection, mirror and all: like butterflies dreaming of philosophers, like abstraction dreaming of painters, like patterns dream of birds, like bathwater dreams of babies. Lovingly.

So remember it's true: *there is no greater love than what I feel for you.*[28]

It's just that I can't wrap it up and give it to you, it is not a gift. It is maybe a pulse, or a current. Or, maybe it is like breathing?

Try this simple breathing exercise: Lay down next to a sleeping person you love, gently without touching or disturbing. (It can be a lover, a friend, a child, or even a parent.) Place your face close to theirs, gently without touching or disturbing. Slow your breathing in sync with theirs, but opposite, so you inhale on their exhale and vice versa, and you let your lungs and nostrils be filled with their sleepy breath.

28 "There Is No Greater Love That What I Feel For You," traditional Jazz Standard.

Heinz Kohut links this light-weight example to the principle of creativity:

> The creative individual, whether in art or science, is less psychologically separated from [its] surroundings than the noncreative one; the 'I-you' barrier is not as clearly defined.[…]The intensity of the creative persons' awareness of the relevant aspects of [its] surroundings is akin to the detailed self-perceptions of the schizoid and the childlike.[…]The indistinctness of 'internal' and 'external' is familiar to all of us in our relation to the surrounding air, which, as we take it in and expel it, we experience as part of ourselves […] a close psychological proximity exists between the coming to life of dust and the creative transformation of a narcissistically experienced material into a work of art.[29]

So, we have a breath, becoming art, so we have a song. It's like music. It's everything, yet it's really no-Thing. Do you get it, this no-Thingness? I don't "get it," but I get it when I hear Donna Summer, that archaic m/other singing "I Feel Love"…that barely there couplet, that is really just an excuse, the lead that is more like a backing vocal, sentient but egoless, multiplying and merging and then…the chorus that just ebbs and flows, libidinous, oceanic, throbbing, endlessly, inwardly, a maelstroem of interiority: *Ooooooooooh, I feel love, I feel love, I feel love, I feel love, I feeeeeeel looooooove*…[30]

And she makes it so palpable, that that's all we can really do with love.

Feel it.

Love,

Mom

---

29 Heinz Kohut, *The Search for the Self*, Vol. 1 (New York: International University Press, 1978), 427, 447–448.

30 Donna Summer, "I Feel Love," *I Remember Yesterday* (Casablanca Records: 1977). The song was originally released as a 7" and 12" single. According to David Bowie, then in the middle of recording his Berlin Trilogy with Brian Eno, its impact on the genre's direction was recognized early on:

> One day in Berlin…Eno came running in and said, 'I have heard the sound of the future.'…he puts on 'I Feel Love,' by Donna Summer…He said, 'This is it, look no further. This single is going to change the sound of club music for the next fifteen years.' Which was more or less right.

(From David Bowie and Kurt Loder, *Sound and Vision*, CD Liner notes, 1989)

MOTHER of PEARL

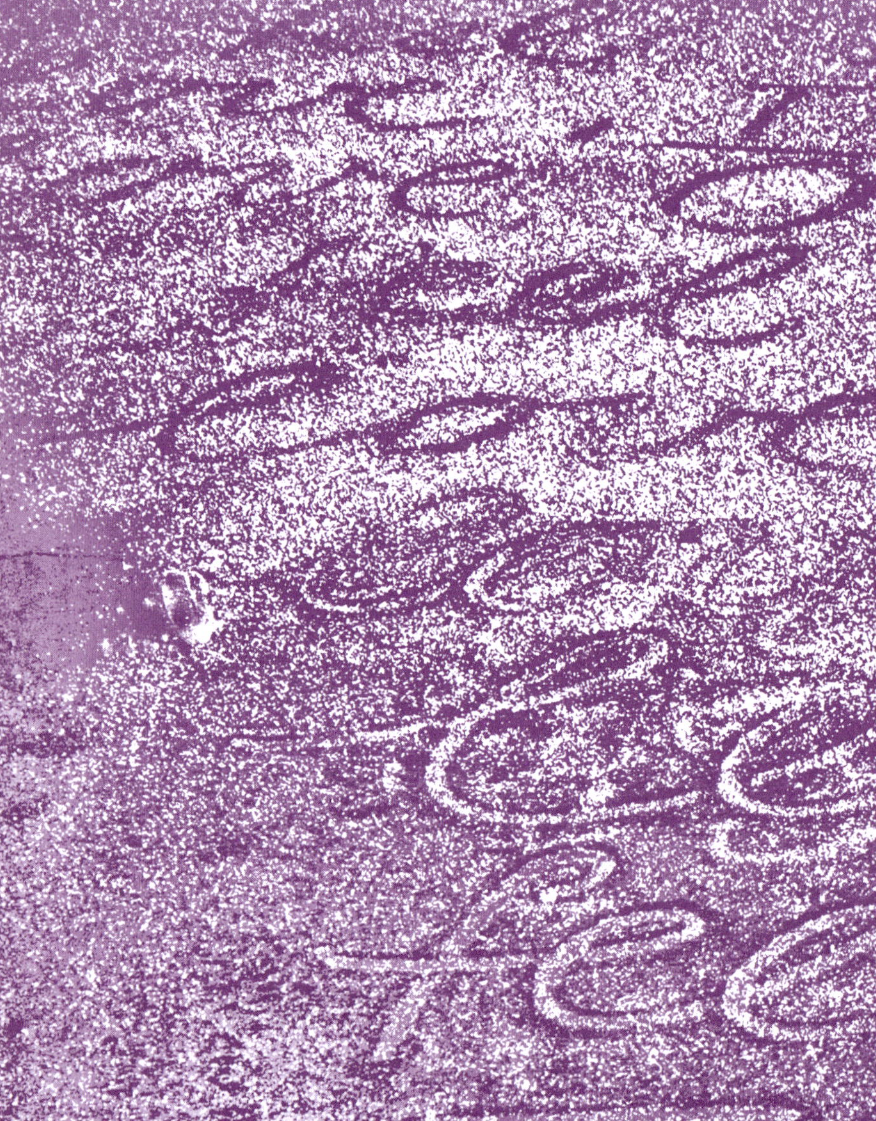

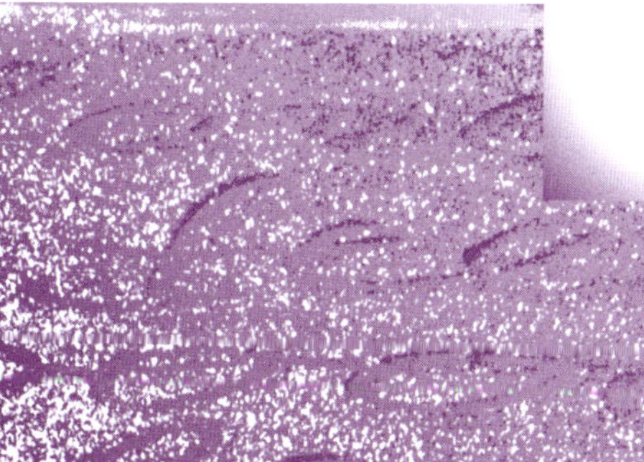

Dear,
Like a pearl, a philosopher's stone, or an everlasting Gobstopper rolling on your tongue, a great lyric operates in layers, through metamorphosis, becoming a mantra, trickling intravenously into your limbic system, entwining with your DNA and connecting the person you are becoming to the person you were.[1]

Consider this:

When I was a very small boy
Very small boys talked to me
Now that we've grown up together
They're afraid of what they see[2]

So, when I was a very small boy, I walked like a boy and I talked like a boy, and my hair was cropped like a very small boy's. Although I was aware I was born a girl, and both very small boys and girls would talk to me as such, I was sure one day I would grow up and marry a woman.

At first I wanted to marry my babysitter, but she was too old, and she was not interested anyway. I knew this because she had a boyfriend I respected; he took me to the ER one time I put a berry up my nostril.

But then, when I was six, we moved to a new town where I met this new girl. *Oh girl, girl, girl*. I introduced myself on her doorstep on the night her family moved into the apartment underneath ours. I cracked a few jokes and made her laugh – baring a still intact row of pearly baby teeth and very pointed fangs, which she quickly covered with a slender hand. From then on, our two young hearts would beat as one, and our great young minds think alike.

She and I decided that we would get married. Unfortunately at the particular time and place we grew up in, same sex marriage

---

1 The everlasting Gobstopper, which first appeared in Roald Dahl's *Charlie and the Chocolate Factory*, is manufactured in Willy Wonka's Chocolate Factory to accommodate children who are given very little pocket money. In real life however, the candy that was produced by Nestlé who later franchised the Willy Wonka name, will only last forever by virtue of you giving up on finishing it, which is likely to happen.

Roald Dahl, *Charlie and the Chocolate Factory* (1964)(New York: Puffin Books, 1998).

2 New Order, "True Faith," single (Factory Records, 1987).

was not yet permitted. While my friend told me this would be a problem, she had also thought of a solution:

She was a believer. Although I wouldn't call her pious, she had a very strong faith for a six-year-old; she told me that if I would only let her pray for me, God would turn me into a boy.

We locked ourselves into her bathroom; I sat on the toilet and watched her kneel by the bathtub with her brown eyes closed in intense focus, muttering under her breath, so absorbed in the magical thinking of play and prayer. I knew intuitively then what I know wistfully now, that only in play can we be really serious… and then I panicked!

I realized that if I had left our upstairs apartment that morning as a girl, only to return that evening as a boy, even if I walked the same and talked the same and looked the same, I wouldn't feel the same because I wouldn't *be* the same, and so my mother would not recognize me. She would turn me away.

This premonition had me practically in tears. Choking up, I asked my friend, Could I think about it? But, she said, she had already asked God!

She said she needed me to understand that this kind of request was a big deal! God was very busy, so she could *maybe* still turn it around, but it was not like I could keep going back and forth over this forever, wasting God's and everybody's time – so could I please just make up my mind?

Divine intervention
Always my intention
So I take my time
I´ve been looking for something
I've always wanted
But was never mine
But now I've seen that something
Just out of reach – glowing –
Very Holy Grail
Oh mother of pearl
I wouldn't trade you for another world[3]

Since I could neither orphan myself at such a young age, nor abandon my parents, I had to tell her that the deal was off, and I decided to be a girl right then and there.

Maybe she was way ahead of me? Maybe she sat there thinking to herself, as I procrastinated:

3 Roxy Music, "Mother of Pearl," *Stranded* (Polydor Records, 1973).

> What is a girl, what is a group of girls? Proust at least has shown us once and for all that their individuation, collective or singular, proceeds not by subjectivity, but by haecceity, pure haecceity. 'Fugitive beings.' They are pure relations of speed and slowness and nothing else. A girl is late on account of her speed: she did too many things, crossed too many spaces in relation to the relative time of the person waiting for her. Thus her apparent slowness is transformed into the breakneck speed of our waiting.[4]

In a sense this could be the mantra for these letters to you—circling around, trying to locate the mother in the girl and the girl in the mother, sussing out questions of haecceity, subjectivity, time, and space: like mother of pearl onto a grain of sand, the girl channels the woman and the woman the girl, until they collapse into one continuous, luminous, layered being.[5]

My own maternal heritage is not very well documented and vanishes quickly in the mist of hearsay: my mother was an occupational therapist and mother of three. Her mother, my grandmother—a petite sweetheart and *baby-woman*—was a sometimes-alcoholic, occasionally suicidal housewife and mother of five. Her own mother, who had more mouths to feed, sent her away to work as a farm hand by age eight and at age eighteen she came to work in my grandfather's grocery store. After he broke his leg, she impressed him by taking charge in the store and they married the following spring. They lost two of their five children to cancer.

Their oldest, likened for her beauty to her namesake Liz Taylor, was a whiz with a sewing machine. She died at thirty-three after a short sick bed and left behind a four-year-old daughter. Number two, less pretty and a spinster, died when she was fifty. She left behind an enormous pile of hand knitted towels in rainbow hues, and a stack of fauna compendia from which she would copy the Latin names of birds and animals in her scrawling handwriting. She was born with both mental and physical handicaps, which were possibly caused by my grandmother skinning a hare while she was pregnant, and possibly not.

I imagine my grandmother, as I am sure she herself oftentimes did, skinning that hare in her kitchen.

(The same kitchen we would later bake cookies for Christmas, where her every embrace would envelop us in a medicinal smell, like cough syrup. A sweetness with a punch thrown in. It mingled

4 Gilles Deleuze and Felix Guattari, *A Thousand Plateaus: Capitalism and Schizophrenia* (Minneapolis: University of Minnesota Press, 1987), 271.

5 This opalescence will attract the eyes of so many people, because nothing attracts the eye like other people!

with the smell of the cookies we baked, the cigarettes she smoked, and the dishes in the sink.)

And I imagine her again months later when – the hare long gone – her baby, my aunt, was born upstairs in the bedroom like her four siblings. My grandmother could see immediately that there was something wrong: those long thin floppy arms, like cucumbers, that high-pitched shrill screaming, but oh, that lovely jet-black hair! She named her Ida after her own mother.

Everybody was kind of relieved when Aunt Ida died. She was still living with my grandparents who were getting really old by then, and nobody wanted to think about what would happen when they couldn't take care of her anymore, since she was unable to take care of herself.

Only my grandparents were devastated, as both children left behind an evenly empty void in their lives.

I guess in looking for the *girl-in-the-mother* and the *mother-in-the-girl* I am also looking for these women – a maternal heritage – in them, in myself, and in you. Their lives span about a hundred years, that saw such big changes in the lives of women, it feels like it may as well have been light years in a sci-fi epic. Today we are faced with so many choices they didn't have a century ago, we can almost forget there is a legacy that made possible these choices we now can, and should, take for granted.

That legacy, from our feminist foremothers and heroines, will tell you that you can be whatever you choose to be – but don't you ever forget that one woman's feminist is another woman's misogynist: although I was a Madonna fan for many years, I have never forgiven her for "Papa Don't Preach." Little did I know in those weeks when that pop-hit topped the radio charts, the fruit of my loins was more the shape and size of a gummy-bear and of the same translucency, than anything resembling a "baby." A gummy-bear with a heartbeat.[6]

I *still* think it's a bullshit song, though perhaps I took it too personally at the time, and that's about all that I will say about that.

(No, I will also say that although I will always defend your right to choose, politically, I hope that you will never need to exercise it, personally.)

You will find enough feminists out there who will tell you that *you* do not qualify as feminist, whereas the misogynists out there will usually tell you that *they* don't qualify as misogynists; meanwhile both will tell you that they really only have *your* best interests at heart!

---

6 Madonna, "Papa Don't Preach," *True Blue* (Warner Bros, 1986).

Oftentimes, when I feel like a disqualified feminist, it helps to recall my relief upon learning that Virginia Woolf was so solidly upper class that she and her husband – with whom she spent a lifelong and poly-platonic relationship – could practically pay for their publishing business out of pocket, while being persistently attacked by her contemporaries (suffragettes and critics alike), as well as literary historians later on, for not knowing the first thing about "real" (read: working class) women's lives.[7]

Or, how disillusioned divorcees were disappointed to discover that Anaïs Nin was still married and supported by her husband, while taking several lovers and writing her five volume coast to coast American odyssey and *fictional* erotic bildungsroman about her sexual and artistic coming of age.[8]

Or, that Suzanne Brøgger married and settled down in the Danish countryside, where she brought up her daughter Luzia, whom she loved to bits and wrote a children's book; becoming, as they say, altogether *boring*, instead of practicing and preaching free sex and to hell with the bourgeoisie and their cannibal monogamy.[9]

Or, that Simone de Beauvoir – rebel, provocateur and one of the greatest intellectuals of the 20th century – moved from her parents' house into a hotel (with a chamber maid) and directly from there moved in with Sartre. He is often described as a big baby, whom she spent her adult life mothering – despite her fierce attacks on motherhood as the destiny of women. She would also share many of her female partners with him – in fact bringing home one budding butt after the other – while condemning housewives for prostituting themselves.[10]

Don't ho' me, if you don't know me, Simone, but seriously:

> With every Goddess a letdown
> Every Idol a bring down
> It gets you down
> But the search for perfection
> Your own predilection
> Goes on and on and on and on[11]

These four women, like all the others who inhabit these letters, whose lifetimes span the same century as my foremothers, also divulge a lineage of sorts, their literary DNA entwined with my own as I write. They are my idols not in spite of their obvious

7 Rumor.

8 Gossip.

9 Hearsay.

10 I heard it through the grapevine.

11 Roxy Music, "Mother of Pearl."

flaws, but because of them—including being accused of whoring—or conversely, accusing others.

And after all, if all our heroes are whores, maybe whoring is heroic?[12]

Whoring; not only in the narrowest sense of the word, as in prostitution, but more broadly—doing whatever you need to do, in order to do whatever you need to do.

Maybe this Cornucopian Principle, the ideal of immensity and endless availability, is the mother lode, the gift that keeps on giving, the good breast that just gets better?

Like Lady Gaga in her meat dress, all the eyes of all her little monsters feasting on her.

Like Janis Joplin singing:

> Come on, come on, cooooooome on and take it, take another little piece of my heart now, baby![13]

Or, Billie Holiday raising her bet with:

> All of me
> Why not take all of me?[14]

Or, like Selma in Lars von Trier's *Dancer in the Dark* who sacrifices her eyesight (and ultimately her life) so that her child can see.[15]

Selma is a compelling figure, but not a new one.

Von Trier could well have gotten his inspiration from Hans Christian Andersen's fairy tale *The Story of a Mother*, in which a mother follows her baby in order to steal it back from Death:

> Then she came to a great lake, on which there were neither ship nor boat. The lake was not frozen enough to carry her, nor sufficiently open to allow her to wade through, and yet she must cross it if she was to find her

---

12 I wonder if the whores of Babylon were multilingual? Maybe translating is the oldest profession in the world?

13 Big Brother and the Holding Company, "Piece of My Heart," *Cheap Thrills* (Columbia, 1968).

14 Billie Holiday, "All of Me," *All of Me* (International Music, 1941).

15 Björk—who famously hated working with Lars von Trier—said afterwards that she believed she was cast for Selma's part after von Trier watched a video in which she attacked a paparazzi photographer trying to take pictures of her son in an airport. Her songs often reflect her own experience of maternal bliss, like this one:

> One breath away from mother Oceania
> Your nimble feet make prints in my sands
> You have done good for yourselves
> Since you left my wet embrace
> And crawled ashore
> Every boy, is a snake is a lily
> Every pearl is a lynx, is a girl

Björk, "Oceania," *Medulla* (One Little Indian, 2004).

> child. Then she laid herself down to drink the lake; and that was impossible for anyone to do. But the sorrowing mother thought that perhaps a miracle might be wrought.
>
> 'No, that can never succeed,' said the Lake. 'Let us rather see how we can agree. I'm fond of collecting pearls, and your eyes are the two clearest I have ever seen: if you will weep them out into me I will carry you over into the great greenhouse, where Death lives and cultivates flowers and trees; each of them a human life.'
>
> 'Oh, what I would not give to get my child!' said the afflicted mother; and she wept yet more, and her eyes fell into the depths of the lake, and became two costly pearls.[16]

This is my favorite of his fairy tales, and the saddest. I cry my eyes out every time I read it, so I read it over and over.

(Like Suzanne Brøgger once said: "Crying is good. It's like an orgasm, just in the other end.") [17]

The self sacrificing mother is a contested figure and has often been interpreted as a misogynist ideal, but she is so powerful also, because she turns the power structures suppressing her, not upside down, but inside out, through the self-sacrifice which in turn becomes the ultimate liberation, a re-birth!

At the end of the story our mother finds her-self in Death's greenhouse, full of potted plants, each of them representing a human life. By the grace of her all-enduring love she managed to outrun him and greets him on his return:

> 'Give me back my child!' said the mother; and she implored and wept. All at once she grasped two pretty flowers with her two hands and called to Death, 'I'll tear off all your flowers, for I am in despair.'
>
> 'Do not touch them,' said Death. 'You say you are so unhappy; and now you would want to make another mother just as unhappy!'
>
> 'Another mother?' said the poor woman; and she let the flowers go.[18]

---

16 Hans Christian Andersen, "The Story of a Mother" (1848), in *Hans Christian Andersen: The Complete Fairytales* (London: Wordsworth Editions, 1997), 398.

17 I read this quote so long ago, I actually don't remember where I read it… but I know that I read it! It's become the kind of knowledge I carry with me, and use to console myself (or you), when unraveling.

Much like the rumor and hearsay I mentioned earlier in the footnotes to this letter, this kind of wisdom layers itself into the narratives we compose about the world around us, and insert ourselves into, hoping to make sense of it all, some day later. This is not traditionally academic or analytical. Nor is it anti-academic or anti-analytical. It is born out of the kind of necessity that is the mother of invention. (See also footnote 3, in the Introduction.)

18 Hans Christian Andersen, "The Story of a Mother," 400.

Death, in return, has a surprise. He gives back her eyes that he fished out of the lake – now even clearer than before – and asks her to look into a nearby well.

> Oh Mother of Pearl
> Submarine lover in a shrinking world [19]

Staring into the depths of the well, she sees the fate of the two flowers: one who lives a full and happy life, spreading joy and happiness in the world, while the other unhappily spreads misery and woe.

> 'Which of them is the flower of misfortune and which is the blessed one?' she asked.
>
> 'That I may not tell you,' answered Death, 'but this much you shall hear, that one of these two flowers is that of your child. It was the fate of your child that you saw – the future of your own child' [20]

The well of destiny, the philosopher's stone, the code-breaker, the DNA: which will tell us if we are children of coincidence or faith? Of haecceity or subjectivity?

Are we so different today than this mother, with our prenatal screening, our prying eye that scrutinizes any fold or flap, in order to predict the future of our unborn?

My mother's generation was handed (or took into their own hands) the speculum, and with it gained a new sense of ownership over their own bodies – that in time led to both a sexual revolution and, with a little help from "the pill," the disconnect between sexual pleasure and reproduction. Along with other events (like the case of Roe vs. Wade) this sense of ownership also paved the way for legal abortion, under the motto "My Body, My Choice."

My generation was handed (or not quite handed and that is the catch) the ultrasound probe.

That diagnostic instrument has become a household commodity in any and all – i.e. not just high risk – pregnancies; the first ultrasound is a rite-of-passage for the expectant parent(s) and the embryonic portraits passed around to friends and family.

Although it may seem innocuous, this "window to the womb" is by no means neutral. As Dutch philosopher Peter-Paul Verbeek points out in his book about the moral agency of the things that surround us:

19 Roxy Music, "Mother of Pearl."

20 Hans Christian Andersen, "The Story of a Mother," 401.

> This technology is not simply a functional means to make visible an unborn child in the womb. It actively helps to shape the way the unborn is humanely experienced.[21]

Ultrasound imaging represents the unborn through a series of interpretative steps, each shaping how the unborn is perceived, for example:

> First of all, the image on the screen has a specific *size*, and even though this representation suggests a higher degree of realism, its size does not coincide with the size of the unborn in the womb. A fetus eleven weeks old measures about 8.5 cm and weighs 30 grams, but its representation on the screen makes it appear to have the size of a newborn baby […] A number of techniques are used to construct a realistic image of the unborn. Further, a sonogram depicts the unborn independently from the body of its mother.[22]

This last point is important, as it redefines not only the status of the fetus, but also the status of the mother. First – because that's what everybody wants to do when having a sonogram – let's take a look at the baby:

> Ultrasound imaging constitutes the fetus as an *individual person*; it is made present as a separate living being rather than forming a unity with its mother, in whose body it is growing. Obstetric ultrasound thus contributes to the coming about of what has been called 'fetal personhood' […] This experience of fetal personhood is enhanced by the possibility of seeing the gender of the unborn; by its ability to reveal the genitals, ultrasound genders the unborn. The expectant parents, as a result, can begin to call the unborn by its name.[23]

Moreover, if you have a name you are *somebody*, and if you are somebody, you live *somewhere*:

> Another effect of this separation of mother and unborn is that the mother is increasingly seen as the environment in which the unborn is living, rather than

---

21 Peter-Paul Verbeek, *Moralizing Technology: Understanding and Designing the Morality of Things* (Chicago: University Of Chicago Press, 2011), 17.

22 Verbeek, *Moralizing Technology: Understanding and Designing the Morality of Things*, 24–25.

23 Verbeek, *Moralizing Technology: Understanding and Designing the Morality of Things*, 25.

> forming a unity with it. And when the fetus is constituted as a vulnerable subject, its environment may potentially be harmful. This opens the way for using ultrasound screening as a form of surveillance, monitoring the lifestyle and habits of expecting women in order to enhance the safety of the unborn.[24]

Accordingly, the ultrasound probe becomes an instrument that effectively hands the (pregnant) female body back to professionals—in this case the medics and the lawmakers—after all, as lay(wo)men we are in no position to interpret these images ourselves.

Furthermore, although there is no medical indication for an ultrasound examination in preparation to a first trimester abortion, several US states require it.[25]

It must be noted that these are not diagnostic ultrasounds, performed to screen for congenital defects that are rarely detectable before twelve weeks gestation, but rather ultrasounds performed solely to establish the "personhood" of the fetus, in a heartbeat.[26]

In the case of a wanted pregnancy however, the ultrasound serves as a *diagnostic* tool, designed to single out fetuses at risk of, for example, Down's syndrome (via neck fold measurements) or spina bifida. This type of prenatal screening frames the unborn as a possible future patient, an interpretive action that is (also) not without moral consequences:

> In translating the unborn into a possible patient, ultrasound makes pregnancy into a medical condition that needs to be monitored and requires professional healthcare. Moreover, ultrasound translates 'congenial defects' into preventable forms of suffering. […] It inevitably becomes a matter of choice now: the choice not to have an ultrasound scan made is also a choice, a very deliberate one in a society in which the norm is to have these scans done, based on the predominant assumption that *not* scanning for

24 Verbeek, *Moralizing Technology: Understanding and Designing the Morality of Things*, 24-25.

25 Guttmacher Institute, "State Policies in Brief, Requirements for Ultrasound as of March 1st, 2014," *Guttmacher Institute*, https://www.guttmacher.org/statecenter/spibs/spib_RFU.pdf (accessed 28 March, 2014).

According to this brief from the Guttmacher Institute, twelve states require that an abortion provider perform an ultrasound on each woman seeking an abortion, while in nine states providers must offer the women the opportunity to see images made as preparation for the abortion and another five states require the provider to offer the woman a voluntary ultrasound before the abortion procedure.

26 In other words, an act of surveillance by the state to protect the safety of the unborn, against the pregnant woman's will; to add to the invasiveness of this procedure, most ultrasounds in the first trimester are performed via the vagina, as the fetus is too small to give "good pictures" via the abdominal wall.

> disease is irresponsible, because you deliberately run the risk of having a disabled or sick child, causing suffering both for the child and for yourself and your family.[27]

When you were about ten weeks inside of me, the doctor couldn't find your head on that scan. She found your heart, but what good is a heart with no head?

I didn't know where to turn. I didn't turn to God. I abandoned the idea of an interventionist God, because what kind of heartless God would put a headless baby inside of me, and then haggle about it through prayer?

I turned to my dad who advised me not to seek knowledge I was not prepared to use, which turned out to be good fatherly advice, so I'm passing this on to you.

And then I turned to you and I asked you; I begged and I pleaded with you, to grow your own head. I wept and implored. I promised I would be the best mother I could ever be, the only mother you would ever need, if you would only grow a head.

Which you did, and how! When I came back the following week to the hospital they told me the images were normal.

I could not believe it. I could not believe it, until many sonogram images and months later I saw it with my own eyes; that in fact your newborn head was not only normal, it was perfect! With your own perfect eyes in it!

Perfectly normal, what else?

Of course during my pregnancy, and some times after, I felt bad for "you," for having considered not to let "you" live, believing "you" had no head and therefor no life outside the womb anyway. (I have since convinced myself…no, it would be more accurate to say that I have since learned, that "you" without "your" head is not the same you I know and love.) But while I didn't feel alright, making that call, I felt like everything would be alright as long as I could only keep you inside of me – but then what?

I am probably neither the first nor the last mother to wish, despite morning sickness, elephant limbs, and deathlike fatigue, to stay pregnant forever. To never have to deliver on the promise of delivery.

The untanglement of the mother-and-child union happens gradually and suddenly, leaving both with an imprint and perhaps a longing, back to this halfway home, where one becomes two? And believe you me; the "Quickening" – the feeling of another life inside you diverging from this point of viability – is a larger-than-life experience.

---

27 Peter-Paul Verbeek, *Moralizing Technology*, 17.

If your *sexual persona*, your womanhood, is layered upon you like mother of pearl, motherhood in turn is layered on you from the inside as it hollows out the shiny phallic object of the female body and turns it into a vessel, a grail, a self-fulfilling prophecy.

(Which is not to be confused with destiny!)

This layering should be taken figuratively, while at the same time quite literally. New scientific research suggests what we perhaps already knew instinctively:

> Women can also gain genomes from their children. After a baby is born, it may leave some fetal cells behind in its mother's body, where they can travel to different organs and be absorbed into those tissues […] It's pretty likely that any woman who has been pregnant is a chimera.[28]

In this way our DNA, like a pearl, a philosopher's stone, or a lyric rolling on your tongue, operates in layers, through metamorphosis, becoming a mantra, trickling intravenously into our limbic system, connecting the person you are becoming to the person I was. And what we look for in this connective tissue is not perfection, but transformation.

It's a lot of information, I know, so much I wanted to tell you, because:

> You are my Favorita
> And a place in your heart dear
> Makes me feel more real[29]

That real feeling of containing and carrying somebody, of the whole oceanic interiority that entails, is a position of hope, but also a position of fear; because something, or somebody, (more precisely that you, you were yet to become and I was yet to know) could be lost, I just had to believe in it, but anyway:

> Even Zarathustra
> Another-time-loser
> Could believe in you[30]

And even so, you can't just take it from me – there is so much I have left out. Like Paula Modersohn-Becker's self portraits,

---

28 Carl Zimmer, "DNA Double Take," *The New York Times*, 16 September, 2013, http://www.nytimes.com/2013/09/17/science/dna-double-take.html (accessed 3 April, 2014).

29 Roxy Music, "Mother of Pearl."

30 Roxy Music, "Mother of Pearl."

Buñuel's *An Andalusian Dog*, or Vermeer's *Woman Reading a Letter*—go see with your own eyes!

Just remember: Seeing is not believing, but it is a practice.[31]

Oh mother of pearl
I wouldn't change you
for the whole world [32]

Amen to that!
Love,
Mom

31 Amelia Charter, note to author, Chicago, March, 2013.

32 Roxy Music, "Mother of Pearl."

outro

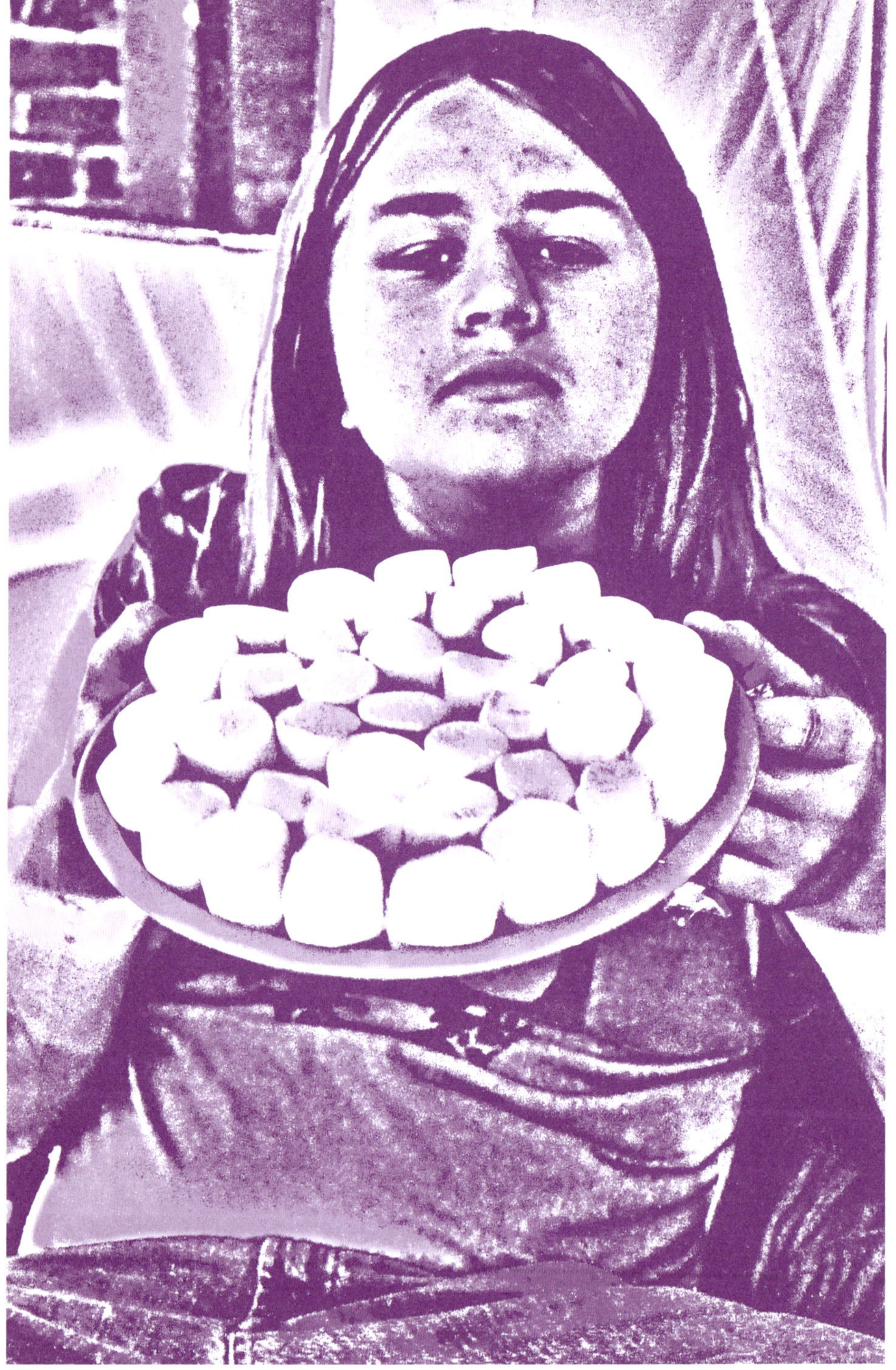

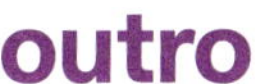

On the Mo(u)rning of Margaret Thatcher's passing.

Dear Reader,
I remember a poster, popular at the time when I was in my preteens and living so close to the Iron Curtain we could see it from our house. In a parody of the movie poster from *Gone with the Wind*, Ronald Reagan carries Margaret Thatcher away from a nuclear mushroom cloud blazing behind them. It reads:

> She promised to follow him to the end of the world,
> He promised to organize it!

It scared the living daylights out of me.

You can argue what came first, the spunk or the egg, but Reagan and Thatcher were made in the boardroom for each other, and they made it clear to the world in no uncertain terms that they would take this new romance to the bunker if needed.

Of course many tried to break them up. In 1982 a crackly tape recording surfaced of a hostile phone call between Thatcher and Reagan. The reason for their fall-out reportedly being the controversial sinking of the Argentine battleship *Belgrano*, which was torpedoed by British nuclear subs as it was sailing away from the Falkland Islands, killing 323 people.[1]

In the recording Reagan accuses Thatcher of being too aggressive and urges her: “Control yourself!”

The tape, delivered anonymously to the office of Dutch newspaper *NRC Handelsblad*, was soon found to be a hoax. Only problem was that nobody knew who had produced the spliced recording of Thatcher and Reagan's voices. A top secret note from the British Foreign Office read:

> There is no information to indicate that any subversive group or individual in this country was involved in making this tape.[2]

---

1 Thatcher was later interrogated about the *Belgrano* incident on the BBC live television program *Nationwide*, by a schoolteacher(!) – an insult that caused Thatcher's husband, Denis, to latch out at the producer of the show that his wife had been ‘stitched up by bloody BBC poofs and Trots.’

BBC News “TV's top 10 tantrums,” *BBC UK*, 31 August, 2001, http://news.bbc.co.uk/2/hi/uk_news/1518975.stm (accessed 30 March, 2014).

2 Nico Hines, “The British Punk Band That Fooled Reagan, Thatcher and the CIA,” *The Daily Beast*, 4 January, 2014, http://www.thedailybeast.com/articles/2014/01/04/the-british-punk-band-that-fooled-reagan-thatcher-and-the-cia.html (accessed 28 March, 2014)

Argentine intelligence was suspected, among others, before it was decided that: "This type of activity fits the pattern of fabrications circulated by the Soviet KGB."[3]

The tape did the rounds for another year or so, before it was discovered to be the brainchild of a little known British anarcho punk band, with a back catalogue of titles like *Penis Envy* and *Christ the Album. Crass.*

If Punk is dad, who will pull this kind of prank, or dress you in a *Ramones* romper and take you out to paint the town black every other weekend, Disco is your eternal mother, into whose pulsating bosom you can always return when he sends you pogoing. Unfortunately they cannot be in the same room with each other.

I thought Thatcher was no dancer. Not true, in fact I've found several photos of her and Reagan waltzing over the world stage, but still – no disco dancer! In fact, I am fairly sure that in Thatcher's universe, disco doesn't even exist. Not even a minuscule degree.

Yet she was instrumental and definitive to my muse and protagonist Queen Leeba. Thatcher became Leeba's antagonist.

In so many ways, 1979 was Queen Leeba's year. It was the Year of the Child. It was the year of Disco Demolition. And it was the year Thatcher was elected into office.

Of course it is just one year of many, but when I think of it now, the transition from the '70s and '80s evokes a shift in the Western paradigm, commencing a retrograde movement away from some of the possibilities and conversations that had been started in the '60s and continued in the '70s – conversations that entertained *The Limits To Growth*, for example, and the redistribution of wealth.[4]

Pretty soon these conversations were to be muffled by ridicule with slogans such as "Greed is Good!" and "The nine most dangerous words in the English language are 'I'm from the government and I'm here to help!'" and the way was paved for Thatcherism and Reaganomics.

As the caption underneath the poster predicted, Reagan and Thatcher's wild romance is *Now Playing World wide*, which is the reason why we are now given all kinds of stuff for free. Not because, as it used to be, the society is you, but because the product is you. Which is great, right? Because we all want free stuff…except the free stuff we get now is not the stuff we need, like education, health care, and affordable housing. No, that

---

3 Hines, "The British Punk Band That Fooled Reagan, Thatcher and the CIA."

4 *The Limits to Growth* is a 1972 book using computer simulations to predict the effect of exponential economic and population growth in a world with finite natural resources. Its first edition bears the subtitle: 'A report for the Club of Rome's Project on the Predicament of Mankind.'

Donella H. Meadows, Dennis L. Meadows, William W. Berens and Jørgen Randers, *The Limits to Growth* (New York: Universe Books 1972).

A PDF of the book can be found here: http://www.donellameadows.org/wp-content/userfiles/Limits-to-Growth-digital-scan-version.pdf (accessed 6 April, 2014).

stuff is really expensive, because it is actually valuable. So what we get instead, for example, is Facebook – *always free and always will be!*

And what we get instead of feminism is the advice to *Lean In*, to take it like a man, to succumb to the prestige of 60+ hour workweeks, with five-hour nights and all-day-care for our kids, to compete and break the glass ceiling. This pseudo-feminism has by now all but cornered the popular imagination of what feminism should be about.[5]

It defines success solely in masculine terms of competing within the existing game, while ignoring that feminism was originally a game changer – aiming at changing the rules, toward equality and (gasp!) solidarity between men and women. What we need according to this breed of "Iron Lady Feminists," are more businesswomen, more momtrepreneurs, more female CEOs and politicians, more world leaders like Hillary Clinton and Margaret Thatcher.

In Leeba's universe, Margaret Thatcher is the "Hannibal the Cannibal" of feminism, butchering the feminist body, and skinning it to sew herself a power suit.

She would probably have loved that idea.

New Statesman's editor Paul Johnson quoted Thatcher as saying:

> The feminists hate me, don't they? And I don't blame them. For I hate feminism. It is poison.[6]

And yet, undeniably, she owed her political career to preceding generations of feminists, just as she made the road to equality and solidarity undeniably harder to travel for any and all subsequent generations (feminists and non-feminists alike).

She basically road-blocked it, or, to borrow her lingo, privatized its infrastructure.

As Russell Brand, ever the voice of reason, remarked in his eulogy for her:

> It always struck me as peculiar […] when the Spice Girls briefly championed Thatcher as an early example of girl power. I don't see that. She is an anomaly; a product of the freak-onomy of her time. Barack Obama, interestingly, said in his statement that she had 'broken the glass ceiling for other women.'

---

5 Except maybe that other popular notion that feminism is about hating men, because yeah really, feminism is really all about men! Really??!? – Oh, please!

6 Jessica Elgot, "Margeret Thatcher Dead: Was the Iron Lady a Feminist?" *Huffington Post UK*, 8 April, 2013, http://www.huffingtonpost.co.uk/2013/04/08/margaret-thatcher-feminist_n_3036864.html (accessed 28 March, 2014).

> Only in the sense that all the women beneath her were blinded by falling shards. She is an icon of individualism, not of feminism.[7]

In keeping with the individualist credo "anything you can do, I can do better!" Thatcher famously hardly ever slept. She got by on catnaps here and there, in boardrooms and taxis for instance, staying up all night, plotting and scheming her new world order.

It makes complete sense to me: I am at my most vitriolic and mean spirited when sleep deprived.

(Although you can wake me up for breastfeeding any time!)

My husband does not understand my passionate resentment toward this woman. Unlike him, I didn't grow up in Britain, where her election was welcomed by his primary school peers with a bemused, "Blimey, now we have a female prime minister! Jolly Good!" before moving along in the lunch queue singing:

> In the gravy, where we can sail the seven peas…

That was before she snatched their milk, of course… and then she snatched so much more than that.

I know it's pathetic, and I know you are going to ask: "Do you have to?" Yes, I have to—because this actually describes the feeling most accurately, and perhaps also underscores that sometimes the pathetic is the perfect antidote to apathy—I have to, have to, have to quote the most pathetic (and therefore one of the greatest) British bands, Pink Floyd. At their most pathetic, on that most pathetic album of theirs, *The Final Cut*, Roger Waters wails:

> Should we shout
> Should we scream
> What happened to the post war dream?
> -Oh, Maggie, Maggie, what did we do?[8]

Maggie should know! She snatched the postwar dream by laying the foundation for a Europe in which the welfare state and the worker's unions—with their credo of eight hours work, eight hours rest and eight hours freedom, of giving what you can and getting what you need, instead of just giving as good as you get—were dismantled and ridiculed.

Instead, groups of people on the periphery of the work market—the immigrants, the unemployed, and most recently, the art-

---

7 Russell Brand, "I Always Felt Sorry for her Children," *The Guardian*, 9 April, 2013, http://www.theguardian.com/politics/2013/apr/09/russell-brand-margaret-thatcher (accessed 30 March, 2014).

8 Pink Floyd, "The Post War Dream," *The Final Cut* (Harvest, 1983).

ists—are singled out and pitted against each other in the name of competition and privatization. Friends of mine who took to the streets in protest of severe budget cuts to the cultural sector of the Netherlands, reported back with shocking accounts: not only of police brutality (which was expected), but also of verbal abuse from spectators of the demonstration. From their front row seats at sidewalk cafés along the route through the pedestrian precinct of the respectable city of The Hague, these *nette burgers* (meaning "good citizens") merrily booed the protesters calling them *Links Tuig!* (Leftist Scum!)

Although, I suspect, Thatcher couldn't care less about Dutch artists, her legacy lives on in the pervasive impulse to ridicule and bully anyone who stands up for their livelihood, or points to the responsibility of the state to the protect its weaker members.

Owen Jones preemptively wrote in *The Independent*, a year before her death:

> Thatcher is reviled by some not just because she crushed the left, the Labour movement and the post-war social democratic settlement. It is because she did it with such enthusiasm, and showed no regret for the terrible human cost […] Perhaps if a Labour government had reduced the prosperous middle-classes of the Home Counties to mass unemployment and poverty, and stockbrokers desperate to save their livelihoods had been chased by police on horseback through the City of London, they would understand the bitterness.[…] But while Thatcher-hate is understandable, it is futile. Celebrating the prospect of her death has become an admittedly macabre substitute for the failure to defeat Thatcherism.[9]

Part of my renewed resentment toward Thatcher was my own bitterness, after seeing friends and colleagues, fellow artists, being bullied into compliance by members of her following, from the wave of neo-liberal government, that washed over Europe since the turn of the millennium.

While that might be futile, an incentive for this book was the unwillingness to accept the neo-liberalist status quo as the end of history.

At the same time, it bothered me that my younger friends did not want to identify with the feminist movement, because in their vocabulary, the term *Feminist* had become attached to the term *Killjoy*.

So, I labeled myself the *Feminist Killjoy* and went on to preach the joys of Feminism.

---

9 Owen Jones, "Not All Socialists Want To Dance On Margaret Thatcher's Grave, I Want Her To Go On And On," *The Independent*, 16 September, 2012, http://www.independent.co.uk/voices/comment/not-all-socialists-want-to-dance-on-margaret-thatchers-grave-i-want-her-to-go-on-and-on-8143089.html (accessed 28 March, 2014).

And Motherhood. And Art. And Disco.

To this end I have been revisiting, reexamining, repurposing, and recycling some of the legacy handed to us from the 2nd wave of feminism from the '70s, and thrown on the landfill of history by *Lean In Feminists*.

There is enlightenment to be found on that tip; although some of this legacy seems quaint and dated now, there is some really good and useful stuff there. As an antidote to the toxic spill of our *laissez-faire* economy, there is also a whole lot of love.

Which makes it clear, perhaps, why Thatcher hated feminism so much. As Russell Brand dryly notes:

> When I awoke today on LA time my phone was full of impertinent digital eulogies. It'd be disingenuous to omit that there were a fair number of ding-dong-style celebratory messages amidst the pensive reflections on the end of an era. Interestingly, one mate of mine, a proper leftie, in his heyday all Red Wedge and right-on punch-ups, was melancholy. 'I thought I'd be overjoyed, but really it's just…another one bites the dust…' This demonstrates, I suppose, that if you opposed Thatcher's ideas it was likely because of their lack of compassion, which is really just a word for love. If love is something you cherish, it is hard to glean much joy from death, even in one's enemies.[10]

Even so, I couldn't but feel a brief elation when I learned of her death. A hope emerged: now that she is gone, perhaps her legacy could rust in peace right along with her.

So I made her a banner and I hung it above my Mothernism tent: a protest-chic *mise-en-scène* – a Femi-Futuristic camp for Queen Leeba and her Mothernists to inhabit. Here, the different parts of the project came together as an audio-visual installation.

The mother-ship of the project, a nomadic tent structure, serves as library, chill room, and gathering point. It contains a selection of Leeba's books along with a soundtrack in the form of recordings of her letters – the letters that were later reworked for this book. Inside the tent, visitors are invited to listen to the audio, to read the books, to think, to talk or to just hang out and eat marshmallows (because we are bad enough Mothers, you can totally eat marshmallows inside our tent!).

The ambience of the space is heavily influenced by the visual language of the futuristic interior design of the '60s and '70s, in particular that of Verner Panton and Poul Gernes. These two

10 Russell Brand, "I Always Felt Sorry for her Children."

influential Danish designers and artists are united in a radical approach to color theory as well as a design philosophy characterized by a social conscience with respect for the ordinary individual, and its right to inhabit a meaningful, stimulating and nurturing, environment. In this so-called *Snoezelen Room*, knowledge transfer is propagated through cross-pollination and exchange – creating a synergy between cerebral and embodied cognition, between "being in it" and "thinking of it."[11]

When the installation was open – both at Co-Prosperity Sphere in Chicago and at the Poor Farm in Wisconsin – I was really happy that people took this invitation to make themselves at home and took the time, both to listen to the audio, but also to each other. Unfortunately, no-one was breastfeeding in the tent yet, but it is my dream that some time in the (not too distant) future, when we get to stake out in the museum, someone will!

Inside and above the tent hang protest-chic banners, sporting Mothernist slogans and symbols, combining the formal language of Hilma af Klint and Kenneth Noland with a disco vibe. They can be worn as scarves and waved like flags, allowing the bearer to protest by day and be chic by night, underscoring that the compromises that you (need to) make as a mother, to accommodate and unite the different spheres of your life, are not signs of weakness but of strength.

Do what you have to do to do what you have to do.

Protest is a position of hope. It hopes to some day make itself redundant. I hope that some day we won't need to point out the legacy of feminism anymore because it has made itself redundant, or self-explanatory.

But, until that day, I have tried to repurpose it for myself and for you, dear reader.

This repurposing took shape as these letters, open letters from a fictional mother to a fictional daughter, sister and mother. But also from myself to my own daughter, or perhaps more accurately, from the girl I was to the woman she will become.

To that girl, the girl I was, 1979 is also a seminal year, as it more or less marks the beginning of my self- identification, at age 10, as an artist and a feminist.

The world I, we, inhabit now, is markedly different from that ten-year-old girl's vision of her own future, so I set out to revision it. To do that, I had to dig up and revise a lot of that good shit on the garbage belt of history, among it what I imagined

---

11 A "Snoezelen Room" is a soothing environment filled with sensory and intellectual stimulation in which the visitor can enter a liminal state of cognitive and aesthetic exploration. The Dutch term *snoezelen* is constructed from two verbs: *snuffelen*, meaning to explore, and *doezelen*, meaning to doze off. The term was invented to describe soothing yet stimulating environments, developed for non-verbal therapeutic treatment of people with severe autism and of demented elderly.

"What is Snoezelen," Holland Bloorview Kids Rehabilitation Hospital, http://www.hollandbloorview.ca/programsandservices/communityprograms/snoezelen/what_is_snoezelen.php (accessed 28 March, 2014).

to be that girl's legacy of feminism –the one we got handed down from our (fore)mothers.

Digging in, I also dug up a lot of stuff I didn't expect, a lot of stuff I didn't agree with and a lot of stuff that I found contradictory, which as it turned out was a great relief.

As I tried to figure out the relationship between the different aspects of my life and this legacy, defining myself as a feminist-academic-artist-mother increasingly felt like playing a complicated game of rock-paper-scissors-boob. I didn't find sufficient space for mothering within the academic feminist discourse I wanted to partake in, just like I had felt discouraged when wanting to include it in my art practice and I felt increasingly provoked at this demand to "check my motherhood at the door." So much so that instead of "covering" that part of my life, I opted to "come out" as a mother, artistically and academically.

One way of reading this book could be as documenting my "coming out" and my attempt to stake out new territory—within this "mother-shaped hole" in art discourse.

This "staking out" should be interpreted quite literally; instead of making work "about mothering" I decided to make a piece that operated "something like a Mama": the installation I described above. I employed my fictive Alma Mater Queen Leeba, as a kind of psychic companion, who would lend me the strength to be fierce, voluptuous, and hysterical.

Together we set out to conquer and inhabit this *terra incognita*, to mine the mother lode, with intent to examine the central hypothesis: If the proverbial Mother is perhaps a persona non grata in the art world, because her nurturing nature is at odds with the hyperbolic ideal of the singular artistic genius.

In its totality *Mothernism* offers a practice-based approach to theoretical research, operating in an organic way more like a sourdough than an archive.

One morning, as I was unloading the *Mothernism* tent in my now empty studio, I had a little cry. I was eating a heart shaped *Mom's Heart* special Mother's Day edition from Dunkin' Donuts, while reading on my cell phone the digital edition of *The New York Times*, about the collapse of a garment factory in Bangladesh.[12]

---

12 CELEBRATE MOM IN SWEET WAYS AT DUNKIN' DONUTS THIS MAY:

> Dunkin' Donuts also has a Mom's Heart Donut, a heart-shaped donut filled with Bavarian Kreme, topped with strawberry icing and festive heart-shaped sprinkles. The Mom's Heart Donut is available at participating Dunkin' Donuts restaurants nationwide for a limited time.

Dunkin Donuts, "Celebrate Mom in Sweet Ways at Dunkin' Donuts this May," *Dunkin' Donuts*, 2 May, 2012, http://news.dunkindonuts.com/Press-Releases/CELEBRATE-MOM-IN-SWEET-WAYS-AT-DUNKIN-DONUTS-THIS-MAY-ec.aspx (accessed 28 March, 2014).

Motherly love, so sweet and yet so raw: you see, a *Mom's Heart* is not only covered in pink glazing and heart shaped sprinkles it is also filled to the brim with the sweetest custard you have ever tasted. While this saccharine goo overflowed and spilled into every cavity of every tastebud I never knew I had and filled it to the brim with some obscene bliss, another mother cried out in another part of the world, holding up the pictures of her two children who had been working in the garment factories on the fourth and the fifth floor of what was now just a giant pile of rubble. She was calling out to them, to the sky and to the world at large and to the void in front of her: "Today, I'm here! But you haven't come back!"[13]

I am here! I am here and you are not! Why are you not here?

In the beautifully raw spring morning light, spilling into my now empty studio (empty but for a ton of stuff), that was too much to bear, and I had to have a little cry.

It was a cry of exhaustion, I guess. The exhaustion of a project nearing its completion, combined with the realization that it can never be completed. The closer I get to the Mother, the closer to infinity.

It's like the world is too large these days for motherly love, and yet too small. Like there is no space for this type of attachment in the digital age.

And in the mental time/space collapse of the here/now and the there/now, it felt so exhaustingly incomprehensible that her kids had to die, *there*, while I could sit *here* and have my donut and eat it too, after dropping my kids off at school where they will hopefully know what to do if an armed lunatic enters the building after the terrifying unannounced lockdown drill they had to endure last week, and me briefly entertaining the question, as I waved goodbye to them, if the security guard was armed, and if it would make me feel safer either way.

The sudden realization that these are the kind of incomprehensible bullshit questions we have to entertain these days, every day – because there is no outside to the vernacular of capitalism – had me in tears. My interest in The Mother stems in part from a defiance to give in to this vernacular, to challenge it. Because, even when you try to squeeze her into a donut, even if the mother lets you do that, she is uncontainable – she runneth over. Her self-sacrifice is a transgression, it breaks the primordial taboo of capitalism, because in capitalism, there is no greater love than what you feel for you, and your infinite individual needs.

---

13 Jim Yardley, "Tears and Rage as Hopes Fade in Bangladesh," *The New York Times*, 29 April, 2013, http://www.nytimes.com/2013/04/29/world/asia/owner-of-collapsed-building-arrested-in-bangladesh.html (accessed 30 March, 2014).

So, I set out to locate the the Mother-shaped hole in contemporary art and discourse. And I realized that the hole *is* the donut, it is the essence of the donut. To paraphrase an old feminist slogan: we don't need another bite of the donut, we need a whole new recipe.

Which is funny because when I started putting this thing together light years ago, it started with a tune stuck in my head.

I was Donna Summer singing what have been dubbed *the worst lyrics in the history of music*:

Someone left the cake out in the rain
I don't think that I can take it
'Cause it took so long to make it
And I'll never find that recipe again[14]

And I thought: what the fuck happened to feminism? And I realized that, to me, feminism had become that cake left out in the rain. It could have been, should have been, the most nutritious and delicious thing, but there it was: all wet and soggy and ruined…and *unappetizing*.

So I looked at it and thought: "If I am to hand this cake down to the next generation, my son's and daughter's generation, what does it need? If I were to bake it again, to change the recipe, what does it need?" And I thought: "It needs a beat, a heart beat and a disco beat."

It needs a future, a future feminism and it needs a space. It needs a space, a liminal space, like a tent, so it can move and move through and be moved through.

A space for mothering and a space in the art world for mothering, because without mothers there will be no next generation of feminists or anybody else.

And without art there will be no future anymore and we will all just be living in the past.

Love,
Lise

P.S. If you mix red, white and blue, it makes lavender.

14 Donna Summer, "MacArthur Park," *On the Radio—Greatest Hits* (Casablanca, 1979).

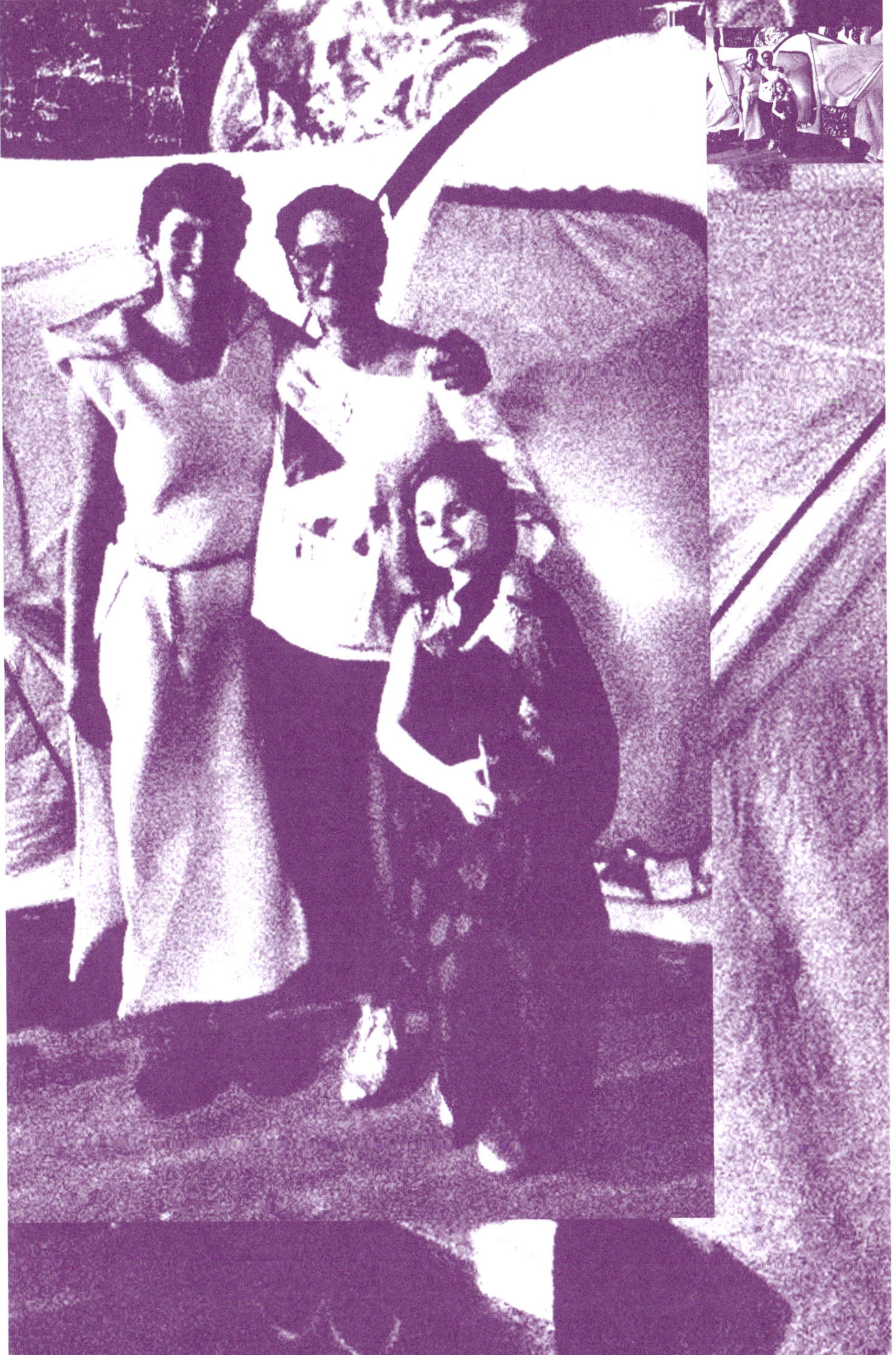

bibliography

Ahtila, Eija-Liisa. *Fantasized Persons and Taped Conversations.* Helsinki: Kiasma Museum of Modern Art and Tate Modern, London, 2002.

Andersen, Hans Christian. *Hans Christian Andersen: The Complete Fairytales.* London: Wordsworth Editions, 1997.

Bennett, Jane. *Vibrant Matter: A Political Ecology of Things.* Durham: Duke University Press, 2010.

Cixous, Hélène. "The Laugh of the Medusa." *Signs* 1, no.4. Chicago: University of Chicago Press, 1976.

——— *White Ink: Interviews on Sex, Text and Politics.* New York: Columbia Press, 2008.

Dahl, Roald. *Charlie and the Chocolate Factory* (New York: Puffin Books 1998).

Davis, Angela. *Women, Race & Class.* New York: Vintage Books, 1981.

Davey, Moyra. *The Mother Reader: Essential Writings on Motherhood.* New York: Seven Stories Press, 2001.

Deleuze, Gilles and Felix Guattari. *A Thousand Plateaus: Capitalism and Schizophrenia.* Minneapolis: University of Minnesota Press, 1987.

Despentes, Virginie. *King Kong Theory.* Feminist Press, New York, 2010.

Dickson, Paul. *Bill Veeck: Baseball's Greatest Maverick.* New York: Walker Publishing Co., 2012.

Ettinger, Bracha. "The Art-and-Healing Oeuvre: Metramorphic Relinquishment of the Soul-Spirit to the Spirit of the Cosmos." *3 Times Abstraction: New Methods of Drawing by Hilma af Klint, Emma Kunz and Agnes Martin.* Edited by Catherine de Zegher and Hendel Teicher. New York: The Drawing Center, 2005.

——— *The Matrixial Borderspace.* Minneapolis: University of Minnesota Press, 2006.

——— "Woman–Other–Thing: A Matrixial Touch." *Matrix-Borderlines.* Edited by David Elliott and Pamela Ferris. Oxford: MOMA Oxford, 1993.

Foucault, Michel. *The Archeology of Knowledge And The Discourse on Language.* New York: Tavistock Publications Limited, 1972.

——— "An Interview by Stephen Riggins." *Ethics: Subjectivity and Truth. The Essential Works of Michel Foucault, 1954–1984.* Volume One. Edited by J. Faubion. Translated by Robert Hurley and others. Middlesex: Penguin, 1997.

Hannula, Mika. "Teaching Discourse (Reflection Strong, Not Theory Light)." *Learning Mind: Experience into Art.* Edited by Mary Jane Jacob & Jacquelynn Baas. Oakland: University Of California Press, 2010.

Klein, Melanie. *Envy and Gratitude and other works, 1946–1963.* New York: Simon and Schuster, 1975.

Kohut, Heinz. *The Search for the Self, Vol. 1.* New York: International University Press, 1978.

Lispector, Clarice. *The Passion According to G.H.* Minneapolis: University of Minnesota Press, 1988.

Müller-Westermann, Iris and Jo Widoff. *Hilma af Klint: a Pioneer of Abstraction.* Stockholm: Moderna Musset and Hatje Cantz, 2013.

Nixon, Mignon. "Bad Enough Mother." *OCTOBER, the Second Decade, 1986–1996.* Cambridge: MIT Press, 1997.

Quetelet, Adolphe. *A Treatise of Man and the Development of His Faculties.* Edinburgh: Chambers, 1842.

Sedgwick, Eve Kosofsky. *Touching, Feeling: Affect, Pedagogy, Performativity.* Durham: Duke University Press, 2003.

Sekula, Allan. "The Body and the Archive." *October 39.* Cambridge: MIT Press, 1986.

Stensgaard, Pernille. *When Louisiana Stole the Picture.* Gyldendal, Copenhagen, 2008.

Suleiman, Susan. "Playing and Motherhood; or, How to Get the Most of the Avant-Garde." *Representation of Motherhood.* Edited by Donna Bassin, Margaret Honey, and Meryle Mahrer. New Haven: Yale University Press, 1994.

Sullivan, Robert. *The Meadowlands: Wilderness Adventures on the Edge of a City.* New York: Random House, 1998.

Summer, Donna with Mark Elliot. *Ordinary Girl, the Journey.* New York: Random House, 2003.

Tuchman, Maurice. *The Spiritual in Abstract Painting, 1890–1985.* Los Angeles: Los Angeles County Museum of Art, 1986.

Various authors. *Kvinde Kend Din Krop –En Håndbog* (5th revised edition). Copenhagen: Tiderne Skifter, 2013.

Verbeek, Peter-Paul. *Moralizing Technology, Understanding and Designing the Morality of Things.* Chicago: University of Chicago Press, 2011.

Wittig, Monqiue. *The Straight Mind and Other Essays.* Boston: Beacon Press, 1992.

discography

Antony & the Johnsons. "Future Feminism." *Cut the World.* Secretly Canadian, 2011.

Big Brother and the Holding Company. "Piece of My Heart." *Cheap Thrills.* Columbia, 1968.

Billie Holiday. "All of Me." *All of Me.* International Music, 1941.

Björk. "Oceania." *Medulla.* One Little Indian, 2004.

David Bowie. "Fantastic Voyage." *Lodger.* RCA, 1979.

——— "Boys keep Swinging." *Lodger.* RCA, 1979.

——— "Rock and Roll Suicide." *The Rise and Fall of Ziggy Stardust and the Spiders from Mars.* RCA, 1972.

Donna Summer. "I Feel Love." *I Remember Yesterday.* Casablanca, 1977.

_________ "Love to Love You Baby." *Love to Love You Baby.* Casablanca, 1975.

_________ "MacArthur Park." *On the Radio — Greatest Hits.* Casablanca, 1979.

Isham Jones. "There Is No Greater Love Than What I Feel For You." Traditional Jazz Standard.

Kiss. "I was Made for Lovin' You." *Dynasty.* Casablanca, 1979.

Madonna. "Papa Don't Preach." *True Blue.* Warner Bros, 1986.

New Order. "Blue Monday." single. Factory Records, 1983.

_________ "True Faith." single. Factory Records, 1987.

Pink Floyd. "The Postwar Dream." *The Final Cut.* Harvest, 1983.

Prince and the Revolution. "Darling Nikki." *Purple Rain.* Warner Bros., 1983.

_________ "If I Was Your Girlfriend." *Sign "O" the Times.* Warner Bros., 1987.

Roxy Music. "Mother of Pearl." *Stranded.* Polydor, 1973.

The Smiths. "How Soon is Now?" *Meat is Murder.* Rough Trade, 1985.

_________ "Panic." single. Rough Trade, 1986.

_________ "Stop Me." *Strangeways Here We Come.* Rough Trade, 1987.

U2. "Even Better Than The Real Thing." *Achtung Baby.* Island, 1992.

online sources

Adams, Tim. "Antony Hegarty: We need more Oestrogen-based Thinking." *The Observer.* 19 May, 2012. http://www.guardian.co.uk/music/2012/may/20/antony-hegarty-interview-meltdown-gender (accessed 30 March, 2014).

Ahtila, Eija-Liisa. "If 6 was 9" (1996). Video. *YouTube.* http://www.youtube.com/watch?v=nSUQcjNvYh8 (accessed 30 March, 2014).

AP/AFP. "Bush and Saddam should Duel: Iraq's challenge." *Smh.com.au.* 5 October, 2002. http://www.smh.com.au/articles/2002/10/05/1033538810033.html (accessed 30 March, 2014).

AR Wear. "AR Wear — Confidence and Protection That Can Be Worn." *IndieGoGo.* 1 October, 2013. http://www.indiegogo.com/projects/ar-wear-confidence-protection-that-can-be-worn (accessed 30 March, 2014).

Bagley, Christopher. "Brad Pitt's Personal Photos of Angelina Jolie." *W Magazine.* November, 2008. http://www.wmagazine.com/people/celebrities/2008/11/brad_pitt_angelina_jolie/ (accessed 26 March, 2014).

Baker, Katie J. M. "Unhappy With Your Gross Vagina? Why Not Try 'The Barbie.'" *Jezebel.* 18 January, 2013. http://jezebel.com/5977025/unhappy-with-your-gross-vagina-why-not-try-the-barbie (accessed 2 April, 2014).

Bassett, Laura. "Susan G. Komen Foundation Elbows Out Charities Over Use Of The Word 'Cure.'" *Huffington Post.* 12 July, 2010. http://www.huffingtonpost.com/2010/12/07/komen-foundation-charities-cure_n_793176.html (accessed 30 March, 2014).

BBC News. "TV's Top 10 Tantrums." *BBC UK.* 31 August, 2001. http://news.bbc.co.uk/2/hi/uk_news/1518975.stm (accessed 30 March, 2014).

BBC Radio 2. "Sold on Song — 'Blue Monday.'" *BBC UK.* April, 2005. http://www.bbc.co.uk/radio2/soldonsong/songlibrary/indepth/bluemonday.shtml (accessed 2 April, 2014).

Blake, William. "Visions of the Daughters of Albion." (1793). *Digital Poet's Society.* http://users.compaqnet.be/cn127848/blake/collected/chap-20.html (accessed 30 March, 2014).

Blas, André. "Niki de Saint Phalle: Introspections and reflections," dir. André Blas, 35 min, *Vimeo,* 2003. http://vimeo.com/35057914 (accessed 28 April, 2014).

Brand, Russell. "I Always Felt Sorry For Her Children." *The Guardian.* 9 April, 2013. http://www.theguardian.com/politics/2013/apr/09/russell-brand-margaret-thatcher (accessed 30 March, 2014).

Clark, Nick. "What's the biggest problem with women artists? None of them can actually paint, says Georg Baselitz." *The Independent.* 6 February, 2013. http://www.independent.co.uk/arts-entertainment/art/news/whats-the-biggest-problem-with-women-artists-none-of-them-can-actually-paint-says-georg-baselitz-8484019.html (accessed 30 March, 2014).

Conway, Megan. "Morrissey's 15 Most Outrageous Quotes." *Rolling Stone.* 16 March, 2013. http://www.rollingstone.com/music/news/morrisseys-15-most-outrageous-quotes-20130306 (accessed 28 March, 2014).

Dahl, Steve and Tom Snyder. "Tomorrow Show with Tom Snyder." 13 August, 1979. *YouTube.* http://www.youtube.com/watch?v=8aU3WIUxLj4 (accessed 28 March, 2014).

Dunkin' Donuts. "CELEBRATE MOM IN SWEET WAYS AT DUNKIN' DONUTS THIS MAY." *Dunkin' Donuts,* 2 May, 2012. http://news.dunkindonuts.com/Press-Releases/CELEBRATE-MOM-IN-SWEET-WAYS-AT-DUNKIN-DONUTS-THIS-MAY-ec.aspx, (accessed 28 March, 2014).

Elgot, Jessica. "Margaret Thatcher Dead: Was the Iron Lady a Feminist?" *Huffington Post UK.* 8 April, 2013. http://www.huffingtonpost.co.uk/2013/04/08/margaret-thatcher-feminist_n_3036864.html (accessed 28 March, 2014).

Emin, Tracey. "Why I Never Became a Dancer" (1995). Video, *YouTube.* http://www.youtube.com/watch?v=2e1SU17plhw (accessed 28 March, 2014).

ESPN. "Disco Demolition Night at Comiskey Park in Chicago 1979." *YouTube*. http://www.youtube.com/watch?v=I1CP1751wJA (accessed 30 March, 2014).

Frank, Priscilla. "Carolee Schneemann, Feminist Performance Pioneer, Talks 'Olympia,' Deodorant and Selfies." *Huffington Post*. 11 December, 2013. http://www.huffingtonpost.com/2013/12/11/carolee-schneemann_n_4415261.html (accessed 28 March, 2014).

Gilson, Dave. "Overworked America: 12 Charts That Will Make Your Blood Boil." *Mother Jones*. July/August, 2011. http://www.motherjones.com/politics/2011/06/speedup-americans-working-harder-charts (accessed 30 March, 2014).

Graff, Amy. "Victoria's Secret employee denies mom the right to breastfeed." *The Mommy Files, SFGate*. 23 January, 2014. http://blog.sfgate.com/sfmoms/2014/01/23/victorias-secret-employee-denies-mom-the-right-to-breast-feed/ (accessed 28 March, 2014).

Greenberg, Clement. "Modernist Painting" (1960/1978). *Clement Greenberg*. (Undated). http://www.sharecom.ca/greenberg/modernism.html (accessed 3 April, 2014).

Guttmacher Institute. "State Policies in Brief, Requirements for Ultrasound As of March 1st 2014." 1 March, 2014. https://www.guttmacher.org/statecenter/spibs/spib_RFU.pdf (accessed 28 March, 2014).

Hannula, Mika. "Mind Mapping: School of the Art Institute of Chicago." 12 October, 2012. *Vimeo*. http://vimeo.com/channels/522660/66763409 (accessed 28 March, 2014).

Hess, Amanda. "The Comfortable, Elegant Chastity Belt for the Modern Rape Victim." *Slate*. 4 November, 2013. http://www.slate.com/blogs/xx_factor/2013/11/04/ar_wear_these_anti_rape_shorts_update_the_chastity_belt_for_the_rape_culture.html (accessed 28 March, 2014).

Hines, Nico. "The British Punk Band That Fooled Reagan, Thatcher And The CIA." *The Daily Beast*. 4 January, 2014. http://www.thedailybeast.com/articles/2014/01/04/the-british-punk-band-that-fooled-reagan-thatcher-and-the-cia.html (accessed 28 March, 2014).

Holland Bloorview Kids Rehabilitation Hospital. "What is Snoezelen?" *Holland Bloorview Kids Rehabilitation Hospital*. (Undated). http://www.hollandbloorview.ca/programsandservices/communityprograms/snoezelen/what_is_snoezelen.php (accessed 28 March, 2014).

Jacobsen, Rebecca. "Slime Molds: No Brains, No Feet, No Problem," *Science Thursday PBS News Hour*. 5 April, 2012. http://www.pbs.org/newshour/rundown/2012/04/the-sublime-slime-mold.html (accessed 30 March, 2014).

Jolie, Angelina. "My Medical Choice." *The New York Times*. 14 May, 2013. http://www.nytimes.com/2013/05/14/opinion/my-medical-choice.html (accessed 28 March, 2014).

Jones, Owen. "Not All Socialists Want To Dance On Margaret Thatcher's Grave, I Want Her To Go On And On." *The Independent*. 16 September, 2012. http://www.independent.co.uk/voices/comment/not-all-socialists-want-to-dance-on-margaret-thatchers-grave-i-want-her-to-go-on-and-on-8143089.html (accessed 28 March, 2014).

Kitestring. "Kitestring: Safety With Strings Attached." *Kitestring*. 2014. https://www.kitestring.io (accessed 21 April ,2014).

Klouger, Jeffrey and Alice Park. "The Angelina Effect: Her Preventive Mastectomy raises important issues about genes, health and risk." *TIME Magazine*. 27 May, 2013. http://content.time.com/time/magazine/article/0,9171,2143559,00.html (accessed 2 April, 2014).

Kolata, Gina. "Vast Study Casts Doubts on Value of Mammograms." *The New York Times*. 11 February, 2014. http://www.nytimes.com/2014/02/12/health/study-adds-new-doubts-about-value-of-mammograms.html (accessed 28 March, 2014).

Kristeva, Julia. "Motherhood Today." *Kristeva.fr*. 2005. http://www.kristeva.fr/motherhood.html (accessed 3 May, 2014).

Lockwood, Patricia. "Rape Joke." *The Awl*. 25 July, 2013. http://www.theawl.com/2013/07/rape-joke-patricia-lockwood (accessed 28 March, 2014).

Magnussen, Anna Knöfel. "My Corona: The Anatomy Formerly Known as the Hymen & the Myths That Surround It." *Scarleteen*. (Undated). http://www.scarleteen.com//article/bodies/my_corona_the_anatomy_formerly_known_as_the_hymen_the_myths_that_surround_it (accessed 28 March, 2014).

Maienschein, Jane. "Epigenesis and Preformationism." *The Stanford Encyclopedia of Philosophy*. Spring, 2012. http://plato.stanford.edu/entries/epigenesis/ (accessed 28 March, 2014).

Miller, Jill. "The Milk Truck." *The Milk Truck*. September, 2011. http://www.themilktruck.org/Info.html (accessed 28 March, 2014).

Mc Nay, Michael. "Helen Frankenthaler Obituary." *The Guardian*. 28 December, 2011. http://www.theguardian.com/artanddesign/2011/dec/28/helen-frankenthaler (accessed 28 March, 2014).

Meadows, Donella H., Dennis L. Meadows, William W. Berens and Jørgen Randers. *The Limits to Growth* (1972). http://www.donellameadows.org/wp-content/userfiles/Limits-to-Growth-digital-scan-version.pdf (accessed 6 April, 2014).

Morrissey in Quotes. "Morrissey In Quotes." *Facebook*. (Undated). http://www.facebook.com/pages/Morrissey-In-Quotes/354253683427 (retrieved 28 March, 2014).

Mumsnet.com. "TRAMP?" *Facebook Timeline Photos*. 10 March, 2014. https://www.facebook.com/photo.php?fbid=10152255954544025 (accessed 3 April, 2014).

Museum of Contemporary Art Chicago. "MCA Chicago Plaza Project: Martin Creed." *MCA Chicago*. August, 2012. http://www.mcachicago.org/exhibitions/now/2012/313 (accessed 28 March, 2014).

Museum of Fine Arts Boston. "International Festival of Films on Art." *Mfa.org*, Undated. http://www.mfa.org/programs/film/niki-de-saint-phalle-and-jean-tinguely-bonnie-and-clyde-art-1 (accessed 21 April, 2014).

National Cancer Institute. "Breast Cancer Prevention." *National Cancer Institute*. (Undated). http://www.cancer.gov/cancertopics/pdq/prevention/breast/Patient/page3 (accessed 2 April, 2014).

National Center for Chronic Disease Prevention and Health Promotion. "Breast Feeding Report Card 2013." *National Center for Chronic Disease Prevention and Health Promotion.* (Undated). http://www.cdc.gov/breastfeeding/pdf/2013breastfeedingreportcard.pdf (accessed 28 March, 2014).

National Geographic. "Great Pacific Garbage Patch (Pacific Trash Vortex)." Encyclopedic entry. *National Geographic Education.* http://education.nationalgeographic.com/education/encyclopedia/great-pacific-garbage-patch/ (accessed 1 May, 2014).

New Order Discography. "New Order: Singles: Blue Monday." *Niagara.edu.* (undated). http://www.niagara.edu/neworder/singles/bm.html (accessed 2 April, 2014).

Orlando Sentinel. Names & Faces. "Pop Artist Says Marriage To Ex-Porn Queen Is Over." *Orlando Sentinel.* 28 February, 1992. http://articles.orlandosentinel.com/1992-02-28/news/9202280604_1_cicciolina-artist-jeff-koons-married (accessed 28 March, 2014).

Pickert, Kate. "Are You Mom Enough?" *TIME Magazine.* 21 May, 2012. http://content.time.com/time/covers/0,16641,20120521,00.html (accessed 2 April, 2014).

Oxford English Dictionary. "Awesome." *Oxford English Dictionary.* (Undated). http://www.oxforddictionaries.com/us/definition/american_english/awesome (accessed 28 March, 2014).

Rabin, Rony Caryn. "A Fresh Case for Breast Self-Exams." *The New York Times.* 17 February, 2014. http://well.blogs.nytimes.com/2014/02/17/a-fresh-case-for-breast-self-exams/ (accessed 2 April, 2014).

Roddy, Michael. "British Artist Tracey Emin's 'My Bed' Heads for Auction." *Reuters.* 28 May, 2014. http://www.reuters.com/article/2014/05/28/us-art-britain-emin-idUSK-BN0E813H20140528 (accessed 30 May, 2014).

Rowher, Susan. "Where are the supportive breastfeeding policies?" *Los Angeles Times: Opinion.* 14 November, 2013. http://www.latimes.com/opinion/opinion-la/la-ol-supportive-breast-feeding-policies-20131113,0,1821022.story (accessed 28 March, 2014).

Saad Nardine. "Gisele Bundchen, Supermodel Mom, Shares Breastfeeding Photo." *Los Angeles Times.* 10 December, 2013. http://www.latimes.com/entertainment/gossip/la-et-mg-gisele-bundchen-breastfeeding-daughter-multitasking-20131210,0,1219750.story (accessed 28 March, 2014).

Saunders, Frances Stonor. "Modern art was CIA 'weapon.'" *The Independent.* 22 October, 1995. http://www.independent.co.uk/news/world/modern-art-was-cia-weapon-1578808.html (accessed 28 March, 2014).

Sclafani, Tony. "When 'Disco Sucks!' echoed around the world." *NBCNews.Com.* 10 July, 2009. http://www.today.com/id/31832616/ns/today-today_entertainment/t/when-disco-sucks-echoed-around-world/ (accessed 2 April, 2014).

Sischy, Ingrid. "Koons, High and Low." *Vanity Fair.* March, 2001. http://www.vanityfair.com/culture/features/2001/03/jeff-koons-200103 (accessed 28 March, 2014).

Staller, Ilona. "Political Woman on LIVE Rome." *YouTube.* http://www.youtube.com/watch?v=EuVG0F_oorM (accessed 28 March, 2014).

Tauber, Michelle. "Angelina Jolie 'I Made a Strong Choice.'" *People Magazine.* 27 May, 2013. http://www.people.com/people/archive/article/0,,20705013,00.html (accessed 30 March, 2014).

TPAF/The Feminist Art Project. "The M Word: Mothers/Artists/Children." Panel discussion. *College Art Association of America conference, Chicago.* 15 February, 2014. https://feministartproject.rutgers.edu/calendar/view/3347/ (accessed 6 April, 2014).

Tracers. "Tracers Take on Feminism: Conversations about Motherhood, LGBTQ and Race." Panel discussion. Threewalls, Chicago. *YouTube.* 14 February, 2014. https://www.youtube.com/watch?v=CqGNvXLgUpg (accessed 2 April, 2014).

U2. "Even Better Than The Real Thing (Official Music Video)." http://www.youtube.com/watch?v=Yrch66gdjjk (accessed 28 March, 2014).

Various Authors. "Kvinde Kend Din Krop." *Kvinde Kend Din Krop.* http://kvindekenddinkrop.dk/ (accessed 28 March, 2014).

Wright, Io Tillett. "The Lowdown on Kembra Pfahler." *The New York Times.* 20 June, 2012. http://tmagazine.blogs.nytimes.com/2012/06/20/the-lo wdown-kembra-pfahler/ (accessed 28 March, 2014).

Yardley, Jim. "Tears and Rage as Hopes Fade in Bangladesh in the *New York Times.*" The New York Times. 29 April, 2013. http://www.nytimes.com/2013/04/29/world/asia/owner-of-collapsed-building-arrested-in-bangladesh.html (accessed 30 March, 2014).

Zimmer, Carl. "DNA Double Take." *The New York Times.* 16 September, 2013. http://www.nytimes.com/2013/09/17/science/dna-double-take.html (accessed 3 April, 2014).

1960geractuell. "Niki de Saint Phalle: Schiessbilder, 1961." *YouTube.* Uploaded 4 March, 2009. http://www.youtube.com/watch?v=jIP5xn0gyDk (accessed 2 April, 2014).

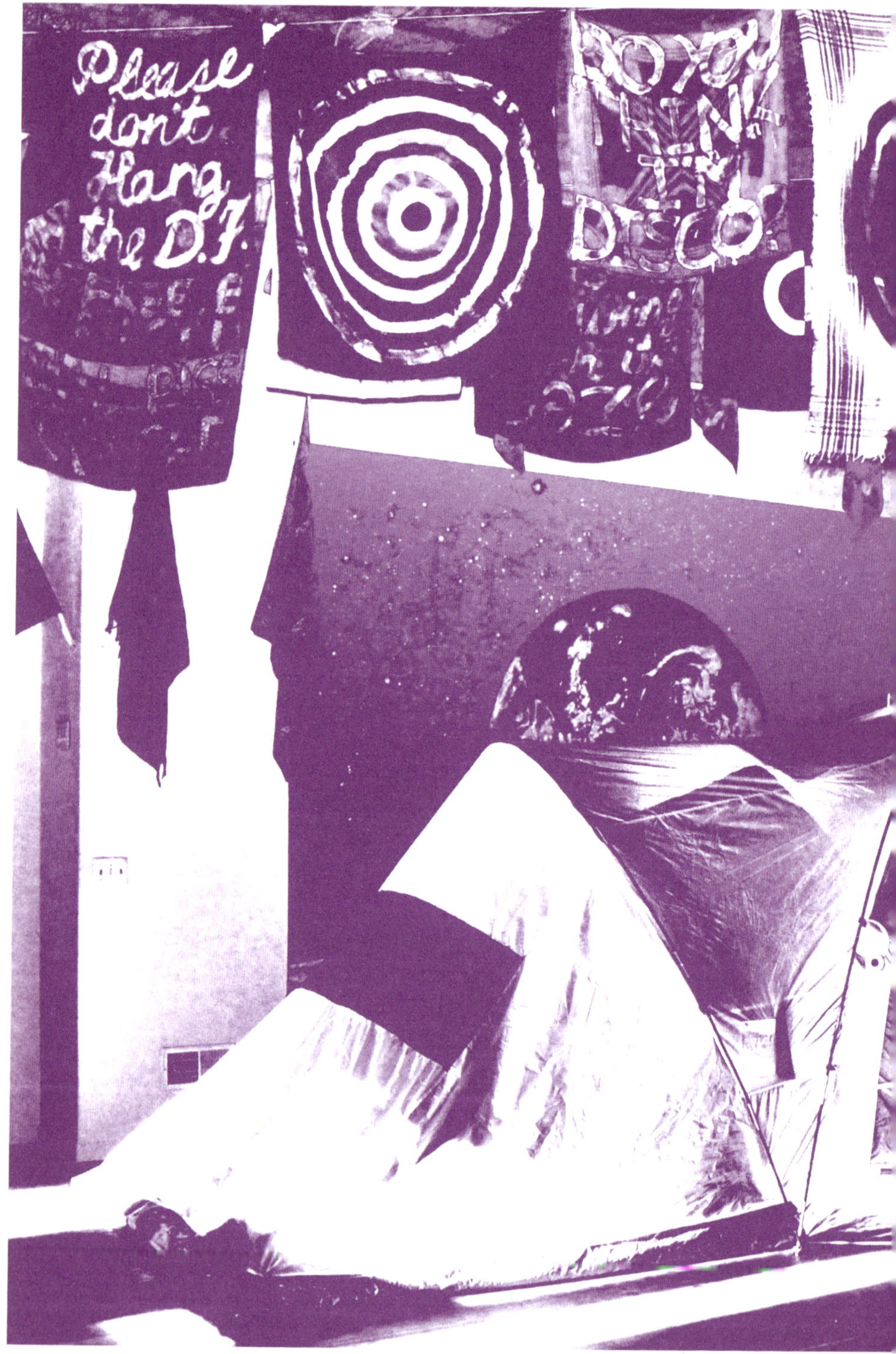
Please don't Hang the D.J.

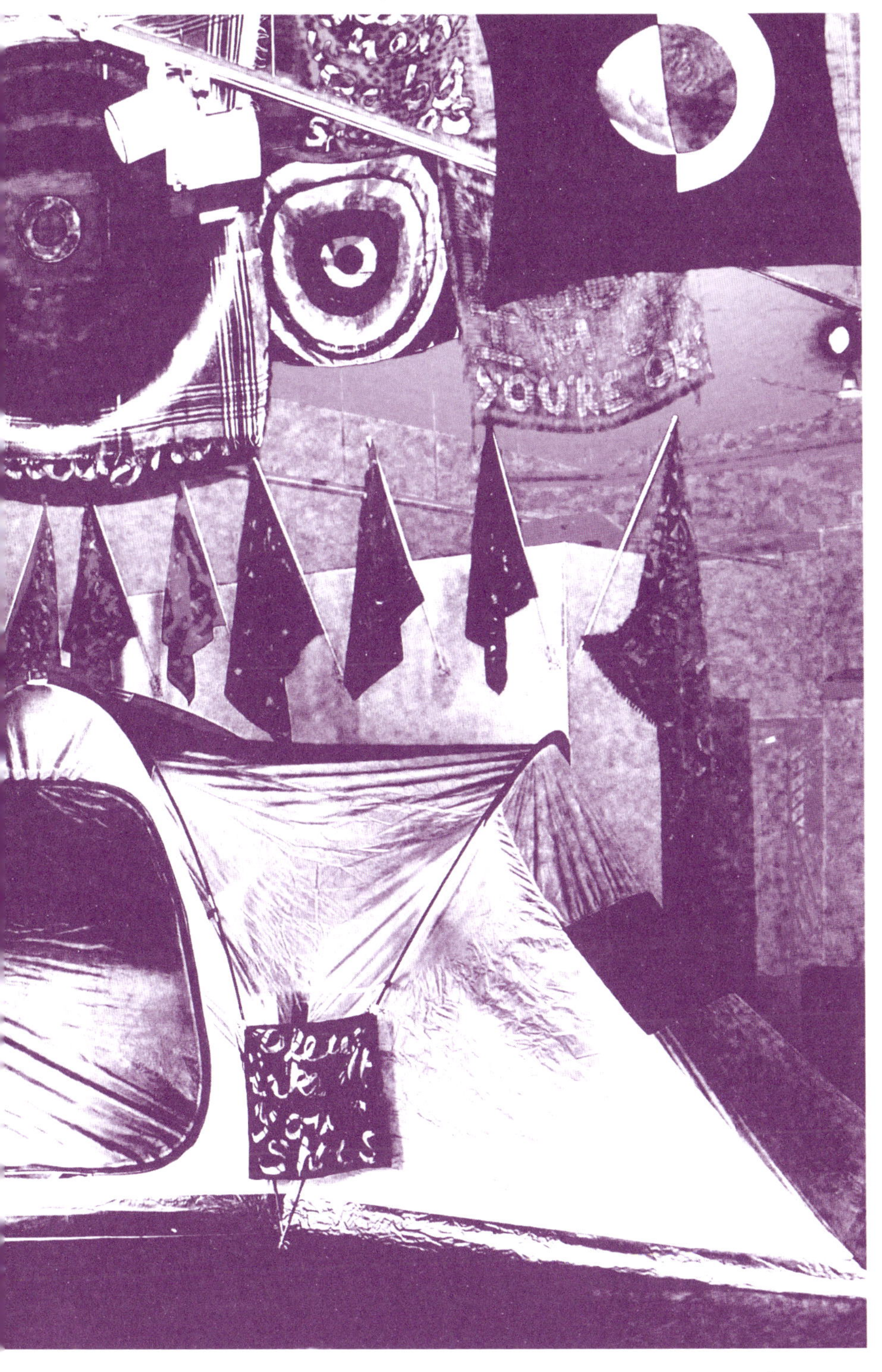

about the author

Lise Haller Baggesen (1969) left her native Denmark for the Netherlands in 1992 to study painting at the AKI, Academy of Art and Industrial Design In Enschede, and the Rijksakademie in Amsterdam. In 2008 she relocated to Chicago with her family, and completed her MA in Visual and Critical Studies at the School of the Art Institute in 2013. Over time, her work evolved from a traditional painting practice toward a hybrid practice including curating, writing, and multimedia installation work.

She has shown internationally in galleries and museums including Overgaden in Copenhagen, the Municipial Museum in the Hague, MoMu in Antwerp, Wurttembergischem Kunstverein in Stuttgart, CAEC in Xiamen, The Poor Farm in Manawa, Wisconsin, 6018 North, Chicago and the Museum of Contemporary Art in Chicago. *Mothernism* is her first book.